Enhance Oil & Gas Exploration with Data-Driven Geophysical and Petrophysical Models

Wiley & SAS Business Series

The Wiley & SAS Business Series presents books that help senior-level managers with their critical management decisions.

Titles in the Wiley & SAS Business Series include:

For more information on any of the above titles, please visit www.wiley.com.

Enhance Oil & Gas Exploration with Data-Driven Geophysical and Petrophysical Models

Keith R. Holdaway
Duncan H. B. Irving

WILEY

Published by John Wiley & Sons, Inc., Hoboken, New Jersey.

Published simultaneously in Canada.

For general information on our other products and services or for technical support, please contact our Customer Care Department within the United States at (800) 762-2974, outside the United States at (317) 572-3993, or fax (317) 572-4002.

Wiley publishes in a variety of print and electronic formats and by print-on-demand. Some material included with standard print versions of this book may not be included in e-books or in print-on-demand. If this book refers to media such as a CD or DVD that is not included in the version you purchased, you may download this material at http://booksupport.wiley.com. For more information about Wiley products, visit www .wiley.com.

Library of Congress Cataloging-in-Publication Data is available:

Names: Holdaway, Keith R., author. | Irving, Duncan H. B., 1971– author.
Title: Enhance oil & gas exploration with data-driven geophysical and petrophysical models / by Keith R. Holdaway, Duncan H.B. Irving.
Other titles: Enhance oil & gas exploration with data-driven geophysical and petrophysical models
Description: Hoboken, New Jersey : Wiley, 2018. | Includes bibliographical references and index. |
Identifiers: LCCN 2017027921 (print) | LCCN 2017040698 (ebook) | ISBN 9781119302599 (pdf) | ISBN 9781119302582 (epub) | ISBN 9781119215103 (hardback)
Subjects: LCSH: Petroleum—Prospecting—Mathematics. | Prospecting—Geophysical methods—Mathematics. | Petroleum—Geology—Mathemaical models. | BISAC: BUSINESS & ECONOMICS / Industries / Energy Industries.
Classification: LCC TN271.P4 (ebook) | LCC TN271.P4 H653 2018 (print) | DDC 622/.1828—dc23
LC record available at https://lccn.loc.gov/2017027921

Cover Design: Wiley
Cover Image: © naqiewei/Getty Images

Printed in the United States of America.

10 9 8 7 6 5 4 3 2 1

Keith Holdaway: To my patient and loving family, Patricia, my wife, and my children, Elyse and Ian.

Duncan Irving: To Sarah, my wife, and my children, Alfred, Edwin, and Ingrid, who have had to put up with less daddy-time than normal during this creation. Sorry, and thank you!

Contents

Foreword

I vividly remember the first time I met Keith Holdaway. It was 14 years ago, and he was standing in the front row of an analytics conference. He cut a distinctive profile as he challenged the speaker at the podium, asserting quite stubbornly that the oil and gas industry could realize huge returns by using a more data-driven approach that exploited the full potential of analytics. As a young man (or so I thought of myself at the time), I had been tasked with selling analytical software to upstream oil and gas companies. Coming from a technology background, I realized that this gentleman was the guide I was looking for and made a mental note to seek him out at the cocktail hour.

Back then, in 1989, the digital oilfield was the topic of the day, promising impressive returns. As the industry embraced the concept more fully over the next decade, I observed companies making significant investments in specific data solutions to automate and solve a broad range of problems. Thought leaders eagerly embraced the application of data-driven analytics, but the adoption was not necessarily as widespread as one would have thought. Scattershot adoption created its issues, with companies sometimes running hundreds of disparate applications and ending up with silos of data across their organizations. The promise remained.

Fast forward to 2014 and Keith's first book, *Harness Oil and Gas Big Data with Analytics*, which arrived just before crude plunged to historic lows. In retrospect his book seems almost prescient as the industry's enthusiasm for data-driven analytics has been driven in part by the potential to generate greater value from its assets in the face of a much lower price per barrel. Many of the leading players—and several influential thought leaders among smaller oil companies—have made substantial investments in this area, and there is more to come.

Increasingly, I am contacted by clients looking for data scientists, asking for training, and seeking guidance on how best to implement advanced analytics programs. We often point them to Keith's book, among other resources at SAS and elsewhere, to help them validate the best path forward.

Hence the genesis of this new book. Interest in his first book has been consistent enough that colleagues implored Keith to write a second volume: a more particular text that digs deeper into applying data-driven approaches across the exploration sector. Keith and his colleague, Dr. Duncan Irving, have written an invaluable book, exploring the data-driven methodologies in the disciplines of geophysics and petrophysics. And the timing is right. We are witnessing an unprecedented convergence of big data and cloud technology with massive increases in computing power at a time when a climate of low prices has made driving efficiencies an absolute requirement. Add to that the influx of technology-attuned Millennials into the workforce, and oil and gas practitioners are on the verge of a new era of opportunity to transform their business.

I have no doubt that this volume will be a valuable addition to the growing body of resources focused on this exciting area. Over years of working at the nexus of energy and technology, Keith has become a mentor and friend. His colleague is a globally recognized geophysicist working in the field of data analytics and brings innovative ideas to the evolving science of data-driven and soft-computing technologies. This new and important book is the result of years of deep work in this area and a real passion for the topic, approached with the same determination I saw at the front of that conference room many years ago. I am honored to introduce this book: *Enhance Oil & Gas Exploration with Data-Driven Geophysical and Petrophysical Models*.

Ross Graham,
Director, O&G Americas
Calgary, June 2017

Foreword

The oilfield is one of the most data-rich industries in the world, and concerning real information (as opposed to virtual data generated by the web and other virtual environments) can lay claim to the most data intensive industry. Most organizations, if they are honest with themselves, rarely capitalize on the potential of analytics and 'big data.' The authors of this book address the most common pitfalls that beset analytics and provide a comprehensive framework and roadmap, from the exploration and production perspective, to achieve the real goal of analytics—simplifying, expediting, or making possible the translation of data into profitable and sustainable outcomes.

To unleash the power of analytics, one must first understand what they are and are not. Analytics are data-centric processes that, if designed and executed properly, will lead to insights and outcomes. Each aspect of the process must receive due diligence, and the focus of the endeavor should always be to add value to the organization.

WHAT ANALYTICS IS NOT

The most common mistake when understanding analytics is to confuse the sizzle with the steak—that is to conflate the perception of a thing with the substance of the thing. Many managers and even technical professionals accept the misconception that analytics is the collation and visualization of data using colorful charts and graphs. This is not only incorrect, but there is a tacit danger in this assumption because it can significantly limit future analytic endeavors that do not, per se, yield an attractive visual. It must be understood, therefore, that dashboards and reports are one of many results of analytics and, while they are the most visible, they may not be the most valuable.

WHAT ANALYTICS ARE

Analytics are multi-step processes which transform data from one or more sources into information which leads to changes in actions and behaviors; and, if an organization is unwilling to do either, investment in analytics should be reconsidered. This book, more than any other before it, details a simple, yet robust, approach to developing an analytics plan that will lead to success. Though analytics methodologies vary depending on query most processes should contain at least the following:

- Data Modeling. Analytics planning should ensure, within practical limits, that necessary and sufficient data are identified beforehand.

- Data Gathering with a focus on quality. Identification and management of adverse data are often far more resource intensive and problematic than data that is missing. Acquiring real data often involves rigorous technical and contract specifications that include detailed definitions of data properties.

- Data Management—how data will be transferred, stored, secured, transformed, and distributed.

- Analysis—Understanding which analytical methods are most appropriate based on types of data and questions asked as well as the speed and accuracy of the desired results.

- Communication—Determining the most efficient and influential modes in which to communicate data to those who should, or could, consume it—whether it is formal reports, presentations, email, social media, audiovisual, or combination of these and other forms.

■ Management of Change. Perhaps the most important, yet sadly overlooked, part of an analytics project involves: identifying, before work begins, who all relevant stakeholder (or customers) are, clearly documenting their needs, and agreeing in advance on if, or how, changes to process might occur based on the results of analyses.

Nathan Zenero
President,
Verion Applied Technologies

Preface

Our motivation for writing this book comes from the professional curiosity and experience we have accumulated over recent years in the Oil and Gas industry. We have noted and continue to witness the struggles between geoscientists and their multiple spatial and temporal datasets. Traditional interpretation can provide certain answers based on Newtonian physics and the fundamental laws of nature, but with so much data being amassed with sensors in this digital age, it is necessary to marry deterministic interpretation with data-driven workflows and soft-computing models.

Owing to the cyclical nature of the Oil and Gas industry, we have seen historically depressed crude prices since 2015. This last downturn, like previous historical downturns, shook the industry to the point of an overreaction: people losing their livelihoods, reduction in OPEX, and cancellation of projects, particularly in exploration. It is at these transition points that oil and gas companies seek more efficient work processes and best practices. This invariably results in the adoption of technologies not necessarily new in other industries. Today we see more adoption of soft-computing and data-driven analytics to complement the traditional interpretation.

Given these cyclical-downturn scenarios, we ask ourselves, being in the trough of a current downturn: What's happening in the Oil and Gas industry today?

We are aware of the dramatic drop in crude oil prices that is a driver behind the industry's march toward adopting new technologies such as analytical and soft-computing workflows. Oil and gas companies realize the climb from the bottom of the cycle is a slow process and has many global and local influences. Too much supply and weak global demand play into a dynamic scenario.

Oil and gas companies are currently contemplating serious near-term investments to develop global assets, but it behooves the industry to move gingerly. We shall witness an inexorably slow increase in oil prices, with global supply bound by the reduction in reserve development projects over the past few years.

Many talented engineers have left the industry, and the internal organizational vagaries, coupled with inflexible and complex systems, processes, and attitudes could put the breaks on any innovative and evolving methodologies and best practices. IOCs and NOCs are looking seriously at a digitization environment using advanced analytics for the new daily workflows. Service companies, analytics vendors, and in-house capabilities are emerging to address these needs. This will enable oil and gas companies to weather current and future industry downturns.

We see this book as a contribution to enabling upstream geoscientists in data-driven analytics in geophysics and petrophysics. We hope it serves to bring together the practitioners of conventional upstream computing workflows with the new breed of data scientist and analyst and generate overlap and common ground so they can understand each other's perspectives, approaches, and role in this new computing landscape.

Acknowledgments

We would like to acknowledge and thank all the contributors to and reviewers of the manuscript, especially Dan Whealing of PGS for running his expert eye across the seismic data portions of the book. Stacey Hamilton of SAS Institute has been an encouraging and patient editor without whom this book would never have been completed. We would like to acknowledge our colleagues in the industry who have given constructive feedback, especially Kathy Ball of Devon Energy and Steve Purves of Euclidity, for ensuring the relevance and applicability of the contents. We wish to recognize the research by Dr. Alexander Kolovos for a section of Chapter 7 ("Knowledge Synthesis") and by Vipin P. Gupta, Dr. E. Masoudi (Petronas), and Satyajit Dwivedi (SAS Institute) for a section of Chapter 4 ("Production Gap Analysis").

Enhance Oil & Gas Exploration with Data-Driven Geophysical and Petrophysical Models

CHAPTER 1

Introduction to Data-Driven Concepts

"Habit is habit and not to be flung out of the window by any man, but coaxed downstairs a step at a time."

Mark Twain

INTRODUCTION

Current Approaches

We wish to air some of the more important practical considerations around making data available for data-driven usage. This could be for static, offline studies or for operationalized, online reviews. We introduce the concept of data engineering—how to engineer data for fit-for-purpose use outside the domain applications—and we take the reader from the first baby steps in getting started through to thoughts on highly operationalized data analysis.

A geoscience team will use an extensive collection of methods, tools, and datasets to achieve scientific understanding. The diversity of data spans voluminous pre-stack seismic to single-point measurements of a rock lithology in an outcrop. Modeling approaches are constrained by:

- Size and scarcity of data
- Computational complexity
- Time available to achieve a "good enough" solution
- Cloud computing
- Budget
- Workflow lubrication

It is this last constraint that has proven the largest inhibitor to the emergence of a data-driven approach in exploration and production (E&P). It is a motif for the ease with which data and insight are moved from one piece of software to another.

These constraints have led to a brittle digital infrastructure. This is problematic not only in the individual geoscientific silos but also across the wider domain of E&P. We can potentially exclude a rich array of data types, and restrict innovative methodologies because of the current hardware/software stacks that have evolved symbiotically. The application-centric landscape undermines E&P solutions that strive to integrate multidimensional and multivariate datasets.

It was not meant to be this way. Back when it all began, it was okay for decisions to be made in an expert's head. High-performance computers (HPCs) were power tools that gave the expert better images or more robust simulations, but at the end of the workflow, all that number crunching led to a human decision based on the experience of that human and his or her team of peers. Currently, there is too much riding on this approach.

So, how do we become data-driven if it's hard to get at the data?

Is There a Crisis in Geophysical and Petrophysical Analysis?

There is a movement to adopt data-driven analytical workflows across the industry, particularly in E&P. However, there is an existing group of Luddites providing not constructive criticism but deliberate and subversive rhetoric to undermine the inevitable implementation of data-driven analytics in the industry. It is true data scientists sometimes lack experimental data of a robust nature. How certain are we that we can quantify uncertainties? How can we understand the things that manifest themselves in the real world, in the hydrocarbon reservoirs? They argue that without concrete experimental evidence, theory harbors the risk of retreating into metaphysics. Predictive and prescriptive models are only the source of philosophical discourse. It is tantamount to solving the problem of how many leprechauns live at the end of our garden. Science is not philosophy. Thus, without recourse to experiment, geoscientists play in the realm of pure speculation and march to the metaphysical drumbeat of ancient philosophers. The slide into metaphysics is not always clear. The language of the perplexing mathematical algorithms can mask it. Theoretical physics, especially quantum physics, and the theories that underpin the geosciences and E&P engineering disciplines can be jam-packed with opaque, impermeable, thorny mathematical structures. The Luddites, looking over the soft computing techniques and data-driven workflows, are betrayed into believing that only the high mathematics and classical physical laws must deliver rigor, a wisdom of the absolute, the lucidity of the variance between right and wrong. No doubt there is rigor. But the answers we get depend so much on the questions we ask and the way we ask them. Additionally, the first principles can be applied incorrectly and the business problem unresolved for the engineers asking the questions.

So, there is no crisis unless we wish to create one. The marriage between traditional deterministic interpretation and data-driven deep learning and data mining is a union that when established on the grounds of mutual recognition, addresses an overabundance of business issues.

Applying an Analytical Approach

The premise of this book is to demonstrate the value of taking a data-driven approach. Put simply, if the data could speak for itself, what would you learn beyond what your current applications can tell you?

In the first place, it is the experience of many other industries that statistical context can be established. This could be around testing the validity of an assumed scientific assumption (for example, water flood versus overburden compaction being the cause of a 4D velocity change) or it could be demonstrating whether a set of observations are mainstream or outliers when viewed at the formation, basin, or analog scale.

The current crop of applications:

- Lack the computational platform for scale-out analysis
- Can only consume and analyze data for which they have an input filter

- Are only able to use algorithms that are available in the code base or via their application programming interfaces (APIs)

We discuss in greater detail ahead how to get G&G (geological and geophysical) data into a useable format, but first let us set the vision of what could be plausible, and this takes us into the world of analytics.

What Are Analytics and Data Science?

Analytics is a term that has suffered from overuse. It means many things in many industries and disciplines but is almost universally accepted to mean mathematical and statistical analysis of data for patterns or relationships.

We use this term in customer- and transaction-rich industries, as well as domains where businesses operate on the thinnest of margins. In the UK in the 1950s, the Lyons Tea Company implemented what we now recognize as centralized business intelligence. It was a digital computer that performed analytics across its empire-wide supply chain: thousands of teashops and hundreds of bakeries. Their business analytics grew from their ability to understand and articulate their business processes regarding a data model: a description of the relationships between entities such as customer and inventory items. The team that built this system (called Leo) went on to create similar platforms for other organizations and even sell computing space. This presaged the central mainframes of IBM by a decade, the supply chains of Starbucks by four decades, and the cooperation/competition of computing resources pioneered by Amazon. This history is well documented (Ferry, G., 2010, "A Computer called LEO") and is worth bearing in mind, as we understand how the paradigm applies to the geoscientific domain.

Let us fast-forward to the late 1990s and the evolution of the Internet beyond its academic and military homelands. Data could be collected from across an organization and transmitted into, around, and beyond its conventional boundaries.

This gave businesses no technical reason to avoid emulating Lyons's example of 40 years before, and those that could exploit the ability to process and assimilate their data for business impact pulled ahead of those that proved unwilling or unable to embrace this technical potential. Davenport's "Competing on Analytics" is a mesmerizing overview of this dynamic period in business history (Davenport, Harris, 2007).

As well as the ability to move data around using well-designed and implemented protocols (i.e., via the Internet), the data was generated by:

- Interactions between people and organizations via interfaces such as point-of-sale terminals or ATMs
- Communications between individuals and agencies via web-based services
- The capture of data along a supply chain as goods and materials—or people in the case of travel and hospitality industries—moved around a complex system

Data arising from a transaction could be captured trivially at sufficient quality and richness to enable statistical insight to be gained, often in real time, in the instance of assessing the likelihood that it is someone other than a banking card's owner using it at a given location and time.

Analytics is provisioned by the integration and contextualization of diverse data types. Moreover, it is predicted by timely access to reliable, granular data. If we look to the downstream domains of our industry, this would be real-time access to real-time data about refinery operations and productivity and passing it through to trading desks to enable capacity to be provisioned against spot pricing options.

The economic luxury of $100 oil insulated a lot of the upstream domain from adopting this type of integration. With the growth of factory-style drilling for unconventional plays, development and lifting costs became a major component of the economics. Since 2014, it has become less unusual (but still not mainstream) for drilling engineers to be guided in their quest for best practices. Such guides include analytical dashboards that are the result of combining petrophysical, technical, and operational data in statistical models. Engineers can use such guidance to characterize likelihoods of bit failure or stuck pipe under given geological and operational parameters.

The big surprise from working on such projects is not the willingness of rough-necked senior drillers to embrace such an approach (money, especially saved costs, always talks), but more that the data types in question could be brought together and used in such a manner. This combined an approach that used to be called *data mining* (it's still an appropriate term but is now deeply unfashionable) and soft computing techniques, which currently fall under the definition *data science*.

To a dyed-in-the-wool data miner (and probably a senior drilling engineer), data science is one of those unpleasant necessities of modern life (so it's probably an age-related thing). *Data science* is an umbrella term embracing mathematics, especially statistical expertise, domain understanding, and an intimate knowledge of the domain data and the different format standards. Clearly, this is beyond the capabilities of one single person, hence the widely circulated concept of the data science unicorn.

However, our experiences suggest that such a team should:

- Be configured as small as possible
- Contain a mathematical component that can cope with the physical sciences
- Deal with the worst of formats and the poorest data quality

Data science, done well, has been the difference between liquidity (and at least the next round of venture capital) and history for startups and mega-scale incumbents in many industries in the twenty-first century. It may seem, on the first encounter, to be an ad-hoc, ungoverned approach to working with data and working in general, but it has yielded dividends when applied formally in an organization.

If there is the political will in an organization to accept and act on findings from data science activities, then it will have a quantifiable business impact. Hence, it is reasonable to assume that data science becomes a measurable and valued capability in that organization. It requires a cultural change to provide pervasive impact, but we all must start somewhere, and small bite-sized projects run with a well-constrained scope in an agile manner can yield impactful results. The endpoint is a continuous conveyor of insight generation, through business validation and into operational usage, the DevOps mindset.

As an industry, we are a long way from A-B testing of our processes in the way that online retailers will test different views of their website on statistically sub-selected groups of their clientele to assess session profitability (yes, they do). There is a lot that can be learned about the behavior of many things that we don't think of in population terms (e.g., wells, formations, offset gathers of traces), and the relationships that may exist within and between such logical or statistical groupings.

Meanwhile, Back in the Oil Industry

With this landscape in sight, let us now turn our gaze to our industry. E&P workflows are designed with the goal of delivering high-value insights into the subsurface world. Data is acquired often at high cost and contains information of potentially enormous economic value. While the general types of data have not changed much since the first seismic surveys were performed and the first wells drilled, the scale of acquisition has increased by orders of magnitude.

We are still trying to measure the properties and behaviors of the subsurface and the engineering developments, interventions, and operations that we apply to the subsurface. But, in contrast, the time available to provide insight has shortened from years to months, or even weeks and days. Workflows are compressed in response to fit more agile portfolio decision making and operationalized development and production environments.

However, the business units involved in the upstream domain have hardened into brittle silos with their disciplines, processes, and technological predilections with data compartmentalization. There is an old approach to data curation, with lineage and provenance often missing, and this leads to a fundamental lack of trust in data on the rare occasion that there is the political and physical will to move it from one business silo to another.

With each silo being driven by its key performance indicators (KPIs), they can often be working at odds with each other. The information technology (IT) and operational technology (OT) capabilities in each domain have prevented data, used at operational and tactical levels, from being given enterprise visibility and value. Hence, there is no analytical culture in the upstream domain of our industry. (We often turn to the refining and trading domains as occasional beacons of good practice.)

With no data-driven culture, there is a weak alignment of business challenges across silos and processes, and no analytical capability has emerged at the enterprise scale. The economic upheaval of the 2014/15 price crash stunned the industry and laid bare its inability to respond to challenges at this scale as the underlying processes were so brittle. However, there is a focus emerging on how cost and value can be tied to processes and activities at ever-more granular scales. This is more predominant in the operations and production domains, but the impact is tangible.

The risk is that the same mistakes are repeated. There is a cultural mistrust between the operational business units and the corporate IT teams that should or could support them. This led to the outsourcing of software development and data processing to proprietary systems from data historians to seismic acquisition and processing. This removal of control over algorithms, data platforms and whole architectures in the case of sensor data yielded control over how data can support a business to the service companies and consultancies and is one of the most notable differences between the Oil and Gas industry and the industries mentioned earlier.

We are in peril of echoing the same mistakes by positioning analytics as point solutions that fail to scale or join up with other analytical endeavors. Without a data-driven culture, there is no strategic ownership of an analytics capability, and it is common to see duplication of effort on the IT and the operational sides of the business with competition for human and platform resources. The same service companies are attempting to fill the void by extending their suites of tools with point solutions, which exacerbates the underlying problem that there is no coupled approach to an analytical culture, the tools used for analysis, or the data that provisions the business insight.

We hope that this book shows how seismic, subsurface, and reservoir data can be used to drive business impact. The techniques that we present cover a broad range of geoscientific problems and while they may be useful in and of themselves, it is the approaches and underlying mindset that are the key messages that we wish to convey.

Depressed oil prices have focused primarily on cost controls and on extracting more value from existing workflows.

How Do I Do Analytics and Data Science?

The fundamental difference between data-driven insight generation and conventional techniques is that the former is labor intensive, whereas the latter usually only requires a software subscription. While there is much value to be had from the range and sophistication of applications, they are limited in the range of data that they can assimilate and the scale at which they can perform this adaptation.

Let's conduct an interesting thought experiment to see how cross-functional insight can be achieved using a data science team. There is the obvious need for business sponsorship via the medium of expected business impact. Delivering a new insight of the behavior of property X in the context of the property of scenario Y is a good place to start. Returning to our driller, it would be insightful to understand the modes of operation to be avoided in each petrophysical and geomechanical context, and base this on experiences gained over several hundred (or thousand) drilling campaigns.

How can this goal be achieved? First, we will consider what resources are needed in a typical endeavor, and when they are deployed along a workflow. At this stage, we concern ourselves with extracting data-driven insights to learn something new. Later we will discuss what we do with this insight and what impact it could have. Will it affect operational processes? Will it drive new technical approaches? Is it something that can be used to generate a rule or parameterize a model? In a continuously evolving deployment, how does the insight become operationalized?

To enable data to be turned into insight, a variety of skillsets is required, which fall into three broad domains:

- The *data domain*—what does the data describe, how is it stored, how can it be accessed, how is it formatted, what does it look like (data demographics and texture—more on this later). We have made this extremely difficult for ourselves in the Oil and Gas industry by keeping everything in application silos and insisting on moving things around using clunky formats specified decades ago (there are good reasons for this, but still).

- The *problem domain*—this is what makes the Oil and Gas industry difficult. The problems are some of the hardest—up there with moon landings—and require some serious brainpower as well as very sophisticated mathematical algorithms to simulate the processes and dynamics of our space. The algorithms have become so erudite that they now drive stovepipe workflows and it is very tough to put context and insights from other domains into play.

■ The *analytical domain* is poorly constrained. We wouldn't be writing a book on data-driven approaches in this industry if it were a well-established discipline. An understanding of statistical methods is a prerequisite. However, the methods that have become conventional in other industries sometimes sit awkwardly and require a practical implementation in the face of ugly data, subtle physical processes, and operational idiosyncrasies that defy characterization.

Each domain contains business-specific challenges as well as technical requirements. Input is needed from the business to ensure effort has validity and impact, as well as providing subject matter expertise.

■ The data is sparse in some dimensions and finely sampled in others (e.g., wells, or seismic volumes). It is often costly to acquire but rarely viewed as an asset, or treated as a byproduct of an expensive activity but discarded as digital exhaust. It requires considerable subject matter expertise coupled with data engineering skills ranging from conventional shell scripting through to XML, JSON, and binary parsing.

■ The problem space demands a strong understanding of the physical sciences and the mathematics to accompany it if the value is to be generated. The level of mathematics usually implies some level of computing ability in most protagonists, but this is rarely formally learned, or scalable, and it rarely has any statistical component to it.

■ Analytics in Oil and Gas has seen a slow adoption rate as analytical and statistical software has found more conducive markets. Many business verticals adopt more consistent data standards, and the business problems appear easier to solve with more tangible and quantifiable results. The key stumbling blocks encountered by the authors in their implementation of analytics have been applying analytics to time series and developing strategies to overcome sparseness in data in one dimension or another. There are also significant computational challenges in driving analytics with upstream data.

What Are the Constituent Parts of an Upstream Data Science Team?

Hence, a team that will work on data-driven projects needs a blend of geosciences, physical sciences, mathematics, statistics, and computer science supported by data architecture. Through experience, it has become clear that a physical sciences background and an average of several years of industry experience is a prerequisite in delivery unless a team is happy to have people learning on the job. This mix of skills and experience is the key ingredient required to perform data science, and it is highly likely that an upstream data scientist would possess most of these skills.

We caution strongly against taking a group of general data science resources and applying them in the upstream domain. There is a definite need to develop strong skills overlap in such a team for productive work to cope with people moving in and out of a project. More specifically, a data science team that does not have significant upstream domain expertise or a mathematical skillset that spans both the physical sciences *and* advanced statistics will fail, generating budgetary and reputational fallout. Correspondingly, there is much to be said for bringing in methods from other industries and problem spaces, but it must be anchored with strong overlap in the data, problem, and analytic dimensions for high impact.

The flipside of this is also problematic. We defined a data-driven study as placing the data and insights of one domain in the context of those from another domain. If a study is too narrow in its scope, it risks being compared unfavorably to well-established applications, algorithms, or workflows. Any new insight will likely be incremental and much groundwork must be applied to the data to establish unique value from the effort derived. Moreover, it will only have business impact at the level where the data is used in isolation. The more data types, the higher the potential impact, as the problem space addresses more of a system or value-chain. Another problem encountered is preconceived notions carried from industry professional training that sometimes lead to acceptance of a process, relationships, or correlations that are not statistically true.

There is a tension or compromise that must be dealt with in repeated data-driven activities. An investment in time and resources is always made in the first encounter with a new data type and problem as a team gets to grips with the data, understands its behavior, and applies appropriate analytical techniques and visualizations. There should be a return on this investment, but at the same time a data science team must retain its objectivity and stay abreast of new approaches and techniques that might be implemented. It is an organizational risk to embed a data science team for an extended period (more than 3–6 months) in any project or domain, and this has long been acknowledged in other industries where "crop rotation" is enforced by strategic KPIs. The upstream space is diverse enough to promote good data science evolution and career paths; individual disciplines such as drilling or reservoir monitoring are too narrow to sustain an intellectually able data science team, however long the wish-list of projects may be.

Strong data science teams are cross-disciplinary, quick to collaborate, business-focused, effective and efficient with the use of technology, and comfortable with failure (it will happen occasionally). It is worth reflecting on whether the upstream domain is currently capable of creating or attracting personnel that could thrive in such teams.

A DATA-DRIVEN STUDY TIMELINE

If you are embarking on a data-driven study for the first time, it is a steep, but exhilarating, learning curve. One of the biggest challenges will be showing value in a specific timeframe. Whether the project is in the commercial or the academic environment, resources are committed as part of an economic consideration and you may only have these resources (people and computational platform) available for a finite period.

The more people are involved in the study, the more dependencies you must deal with on their engagement. Also, there is often the need to ensure that all team members are aligned in progress and vision, so regular review, refocusing, and planning must take place. An agile methodology works well in this context as a good compromise between experimentation and productivity. The three core activities are to:

1. *Learn something new from your data assets:* Is there a pattern, trend or relationship in your data that is telling you something that no one has seen before?
2. *Place that knowledge in a business context:* Does it add value, save cost, change operational process?
3. *Document everything:* The chances are that this will not be the last time you do this. Record code, methods, problems, figures, and reports.

All three areas should be viewed as areas of outcome and should be explicit in the planning, funding, execution, and reporting of a project. At the scale of a large organization, if data-driven methods are being deployed to complement and enhance existing approaches, then a longer-term view on sustainable and scalable implementation must be developed. Smaller studies are the leading edge of this movement and are a way of learning how to perform data-driven techniques, hence the need to understand the business, technical, and process challenges and benefits.

Realistically, a small data-driven study is anything from one to eight weeks. A one-week study is at the same scale as a coding "hackathon." This is an event that has become popular in many organizations where the use of technology is a competitive differentiator. It allows low-risk experimentation with software (and often hardware) by teams of professionals (e.g., mathematical modelers) and business stakeholders (e.g., drilling engineers) to test ideas. This general premise is extended to longer time frames based on considerations around data engineering, projected time to business value, and complexity of analytical tasks. In our experience, six to eight weeks is a typical timeline for a successful discovery project.

For a pure discovery-style study, a simple set of workflow gateways should be constructed, which are typically as follows:

- Pre-project work:
    - Identify use case.
    - Define data.
    - Agree on success criteria.
- Data preparation:
    - Acquire data.
    - Load data to a staging area.
- Work preparation:
    - Understand toolsets.
    - Identify analytical packages.
- Work packages:
    - Execute analytical packages.
    - Continuous documentation.
    - Review, obtain feedback, and plan next package.

- Review:
  - Present to stakeholders.
  - Review and obtain feedback.

The pre-project work could take several weeks of meetings and requests for data until there is agreement across all parties concerned that sufficient data is available to enable outcomes that justify the effort and the resourcing. The data preparation and data engineering are often the most poorly scoped aspects of projects. If a team is meeting a data type for the first time, then it is not unusual for a few hundred person-hours to be devoted to unlocking the structure and behavior of the data; pre-stack seismic would fall into this category. Conversely, parsing a few thousand Log ASCII Standard (LAS) files out into a useable form is often a matter of hours as the format is well understood and tools freely available.

Once the study has been defined and the data loaded and understood, the analytical work can begin. A shared understanding of the potential business questions across the team performing the analysis and any stakeholders is vital, even if it is simply "What is there in my petrophysical data that I haven't spotted when viewed at the basin scale?" The analytical tools will likely be agreed at this stage, and an understanding of the shape and size of each of the steps should be developed. An agile methodology of planning, sizing, and execution could be applied if the study is to run for more than a few days.

Regular regrouping to ensure alignment of effort is vital, and if running for several weeks, then periodic reviews with stakeholders are necessary to ensure expectations are managed, the value is communicated, and new ideas can be drawn if progress permits. All the time, documentation should be a background activity. There are several tools available that allow code to be stored and shared in online repositories (public or private, e.g., Github). There are simple platforms and a service that teams can use to document their work (e.g., Jupiter,

Apache Zeppelin) with working code and statistical algorithms. It is necessary to provide interactive visualizations to help with communicating the outputs from their analysis. This ensures that the insights can live on well beyond the completion of the project as opposed to fossilizing them in PDF and PowerPoint.

What Is Data Engineering?

For this book, we view data engineering as the design and implementation of a data access framework. It covers the extraction of data, metadata, and information from source files and transforming them into a form, view, or analytical dataset to enable data-driven analysis. It should consider governance around security, quality, and lineage and engineering, data reuse, extensibility and scalability in size, complexity, and execution speed may also be considerations. Crucially, it is the cultural bridge between the curational world of subsurface data management and the insight-producing domain of analytics and data science. As in a construction project, where an architect must listen to the client and create a building that at the same time is aligned with a shared vision and meets the customer's needs, so the engineer must execute against these requirements using his or her understanding and experience with the practicalities of the materials to be used.

So, in a data-driven analytics environment, matters could be as simple as lining up a collection of time series samples from disparate data domains along a consistently tested timeline, or they could be challenging as ingesting passive seismic data from hundreds of sensors and extracting patterns and features for operationalized analytics.

If the data-driven study is a one-off activity, then shame on you for lack of vision. Let us explore this road momentarily and then move on. Data must be extracted from a native file format, an application database, or some other form of transfer mechanism (Excel, plain text) and then cleaned, validated, and placed into some structure that allows analysis. This could be a table in a database, a data frame in R or Python, or some custom structure in any one of the many big data number-crunching platforms. The effort has been expended with no value to show.

Before spending the energy, think of the future and consider what might happen if the insights of your data-driven analysis are considered valuable. You will be asked to repeat it with a larger dataset, more sophisticated algorithms, combined with other data types, and more—will you have to repeat all the steps and expend the same effort, or can you repeat, reuse, scale, and extend your efforts with ease? If we answer in the negative, then you need to consider your approach to data engineering.

A Workflow for Getting Started

We offer a set of guiding principles rather than a rigid methodology. The amount of time spent in preparing the data for use and engineering more robust functionality around your work is governed by the quality of the data, the volume and structure of the data, how much integration is required, and how quickly the whole workflow needs to be performed—from one-off to continuously streamed data.

We will stay away from stream processing architectures and remain in the shallow end of the analytics pool in trying to expose data at its most granular level, bring it to a level of quality that is fit for analytics, and apply context using any metadata and by integration with other data. What follows is a roughly linear workflow with the caveat that you should expect iterations through it until you arrive at a dataset and resulting insights that are robust enough to drive a business decision.

Opening the Data

The first practical step is getting hold of the data. Often this is a political challenge as much as a practical one. Confidence must be won, usually with the promise of a stake in the project and a sharing of outcomes. When requesting data, ask for as much as possible. That's not idealism speaking; that's a request for metadata. When you ask for "everything" you can then ignore unimportant data at your leisure; but when asking for the "raw" curves you realize that you forgot to call for the well headers, and so on, you get the idea. You'll understand that you need data about the data (metadata) and some reference data (master data) such as the Master Curve List of well curves or the official stratigraphic terms used by your organization or client. This is your first step on the road to context and hence enlightenment.

In many Oil and Gas companies, it's hard to locate, or sometimes access, the "official" or "correct" version of such data and a gray area exists that is inhabited by people's favorite or most trusted version of a given dataset or reference table. We have all seen examples of this murky world, and checking the veracity of data as it moves from one domain application to the next is one of the major time-sinks in subsurface analysis workflows.

Metadata, Master, and Measurement Data

Metadata is a necessity in the subsurface data world. It is the anchor for all those physical measurements and interpretations. As geoscientists, we like to think that we know exactly when and where all our costly measurements were made. In the real world, it is customary to hear anecdotes about the geodetic baseline and reference ellipsoid being lost when a system is migrated from one database to another as part of technology refresh or when undergoing acquisition by another organization.

Fortunately, our subsurface data managers are smart people even if the systems that they must use are not, and their technical committees created data exchange formats for various data types that have stood the test of several decades (something that nearly all other file formats have failed to do!). Seismic, well, and production datasets all contain data that tell the user (in human-readable text) how to unpack the data and what each field means. At the very least we have a logical framework, if not a spatial or chronological one, from which to set out. If you're lucky, you will then have enough metadata in the form of headers, comments, and accompanying master data that will allow you to place your measurement data in the correct spatial and logical context.

The location of this metadata is well defined (and well adhered to, usually) in formats such as SEG-Y (seismic) and LAS (well log), and what is easily readable by the human eye is now easily assimilated by parsing scripts in a variety of languages. A consistent data science team should find it simple to parse trace headers, well headers, or any other industry metadata to extract necessary information about survey/well names, and common-depth point (CDP)/well header locations. Several open-source projects are now hosted on public code bases such as "Github" to get started.

Data Types

Let us briefly consider the three main classes of data that are encountered in the subsurface domain and reflect on the challenges of each class. Our data is usually a measurement or collection of measurements at a location and a particular time. We take raw physical measurements and perform all manner of cleaning, interpolation, and refactoring to give a better measurement but, raw or synthetic, we are trying to describe the subsurface in space and time. There will also be contextual information contained in the text that may need to be extracted and integrated at scale.

Chronological Data

Beyond single-point measurements, time series are the simplest data types. Typically, they are measurements of the same property at the same location, ideally at regular intervals. If the interval is irregular, then some interpolation and resampling strategy are often required to provide a consistent dataset (computers and more importantly our algorithms prefer regular sampling). Analytics often requires asking a system what is happening at a point in time, or across a discrete window if the concurrence constraint can be justifiably relaxed.

Chronological data is best converted to an International Organization for Standardization (ISO) timestamp data type, which requires some careful parsing, conversion, and concatenation of data that often comes in Julian Day format if a boat has been involved in its acquisition (e.g., seismic data).

As a special case of temporal data, well logs represent a time series, masquerading as a simpler 1D dataset. Remember that well logging is a collection of rock properties sensed at a regular sampling rate while a logging tool is pulled up a borehole. This is then converted to a down-hole depth, but it should be noted that mismatches can occur, and composite logs are not immune to errors creeping in where logging has taken place at different rates by different contractors.

Similarly, seismic imaging data is also a collection of discrete time series windows. The time is two-way travel time, and the data is presented as bunches of time series attached to fixed points on a survey. Pre-stack seismic data is more complex since the time becomes a critical access path when assembling simultaneous events such as a shot gather.

While these last two examples of time series may seem contrived, they illustrate the fact that there needs to be careful thought as to what questions we are asking of our data before we plan how to store and access our data for analysis. The industry standards for data formats were developed for robust and fool-proof *transfer* of data, and not for ad-hoc access to granular data at scale.

Let us consider the simplest case more closely. Imagine that we have a single sensor taking a measurement at frequent and regular intervals (one second, for the sake of this example). Let us assume that we measure a property that changes rapidly enough that we need to sample it every second, and is part of an operational control system that we can tap into for logical reasons. We would like to understand the longer term (e.g., week–month) scale behavior of our property. We will address the types of analysis that are appropriate for this later; suffice to say we will have a very long, thin dataset. We shall quickly fill a spreadsheet beyond the point that a human brain and eye can extract meaningful insight, and moreover, it will present an indexing challenge if stored as a single physical file.

For accurate time series, it may be necessary to resample to a standard timestamp for analysis or—better—use a time series database. This is an emerging class of databases that allows ranges of historical data to be extracted and compared even when events do not fall on exact timestamps. This was until recently not engineered into mainstream databases, but the rise of the Internet of Things (IOT) agenda and its industrial equivalent have seen considerable investment in time-based analytical capabilities.

For 1D data that happens to be a discrete time series—seismic traces and well logs—there are still decisions to be made about how to access data in the time series. However, this needs to be balanced with how each measurement is indexed. Adding additional indexes for easting, northing, acquisition time (or survey identifer for 4D seismic), parameter name (for well logs), and offset (for pre-stack seismic) require extra storage. Such storage needs have to be justified as regards the value of provisioning so many ways of accessing the data for instant analysis.

Spatial Data

Spatial data presents its class of problems, which are dealt with efficiently in many other publications. For a thorough grounding in the theory, we recommend *Spatial Data Modelling for 3D GIS* (Abdul-Rahman and Pilouk, 2008) as a starting point. Most analytical approaches should support some spatial representation of relationships between data. It is possible to decompose any 2D or 3D dataset into its most granular form where the analytical value requires it. As with time series data, it then becomes a series of design decisions on how to provision access at scale and a degree of performance.

The ability to access geospatial subsets of contiguous data is often used for specific geological data. We shall see in the petrophysical use cases that it is more often the case that there are relationships at play in the data that are hidden from us. We insist on storing and manipulating the data as a 2D or 3D unit rather than letting the data show us the dimensions in which it contains the most information.

As long as data governance is strong, that is, you don't lose the information (aka master data) about coordinate reference systems, reference ellipsoids, and the reference datum of a dataset, then it is possible to take more abstract relationships in the data and project them faithfully back into our physical world.

Textual Data

Textual data in this sense refers to documents, as well as comment fields within applications, that contain written information that can be incorporated into a data-driven study. This is more typically to add context to numerical data rather than as a source of statistical or measurement data in its own right. Text analysis is a massive area of research and we introduce it here to signpost its applicability and low barrier to entry.

At its simplest text analysis looks for words and clusters of words in a document. The end goal is to distill a document into a reduced vocabulary that can be extended to other data types. Examples are equipment inspection and operational notes, geological interpretation, or observations during seismic acquisition. Commonly occurring words are identified and then tuples of two, three, and four words are inspected for deeper context (e.g., sandstone, fine-grained sandstone, fine sandstone).

Adjustments for spelling can be made, and eventually, a reduced vocabulary can be derived. Where the data quality is high, it has been possible to develop predictive models of varying validity, and more sophisticated statistical approaches in this area are discussed by Chen et al. (2010).

Hence, the transformation is not a simple geometric or structural manipulation of the data. It is the extraction of information contained in the data—information that is then becoming a property or attribute to provide context about a location, area, event, period, and so on. Hold this thought as we progress through feature engineering.

Making Your Data Useable

A critical capability in your data science skillset is the ability to understand when you have a data quality issue. It is straightforward to inspect data and see where non-numerical characters occur where you expect to see a number. However, it requires increasing degrees of sophistication to establish what a range of allowable values are; what the expected precision should be; or whether a blank, a null, an NaN (not a number), or a value (e.g., −999 in LAS files) should be respected and resolved by imputation. Data should be engineered such that rules are developed and applied consistently—in agreement with a domain expert where necessary—to ensure that insight is robust from the first pass and that any future work builds on strong foundations.

Dealing with poor-quality data by removing values can lead to another problem—data sparsity. Is there enough information contained in a dataset for meaningful insight? Sparsity also requires rules. If data is missing, then should the last value be used, or a null value, or an interpolated value? If it is interpolated, then what approach should be utilized?

If data is prone to error—mainly instrumental error—then statistical methods should be used to smooth it. Such approaches could be as simple as a running mean, applied by passing a window along a dataset, to more sophisticated statistical techniques, including *statistical process control* and *moving-window principal component analysis* (PCA). This is entering the territory of time-series analysis, and there are a multitude of techniques that can be deployed. As in the real world, it is feasible to clean data too much; a smoothing filter or overly aggressive interpolation will remove the very detail and variability that contains the information required for the analysis. This is where an iteration through domain expertise is vital to ensure that data and insights are statistically valid while retaining as much information in the source data as possible. Good data engineering will then allow this to be built up and appended efficiently.

The Road to Data Science Perfection

We apologize for the tongue-in-cheek heading, as perfection is something that we see as a long way off at the time of writing—and something we hope to see changing in our geoscience world quite soon. We hope that the following reasoning—based on many analytical projects executed by the authors—shows the value of getting the data preparation workflow as robust as possible before embarking on what may seem to a business stakeholder as the high-value activity of analysis. Our experience gives rise to a cautionary and measured approach.

Data Profiling

Data profiling goes beyond basic error checking to tell us something about the behavior or character of the data. Simple metrics such as its variability or standard deviation are useful, as are ranges, means, and medians. This is elementary statistics, but it is a mathematical domain that many geoscientists may not have encountered for some time. We illustrate this with well-logging data in Chapter 3, concerning petrophysical data, where statistical profiling at the formation level is a simple and efficient metric that can be stored alongside the raw data.

At a more generalized level, consider an infinitely long time series of data. There is a signal contained in the data, and for a thought experiment it can be a simple harmonic signal with a lot of background noise. Imagine you are listening to a flute being played through a thin wall and the window is open so traffic noise is there in the background and must be filtered out. Suppose a flute plays a concert pitch note of A above middle C (440 Hz) and the sound is being sampled 1 ms; then you acquire 1000 bytes per second. We are assuming that you can describe the amplitude of your microphone in a 32-bit byte (this is reasonable, so don't think too hard about it).

Now, what if the pitch of the flute rises and falls for whatever reason. As a subject matter expert (i.e., you're the neighbor who listens to this all day and every day) you observe that this rising and falling off a constant note is not abrupt but changes slightly over a period of many seconds. Continuing in this imaginary world and pretending that we are set the task of monitoring the pitch of the flute over the course of several hours, let's say that we only have a spreadsheet for the purpose. It becomes apparent that we will overcome the size limitations within a matter of minutes if we attempt to record sound intensity as measured by a microphone every millisecond.

This is the idea of profiling surfaces. It is not the raw data, but the frequency (or pitch) of the data at any given instant that interests us. Moreover, as the frequency is varying slowly, it only requires samples every ten seconds, per our subject matter expertise. Hence we now have one number—pitch—that describes the data at a given period, say every second. This provides all relevant information but reduced bin volume by three orders of magnitude. Signal processing may be required to extract this from the background noise, but judicious filtering will achieve this and leave the necessary signal intact.

Now consider the background noise. There is the steady hum of traffic and potentially the odd aircraft. We notice that as an airplane passes overhead, the music becomes livelier with sequences of notes being played. Our flutist neighbor is an aircraft fan and the sight of a plane lifts the music. If we are calculating the standard deviation (a measure of the variability) in the data through time, we see that it has a higher range and standard deviation of its pitch at such times and a linear regression performed by the data scientist backs this up readily.

Is there a way of characterizing what our neighbor plays when a plane is sighted? There is, and this is feature engineering. We see that there is a characteristic pattern of the notes, for instance, and we always hear a progression of the same four notes when sighting a plane. This progression is a pattern or feature that we should keep as we now have an early warning that an aircraft is approaching and we should close our windows to avoid the deafening noise. We have just performed a feature engineering thought experiment.

Feature Engineering

Using the example of a set of notes to define a feature, it should be evident that there are many applications to this in geosciences data. This could be the sea state or tidal behavior in maritime operations, a litho-facies in a well log, acoustic facies in a seismic survey, or a dynamic reservoir effect seen in production response.

Put simply, feature engineering allows a geoscientist to identify and capture all the exciting aspects of a dataset that would have been sketched and noted in a field notebook in the physical world. Data science techniques lead to the prominent features, and it is the subject matter expert—in this book, the geoscientist—who then assigns context or meaning or otherwise. Even better is to allow other data to provide the context.

It is beyond the scope of this chapter to review specific use cases or algorithms as data, and mathematical approaches display so much diversity across the E&P domain. The purpose of this extended thought experiment is to show that it is at least equally useful—if not more so—to present the raw data in an accessible and well-curated form. We must also keep profile data and key features of the data alongside it. It is the features that provide the analytical hooks: "Where do I hear this sequence of notes?" becomes "Where do I see these facies?"

Analytical Building Blocks

These features and statistical parameters become analytical building blocks. As familiarity with your data evolves, so the statistical methods become more sophisticated and more abstract. It is at the feature engineering level that the subject matter expertise needs to bake in a lot of the scientific relationships in the data. At risk of laboring the point, the data quality and data preparation strategies are vital if the features are to be useful for longstanding analytical deployment in a business context.

In many cases, it is these features rather than the raw data itself that become the starting point for regression and machine learning (ML) algorithms. If the subject matter expert has validated that the features and statistical metrics contain sufficient information about the data, then there is a much higher likelihood of running successful ML workflows on the data at scale as opposed to developing an architecture for data mining, statistical processing, and ML workflows of granular data at scale.

It should become the norm for dimension reduction and characterization steps to be performed, and the benefits of good data governance become apparent if these features are to be reused across several studies at the scale of a large organization like an oil company or the academic community. Equally, well-crafted and -engineered features may well become the intellectual property of an organization if the competitive benefit can be derived from their ownership. This question is likely to vex the industry for several years hence!

IS IT INDUCTION OR DEDUCTION?

"Though this be madness, yet there is method in it."

Hamlet

The objective behind *deep learning* (DL) is without question the art form that is *induction*. How does it differentiate from *deduction*?

- *Induction:* the cerebral path from factual minutiae to general principles.
- *Deduction:* traveling in the opposite direction to induction, it follows the reasoning from the general to the specifics or from cause to effect.

Through induction in deep learning we are striving to make sense of the big data accumulated across disparate engineering sources: data from multiple sensors that record what has happened in the system under investigation. We then draw grandiose conclusions as we identify trends and patterns in these datasets. Essentially, we are reverse-engineering Mother Nature's physical laws and first principles. As Polonius observed in Hamlet: it is the uncovering of the *method* in the *madness*.

We must make assumptions during our induction process since there are many irrational behaviors noted in the data. There is no such thing as a perfect understanding of the way a system works. Hence the learning method is based on simple assumptions that are an intelligent way to identify patterns that are useful in our DL methodology.

It seems the Oil and Gas industry is riddled with engineers and geoscientists who are tightly anchored to the deductive reasoning espoused by Aristotle and posited by Hobbes in his arguments with Wallis in the 1600s. If the analytical methodology is deficient in rigor and invariably takes you down the road to paradoxes, then it is *not* precise and scientifically acceptable. Zeno's famous example of contradictions, illustrating the celebrated "Achilles and the Tortoise" enigma, adds substance to contemporary attitudes against inductive logic. Why was the

Royal Society initially distrustful of mathematics when established in England during the 1600s? Because of the illustrious founder, fellows such as William Ball, Sir Robert Moray, and subsequently Wallis and Wren revered experimental science. Of course, much of the argument for inductive as opposed to deductive reasoning was born from the liberal ideals of the day that fought the Jesuit iron fist that seemed to be choking society in the seventeenth century.

However, Wallis, who stood as the single mathematician in the hallowed corridors of the Royal Society, took up the mantle to merge mathematics with the life force of the Society. He claimed, "Mathematical entities exist not in the imagination but reality." In short, he supported the experimental methodology that has since evolved into today's data-driven analytical workflows under the banner of *data science*. This is in stark contrast to the Euclidean perspective of geometry. Wallis argued that constructing geometrical objects from the first principles is contrary to the natural world order where such geometry exists in Mother Nature. He stated that the study of geometrical figures was analogous to examining the geologic strata in the subsurface. Like Wallis, the modern geoscientists should rely more on inductive logic and hence integrate data-driven methodologies within the rigorous context of the first principles. Why? Because simple deduction stifles new ideas and induction paves the way to revolutionary ideas being seeded as we toy with new perspectives that reflect the reality of nature. Without induction, Newton would not have invented calculus as a branch of mathematics to address the issues generated by the "method of indivisibles," a suspicious technique per the Jesuits who poured scorn on those striving for an explanation of "infinitesimals." So, let us not reject induction when applying a reasoned and logical approach to solving reservoir characterization or simulation across the geophysical and petrophysical sciences. Stuck in deduction just to adhere to the first principles will deflect from the realistic, even if probabilistic, results garnered from a data-driven methodology born in induction.

The Oil and Gas E&P activities are at an intersection. There is an increasing strain between the accepted and prevailing image of mathematics as an assemblage of eternal and unchanging truths and its actual implementation in the global reservoirs replete with uncertainties, frustrations, and failures. Do we as geoscientists wish to perpetuate, like the Jesuits in the 1600s, the appearance of academic infallibility at the expense of exploring new ground and innovative techniques? Remember theoretical and practical advancements in all sciences are invariably engendered from bizarre ideas.

With that in mind, let us uncover the probabilistic insights from some advanced data-driven techniques applied across the geophysical and petrophysical sciences when applied to data generated in these silos.

REFERENCES

Abdul-Rahman, Alias, and Morakot Pilouk, *Spatial Data Modelling for 3D GIS* (2008). DOI: 10.1007/978-3-540-74167-1.

Amir, Alexander, "Infinitesimal: How a Dangerous Mathematical Theory, Shaped the Modern World," *Scientific American*/Farrar, Straus & Giroux (April 2014).

Boman, Karen, "Study: Low Oil Price Gives Industry Chance to Pursue Digital Transformation," *Rigzone*, May 12, 2015, www.rigzone.com/news/oil_gas/a/138503/Study_Low_Oil_Price_Gives_Industry_Chance_to_Pursue_Digital_Transformation, accessed July 27, 2015.

Chen J., Z. Li, and B. Bian, "Application of Data Mining in Multi-Geological-Factor Analysis." In: Cai Z., C. Hu, Z. Kang, and Y. Liu (eds.), "Advances in Computation and Intelligence," ISICA 2010, *Lecture Notes in Computer Science*, vol. 6382, Springer, Berlin, Heidelberg. DOI: 10.1007/978-3-642-16493-4_41.

Davenport, T. H., Harris, J. G., *Competing on Analytics: The New Science of Winning*, 2007.

Ferry, G., *A Computer called LEO: Lyons Tea Shops and the World's First Office Computer*, 2010.

Jacobs, Trent, "High-Pressure/High-Temperature BOP Equipment Becoming a Reality," *Journal of Petroleum Technology*, 67, no. 7, www.spe.org/jpt/article/6707-ep-notes-5/, accessed July 27, 2015.

Kane, Gerald C. et al., "Strategy, Not Technology, Drives Digital Transformation," Deloitte University Press, Summer 2015, http://52.7.214.27/articles/digital-transformation-strategy-digitally-mature/, accessed July 27, 2015.

Slaughter, A., G. Bean, and A. Mittal, "Connected Barrels: Transforming Oil and Gas Strategies with the Internet of Things" (2015), https://dupress.deloitte.com/content/dam/dup-us-en/articles/iot-in-oil-and-gas-industry/DUP-1169_IoT_OilGas.pdf.

Teradata, "Reduce Operational Complexity to Cut NPT," www.teradata.com/industry-expertise/oil-and-gas/, accessed July 27, 2015.

CHAPTER 2

Data-Driven Analytical Methods Used in E&P

"There is a tide in the affairs of men. Which, taken at the flood, leads on to fortune; Omitted, all the voyage of their life is bound in shallows and in miseries. On such a full sea are we now afloat, and we must take the current when it serves, or lose our ventures."

William Shakespeare
Julius Caesar, Act 4, Scene 3, 218–224

INTRODUCTION

Generations of geoscientists have passed through the scholastic corridors of global institutions for advanced learning to achieve their graduate and post-graduate degrees. The syllabi have been based on first principles and engineering concepts. These empirical algorithms are underpinned by pure and applied mathematics, the observations made by Newton, the genius of Einstein, and many theoretical physicists driven to understand the subatomic world of quantum physics.

We need to find common ground where physics and mathematics can play with the ever-increasing datasets, both hard and soft measurements, to enable predictive and prescriptive analytical methodologies. Let us start with the premise that soft computing techniques such as artificial neural networks and decision trees, just two examples among a litany of different probabilistic models, can be more useful and potentially far more robust by feeding them with a physics or mathematical model. In the oil and gas field evaluations, it is imperative to estimate unknown values for the primary parameters and quantify the uncertainty inherent in these parameters. We can determine these parameters using correlations or estimates determined by third-party vendors or even make our calculations via statistical algorithms. But there are traps hidden along the path to identifying functional relationships that yield these measurements. There are higher risks associated with decisions dependent on the knowledge garnered from the raw datasets.

Be aware that not everything you do results in an actionable impact on your business objective. The three broad, interrelated systems witnessed in oil and gas activities, namely, *reservoir, wells,* and *surface facilities,* are complex and heterogeneous by nature and determining those parameters that cause changes within each system and across systems is, even under ideal conditions, nearly impossible and subjective.

The Oil and Gas industry is piecemeal adopting the concepts that underpin big data and data-driven methodologies. Real-time data flows from intelligent wells equipped with multiple sensors are aggregated with myriad sources of different structured hard and soft data. It is very apparent that a comprehensive suite of data-driven workflows is required to gather actionable knowledge from the tsunami of raw data now in the pipeline. To clarify and expand the data landscape, we now have a toolbox replenished with solutions that can gain insight and surface patterns from unstructured data. Data mining techniques are no longer an interesting study; they have manifested into a de facto standard that engineers ignore at their peril as they struggle to make sense of the big data analytics paradigm.

In oil and gas exploration we have both *spatial* and *temporal* datasets. Let us define these two perspectives from a geophysicist's and petrophysicist's perspective:

Spatial Datasets

The strength of the correlation between two random geophysical or petrophysical properties is reflected in probability theory as the covariance measure. Such linear relationships underpin the spatial dimension of an *exploration and production* (E&P) model. These geophysical attributes or petrophysical properties at proximal points in space can be correlated from a positive or a negative perspective. Autocorrelation in the spatial domain, like temporal autocorrelation, contravenes basic statistical procedures as there is an expectation of independence across all observations in a spatial dependent model.

Temporal Datasets

When we study time series data, it is advantageous to perform analytical workflows in either the time-offset domain or post-Fourier Transform, in the frequency-wavenumber domain. It is feasible to run spectral analysis as well as wavelet analysis and determine autocorrelation and cross-correlation analyses to garner insightful characteristics that shed light on the complexity inherent in reservoir data, both geophysical and petrophysical.

There are two distinct families of time series analytical methods, namely parametric and nonparametric. The former assumes a particular structure underpins a stationary stochastic process. You only need a small number of parameters to define the structure. Autoregressive (AR) and moving average (MA) processes are parametric. Both methods estimate the model's parameters detailing the stochastic process. By contrast, non-parametric methods explicitly evaluate the process's covariance with no preordained assumption regarding the internal structure of the process. We can also divide time series algorithms into linear or nonlinear, and from a univariate and multivariate perspective.

With the growth of connected sensors and the ever-increasing data landscape of diverse sources, both unstructured and structured, we are witnessing an acceleration of adoption across automated and related assets. Both batch and real-time data mining are critical methodologies to surface hidden patterns and turn raw data into actionable knowledge. Three key business sectors impact E&P: data management, quantification of uncertainty, and risk assessment. And the two major analytical workflows implemented to address these three areas are named exploratory and predictive data analysis. The former identifies hypotheses worth modeling to refine the multivariate, multidimensional, and complex input space. The latter builds on the model datasets generated by and the lessons learned from the exploratory data analysis (EDA) to map business issues to objective functions. This process enables the development of predictive models that are operationalized in real-time data streams to identify hidden signatures.

Resources such as engineers, technology, and analytical methodologies underpin a comprehensive reservoir management platform. The ideal time to start managing a reservoir is at the discovery stage. However, a well-thought-out, coordinated reservoir management program is always topical and enriched by data-driven time series analytical methodologies.

Reservoir characterization and simulation are two workflows that underpin a 3D model of oil and gas fields. The model is used for reserves estimation, for cost-effective well placement and enhanced oil recovery strategies in a mature field. Soft computing techniques such as neural networks, fuzzy logic, genetic algorithms and pattern matching data-driven models have demonstrated that it is feasible to get more active models compared with conventional interpretive methodologies.

Seismic analytical workflows implementing soft computing techniques such as artificial neural networks have been established for several decades. There are multiple examples of case studies that map seismic attributes to rock properties. We shall create critical bedrock methodologies to delve deeper into seismic attribute analytical workflows taking advantage of data-driven models implementing data mining techniques to surface hidden patterns and trends in exploration.

It is imperative to understand the historical context that has inexorably led to the current adoption of data-driven models to supplement the traditional deterministic methodologies as we walk through some of the cornerstones of soft computing techniques in the Oil and Gas industry.

SOFT COMPUTING TECHNIQUES

Data mining is often defined as the process of finding patterns in datasets. This definition has many implications. One is that the data is mostly opportunistic, in the sense that it was not necessarily acquired for statistical inference. A significant part of a data mining study is devoted to iterative cycles of data investigation: cleansing, aggregation, transformation, and modeling. Another implication is that models are often built on data with scores of observations or variables. Statistical methods must be chosen and implemented carefully for scalability. Finally, a data mining model must be actionable.

In the E&P domain, there are multiple scientific disciplines. They could all benefit from the various soft computing technologies derived as data mining workflows, as depicted in Figure 2.1.

Stable rules (models) can predict the values of target variables dependent on the values of the different independent variables for each dataset observation. After establishing useful rules, we can apply them to new datasets (scoring) that might contain the variable or variables to be predicted.

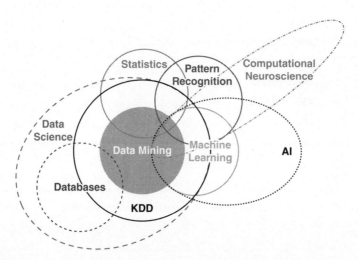

Figure 2.1 Multidisciplinary nature of soft computing technologies

There are many tools for predictive modeling. Regression, decision tree analysis, and artificial neural networks are familiar to most geophysicists and petrophysicists. But soft computing techniques seem to grow in number inexorably as innovative algorithms become part of the everyday vernacular. Machine learning (ML) and deep learning (DL) methods tempt our interests daily and educate us as to their adoption across different vertical businesses. So before discussing predictive modeling methods in geophysics and petrophysics, it will be helpful to clarify the terms under discussion.

Data Mining Nomenclature

- **Model:** A model is a class of algorithms that computes outputs from inputs. A statistical model includes knowledge of the conditional distribution of the dependent variables based on the independent variables ingested by the model. See the definition for trained model.
  Synonyms: classifier, equation, function
- **Weights:** Weights are typically unknown quantities used in the models before any analysis is carried out on the data under study.
  Synonyms: estimated parameters, regression coefficients
- **Training:** The process of computing real values for the model's weights. Tree-based models require training based on optimum split variables and associated values.
  Synonyms: estimation, fitting, learning, adaptation, induction, growing
- **Trained Model:** A trained model computes outputs given specific inputs. A training algorithm selects all the weights or parameter approximations in the model based on a class of designer algorithms.
  Synonym: fitted model

- **Noise:** Noise, be it random or coherent, represents an unpredictable discrepancy found in a dependent variable. If a petrophysicist modeled identical input parameter values and assigned various target parameters, the disparity in those different target values is unpredictable by any model ingesting only those inputs. The variation is noise. Noise, if random, is inherently unpredictable. Since noise prevents target values from being accurately predicted, the distribution of the noise can be estimated statistically given enough data.

  Synonym: error

- **Signal:** Target variables sometimes have predictable variation, and this is called a signal. It is often assumed that target values are the sum of signal and noise, where the signal is a function of the input variables.

  Synonyms: function, systematic component

- **Training Data:** Data consisting of dependent and independent parameter values, used for training to approximate weights and values of other parameters.

  Synonyms: training set, design set

- **Test Data:** Data consisting of dependent and independent parameter values, not used during training, but used to approximate generalization errors.

  Synonym: test dataset

- **Validation Data:** Data consisting of dependent and independent parameter values used indirectly during training for model selection.

  Synonym: validation set

- **Scoring:** We apply a trained model to our data to calculate outputs.

  Synonyms: running (for neural nets), simulating (for neural nets), filtering (for trees), interpolating, extrapolating

- **Interpolation:** Interpolation is an approximation of a value between two identified measurements of a localized property. Petrophysicists determine permeability at the well locations and then estimate the permeability between the wells.

- **Extrapolation:** By extrapolating an approximation of a parameter value, such as a rock property measured in cores, we are extending an identified sequence of values beyond the localized value.

- **Operational Data:** Data to be scored containing independent variables but not dependent variables. Operational data in the Oil and Gas industry can also refer to those parameters under control of engineers. Reservoir properties are the domain of Mother Nature and hence are coined as nonoperational.

    Synonym: scoring data

- **Categorical Variable:** A categorical variable is used for mutual exclusivity. It is not an ordered category. For example, geophysicists might compare different seismic attributes. We can code these attributes with numeric values as long as the order is arbitrary and any estimates are worthless.

    Synonyms: class variable, nominal variable, label

- **Category:** One of the probable values of a categorical variable.

    Synonyms: class, level, label

- **Class Variable:** A class variable is a categorical target variable, and classification means assigning cases to categories of a dependent variable. A class variable is a categorical variable, either an input or a target.

- **Measurement:** The process of assigning numbers to a characteristic of an object. The numbers' properties reflect an attribute of the object or events in the case of a time series.

- **Measurement Level:** One of the several ways in which properties of numbers can reflect attributes of things. Standard measurement levels are nominal, ordinal, interval, log-interval, ratio, and absolute.

- **Nominal Variable:** A numeric or character categorical variable. The categories are unordered. The values of each category carry no supplementary information beyond the category membership.

- **Ordinal Variable:** The order is important, but any differences between the values are immaterial. For example, a petrophysicist might express the hardness of a rock using Moh's scale of 1 to 10. However, a score of 8 means a harder rock than one scored at 6, and that is more than 4, but the difference between 8 and 6 is not the same as that between 6 and 4.

- **Interval Variable:** An interval variable reflects a meaningful difference in measurement between two variables.

- **Ratio Variable:** A ratio variable is similar to an interval variable and carries a defined value of 0.0. The weight of proppant in a hydraulic strategy is a ratio variable, but the temperature is not, as $100°$ C is not twice as hot as $50°$ C, but 1000 lbs is twice as much a 500 lbs.

- **Binary Variable:** A binary variable has only two distinct values. A binary variable can be legitimately treated as nominal, ordinal, interval, or sometimes ratio.

Some of the soft computing techniques discussed in this book are summarized here for useful reference.

Decision Trees

We can represent the segmentation or breakdown of the data by a decision tree, guided by a suite of simple rules. The stipulated rules look at each observation or row of data and allocate it to a section based on the value of one input. The iterative application of rules results in a hierarchy of segments within segments. A decision tree is a hierarchy, and each segment is called a node of the tree. All the data makes up the original segment and represents the root node of the tree. Branches grow from the nodes, and leaves represent the terminal nodes. At the lcaf level, a decision is made and applied to all observations in the leaf. Contextual data determines the kind of decision. In predictive modeling, the decision is the predicted value.

You use the *decision tree* to create a model that does one of the following tasks:

- Classifies observations based on the values of nominal, binary, or ordinal targets
- Predicts outcomes for interval targets
- Predicts the appropriate decision when you specify decision alternatives

An advantage of the decision tree over other modeling techniques, such as the *neural network*, is that it produces output that describes the scoring model with interpretable rules. Another advantage of the decision tree is the treatment of missing data. The search for a splitting rule uses the missing values of an input observation. Surrogate rules are available as a backup when missing data prohibits the application of a splitting rule.

RULES-BASED METHODS

Rules-based techniques fall into the same family of soft computing methods as the decision trees. However, there is no rigid hierarchical partitioning of the training set for rules-based workflows. The lack of rigidity enables an overlapping option to generate a more robust training model and a more general predictive model. This approach is suitable for analysis of petrophysical datasets to classify rock characteristics of subtle facies changes in complex structural reservoirs.

Regression

You use regression to fit both linear and logistic regression models to a predecessor dataset. Linear regression strives to predict the value of an interval target as a linear function of one or more independent inputs. However, the logistic regression method predicts the probability that an ordinal or binary dependent variable will attain the event under study as a function of one or more independent inputs.

You can also use a neural network to build regression models. In this case, you should configure the network to have direct connections between the input units and the output unit(s) without including any hidden units. Direct connections define linear layers, whereas hidden neurons define nonlinear layers. The neural network supports more link functions (such as identity, logit, log, square root, and reciprocal) and more error functions (such as normal, Poisson, and gamma) than does regression. Neural networks also have robust estimation capabilities (such as Cauchy, logistic, and Huber).

Regression uses an identity link function and a normal distribution error function for linear regression. Regression uses either a logit, complementary log-log, or binomial distribution error function for a logistic regression analysis. A disadvantage in using the neural network for a regression analysis is that it does not provide p-values for testing the significance of the parameter estimates.

Classification Tasks

In classification tasks, we are trying to produce a model that can give the correlation between the input data X and the class C to which each input belongs. This model is formed with the feature values of the input data. For example, the dataset contained data points belonging to the classes Apples, Pears, and Oranges, and based on the features of the data points (weight, color, size, etc.) we are trying to predict the class.

The classifier requires a certain amount of training data to generate a reliable model. The trained classifier is then ideally suited to categorize new observations. The well-trained classifier can predict the class probabilities of new data within stipulated confidence intervals.

There are four traditional classifiers that use different mathematical approaches to classifying data:

- *Naive Bayes*, which uses a statistical (Bayesian) method
- *Discriminant analysis*, which uses quadratic, linear, regularized, and wide linear fitting methods
- *Logistic regression*, which uses a functional approach
- *Support vector machines*, which use a geometrical methodology

Bayes' Theorem

From a purely statistical perspective, we would implement the Bayes' classification technique. There are several basic data classification methods, and the probabilistic approach underpins all the techniques. The probabilistic classification adopts a statistical inference method to ascertain the most suitable class for the data under study. Beyond optimum class assignation, the probabilistic classification technique delivers an equal posterior probability of the trial instance being a participant of all possible classes. The prior probability represents that fraction of all the training observations that are members of each class, regardless of any knowledge inherent in the trial instance. Decision theory is the preferred choice to implement class membership identification for all new instances, based on the posterior probabilities.

Discriminant Analysis

Discriminant analysis endeavors to classify rows of data defined by values of continuous variables into clusters. Group affiliation, identified by a categorical variable X, is predicted by the continuous variables. These variables are called covariates and are denoted by Y. In discriminant analysis, the classifications are fixed and the covariates (Y) are realizations of random variables. However, like logistic regression, the categorical value is predicted by the continuous variables.

The four fitting methods are:

1. *Linear:* Assumes that the within-group covariance matrices are equal. The covariate means for the groups defined by X are expected to differ.

2. *Quadratic:* Assumes that the covariance matrices differ within the group. A quadratic method estimates values based on more parameters than a linear method. Small group sample sizes tend to generate unstable estimates for quadratic fitting.

3. *Regularized:* Provides two methods to ensure stability on estimates when the within-group covariance matrices differ. This is useful if group sample sizes are small.

4. *Wide linear:* This method is most appropriate when fitting models based on a large number of covariates. There is an assumption that all covariance matrices are equal.

Logistic Regression

Logistic regression is a method to identify a binary outcome variable (e.g., good/bad). In the world of geophysics or petrophysics, the X-variables may be seismic attributes or rock properties used to build a mathematical algorithm to predict the probability that the Y-variable, direct hydrocarbon indicator (DHI) or reservoir rock, takes on a value of 1 or 0. So, we implement logistic regression workflows when it is feasible to address a business problem in E&P with the knowledge of a Y-variable being 0 or 1. Like flipping a coin, there is a likelihood of seeing a "heads" or a "tails" based on the X-variables. But, unlike tossing a coin, the probability of seeing tails is not always 50/50, since the result is dependent on the multivariate, multivariant, and stochastic values of all the X-variables.

Support Vector Machines

Super vector machines (SVMs) use linear conditions to isolate classes from each other. The methodology known as SVM executes binary linear classification as well as a nonlinear classification. It uses a mapping of the input geophysical and petrophysical data into a high-dimensional feature space.

We can map rows of data as points in a hyperplane or even a suite of hyperplanes in a multidimensional input space. When trying to resolve data-driven workflows with both geophysical and petrophysical data, we find that the information space is invariably both multidimensional and multivariate. The mapping process allows us to distinguish the separate categories by the largest distance or functional margin. As we introduce new data points into the SVM workflow, the algorithm maps these points into the same space. The predictive component then associates the new observations to a category that reflects the side of the margin most appropriate.

Ensemble Methodology

The ensemble methodology generates models by uniting the posterior probabilities or the predicted values from multiple precursor models. The ensemble model is used to score new data. The ensemble workflow supports group processing options of indexing, stratifying (looping over variables), cross-validating, stacking, bagging, and boosting.

The bagging aggregation approach diminishes the possibilities of overfitting a model. The process, also known as bootstrapping, averages the models under consideration by creating more learning datasets of the same size in various combinations, developed from the original input dataset. The bagging or bootstrapping methodology determines probabilistic estimates within a predefined confidence interval. So, it is deemed a statistical method to evaluate the uncertainty inherent in the estimates objectively.

A bootstrap forest, for example, averages the predicted values of multiple decision trees. Thus, we only consider an arbitrary population sampled from the observations for each of the trees under study to generate a "forest" perspective. This methodology ensures that most of the independent variables under consideration carry a statistical benefit to predict the target or response variable. Row and column exclusion empower the bootstrap forest to surface correlations hidden in the data. Studying those variables that are populated by non-zero values across the observations allows us to detect the factors that statistically impact the target variable, even if by a subtle quantity. It is important to identify the factors that have the most predictive power and hence the highest contribution to the ensemble model, in this case the bootstrap forest.

Boosting is implemented to diminish data variance and bias. It is an iterative process to learn from weighted-average datasets to evolve from a weak to a strong learning dataset. To avoid a misclassification of the weight change, we compute the weight after each weak learner step.

Another methodology is stacking. This approach mingles several models to endorse a concept known as meta-learning. These are typical phases followed by a stacking process to deliver an ensemble model:

1. Divide the training set into two parts.
2. Use one part to train a few base learners.
3. Measure the base learners against the second part.
4. Prepare a learner at a higher and more robust level with the predictions calculated from the previous phases and with the accurate responses as the outputs.

The cross-validation methodology splits the data into multiple k-sets or k-folds, often referred to as k-fold cross-validation.

We can then estimate k models, where each model is generated with the data that is residual, after a single fold from the existing data. This allows us to score the fold excluded when estimating it. The final ensemble model characterizes an averaging process of all the k models under study from both a predictive perspective and a statistically evaluated perspective. The cross-validation approach is conducive to studies populated by small datasets, but the drawback is probably the ensemble model's weakness for generality.

One ensemble method is to aggregate several modeling methods, such as a decision tree and an artificial neural network, to get separate models from the same training dataset. The component models from the two complementary modeling methods are integrated into an ensemble model to form the final solution, as depicted in Figure 2.2.

An ensemble model is more accurate than the constituent models only if the individual models are in disagreement. It is critical to compare the ensemble model performance with the efficacy of the individual models.

Partial Least Squares

Data mining problems that might traditionally be approached using multiple linear regression techniques become more complicated when there are many input variables or there is significant collinearity between variables. In these instances,

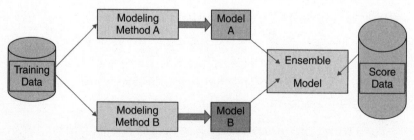

Figure 2.2 Analytical workflow demonstrating an ensemble model

regression models tend to overfit the training data and do not perform well when modeling other data. Often this is the case when just a few latent variables among the many input variables are accountable for most of the variation in response or target variable values.

Partial least squares is a methodology that is useful for extracting the latent input variables that account for the greatest variation in the predicted target. PLS means "projection to latent structures" and is helpful for identifying latent variables from a large pool. But, the analytical results of the PLS workflow are not useful in identifying variables of minor or no importance.

Traditional Neural Networks: The Details

Units and Connections

A neural network consists of units (neurons) and connections between those units. There are three kinds of units.

1. Input units obtain the values of input variables and optionally standardize those values.
2. Hidden units perform internal computations, providing the nonlinearity that makes neural networks compelling.
3. Output units compute predicted values and compare those predicted values with the values of the target variables.

Units pass information to other units through connections. Links are directional and indicate the flow of computation within the network. Connections cannot form loops since the neural network node allows only feedforward networks.

The following restrictions apply to feedforward networks:

- Input units can be connected to hidden units or output units.
- Hidden units can be connected to other hidden units or output units.
- Output units cannot be connected to other units.

Predicted Values and Error Functions

Each unit produces a single computed value. For input and hidden units, this calculated value is passed along the connections to other hidden or output units. For output units, the estimated value is what statisticians call a predicted value. The predicted value is compared with the target value to calculate the error function, which the training methods attempt to minimize.

Weight, Bias, and Altitude

Most connections in a network have an associated numeric value called a weight or parameter estimate. The training methods attempt to minimize the error function by iteratively adjusting the values of the weights. Most units also have one or two associated numeric values called the bias and altitude, which are also estimated parameters adjusted by the training methods.

Combination Functions

Hidden and output units use two functions to produce their computed values. First, all the calculated values from previous units feeding into the given unit are combined into a single value using a combination function. The combination function uses the weights, bias, and altitude.

Two general kinds of combination function are commonly used.

1. *Linear combination functions* compute a linear combination of the weights and the values feeding into the unit and then add the bias value (the bias acts like an intercept).
2. *Radial combination functions* compute the squared Euclidean distance between the vector of weights and the vector of values feeding into the unit and then multiply by the squared bias value (the bias acts as a scale factor or inverse width).

Activation Functions

The value produced by the combination function is transformed by an *activation function*, which involves no weights or other estimated parameters. Several general kinds of activation functions are commonly used.

- Identity function is also called a linear function. It does not change the value of the argument and its range is potentially unbounded.
- Sigmoid functions are S-shaped functions such as the logistic and hyperbolic tangent functions that produce bounded values within a range of 0 to 1 or −1 to 1.
- Softmax function is called a multiple logistic function by statisticians and is a generalization of the logistic function that affects several units together, forcing the sum of their values to be one.
- Value functions are bounded bell-shaped functions such as the Gaussian function.
- Exponential and reciprocal functions are bounded below by zero but unbounded above.

Network Layers

A network may contain many units, perhaps several hundred. The units are grouped into layers to make them easier to manage. Invariably there is an input layer, a hidden layer, and multiple output layers. In the neural network, when you connect two layers, every unit in the first layer is connected to every unit in the second layer.

All the units in each layer share certain characteristics. For example, all the input units in each layer have the same measurement level and the same method of standardization. All the units in each hidden layer have the same combination function and the same activation function. All the units in an output layer have the same combination function, activation function, and error function.

Simple Neural Networks

Overview

The simplest neural network has a single input unit (independent variable), a single target (dependent variable), and a single output unit (predicted values), as depicted in Figure 2.3.

The slash inside the box represents a linear (or identity) output activation function. In statistical terms, this network is a simple linear regression model. If the output activation function were a logistic function, then this network would be a logistic regression model.

When a neural network is applied to seismic data to identify reservoir properties, we must be cognizant of two critical steps that are potential traps:

1. Selection step
2. Learning step

Both these steps have a significant influence on the network efficiency and the credibility and robustness of the results. Per Romeo (1994), there are three explanations for poor performance:

1. Inadequate network configuration
2. Training algorithm confined to a local minimum
3. Incongruous training dataset

Network configuration or architectural design is critical. One of the key drivers behind the architecture of a deep neural

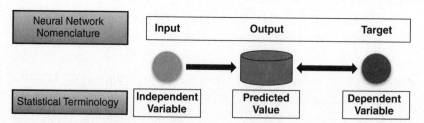

Figure 2.3 Simplest expression of a neural network

network, no matter its algorithm, is the number of hidden layers and the number of neurons in each layer. We are striving to describe the underlying statistical distribution of the input data spread. There are no rigid rules governing the number of layers and neurons, but Huang and Huang (1991) illustrate that the ceiling for the number of neurons per hidden layer should not exceed the number of training samples. And to constrain the training, the number of training samples must exceed the number of internal weights. By limiting the number of neurons, we can avoid overfitting.

The misfit function is invariably very complex (Hush et al., 1992). Such a phenomenon will trap the network in a local minimum instead of attaining a global aspect. It is important to initiate weights via random and non-random techniques and test several inversion algorithms.

The training set must be representative of the solution sought by the network. Too many bad patterns could be identified if the training set is incongruous to the desired output. The other negative impact is overtraining the network, resulting in a memorized set of patterns only appropriate for the training dataset. This behavior necessitates adequate splitting of the dataset into a training and validation dataset.

Perceptrons

One of the earliest neural network architectures was the *perceptron*, which is a type of linear discriminant model. A perceptron uses a linear combination of inputs for the combination function. Initially, perceptrons used a threshold (Heaviside) activation function, but training a network with threshold activation functions is computationally demanding. In current practice, the activation function is almost always a logistic function, which makes a perceptron equivalent in functional form to a logistic regression model.

As an example, a perceptron might have two inputs and a single output, as shown in Figure 2.4.

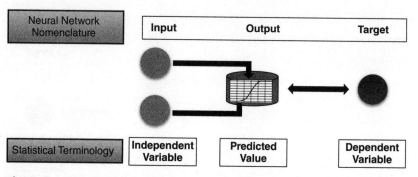

Figure 2.4 Perceptron architecture for a neural network

In neural network terms, the diagram shows two inputs connected to a single output with a logistic activation function (represented by the sigmoid curve in the box). In statistical terms, this diagram shows a logistic regression model with two independent variables and one dependent variable.

Hidden Layers

Neural networks may apply additional transformations via a hidden layer. Typically, each input unit is connected to each unit in the hidden layer and each hidden unit is connected to each output unit, as illustrated in Figure 2.5. The hidden units combine the input values and apply an activation function, which may be nonlinear. Then the values that were computed by the hidden units are combined at the output units, where an additional (possibly different) activation function is applied. If such a network uses linear combination functions and sigmoid activation functions, it is called a multilayer perceptron (MLP). It is also possible to use other combination functions and other activation functions to connect layers in many other ways. A network with three hidden units with different activation functions is shown in the following diagram.

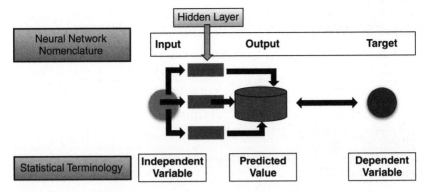

Figure 2.5 Hidden layer within the neural network architecture

Multilayer Perceptrons (MLPs)

The most popular form of neural network architecture is the *multilayer perceptron* (MLP), which is the default architecture in the neural network node.

A multilayer perceptron:

- Has any number of inputs
- Has a hidden layer with any number of units
- Uses linear combination functions in the hidden and output layers
- Uses sigmoid activation functions in the hidden layers
- Has any number of outputs with any activation function
- Has connections between the input layer and the first hidden layer, between the hidden layers, and between the last hidden layer and the output layer

The neural network node supports many variations of this general form. For example, you can add direct connections between the inputs and outputs, or you can cut the default connections and add new connections of your own.

Given enough data, enough hidden units, and enough training time, an MLP with one hidden layer can learn to estimate any function to any degree of accuracy. (A statistical analogy is approximating a function with nth-order polynomials.) For this reason, MLPs are called *universal approximators* and can be implemented based on limited prior knowledge of the relationship between inputs and targets.

Error Functions

A network is trained by minimizing an error function (also called an estimation criterion or Lyapunov function). Most error functions are based on the maximum likelihood principle, although computationally it is the negative log likelihood that is minimized. The probability builds on a family of error (noise) distributions for which the resulting estimator has various optimality properties. M-estimators are formally like maximum likelihood estimators, but for certain kinds called redescending M-estimators, no proper error distribution exists.

Some of the more commonly used error functions are:

- *Normal distribution*—also known as the least-squares or mean-squared-error criterion. Suitable for unbounded interval targets with constant conditional variance, no outliers, and a symmetric distribution. Can also be used for categorical targets with outliers.

- *Huber M-estimator*—suitable for unbounded interval targets with outliers or with a moderate degree of inequality of the conditional variance but a symmetric distribution. Can also be used for categorical targets when you want to predict the mode rather than the posterior probability.

- *Redescending M-estimators*—suitable for unbounded interval targets with severe outliers. Can also be used for predicting one mode of a multimodal distribution. It includes bi-weight and wave estimators.

- *Gamma distribution*—suitable for skewed, positive interval targets where the conditional standard deviation is proportional to the conditional mean.
- *Poisson distribution*—suitable for skewed, nonnegative interval targets, especially counts of rare events, where the conditional variance is proportional to the conditional mean.
- *Bernoulli distribution*—suitable for a target that takes only the values zero and one. Same as a binomial distribution with one trial.
- *Entropy*—cross or relative entropy for independent interval targets with values between zero and one inclusive.
- *Multiple Bernoulli*—suitable for categorical (nominal or ordinal) targets.
- *Multiple entropy*—cross or relative entropy for interval targets that sum to one and have values between zero and one inclusive. Also called Kullback-Leibler divergence.

Random Forests

A random forest collates a group of decision trees that each represent a randomly associated subset of the original data and then determines a predictive result from the ensemble methodology. Quite often we can witness overfitting in individual decision trees, but the random forest dramatically reduces such poor model behavior. How many trees make a forest? In the geophysics and petrophysics world of high-dimensional datasets, we could aggregate hundreds of decision trees.

All the decision trees within the random forest use diverse sets of data, each a subset of the original dataset.

1. Divide the rows containing the observations to form training datasets.
2. Make the columns representing the variables or factors available to each splitting node.

Gradient Boosting

Another example of an ensemble methodology is gradient boosting, which generates a resultant model from a suite of weak predictive models in a stepwise and sequential process. The algorithm is implemented to transform weak learners into stronger representations. In supervised learning, we see this technique reduce variance and bias hidden in the original data. We initialize the gradient boosting algorithm with weights of equal measure across all points. During the implementation, those points that are correctly categorized are then allocated a lower weight, and conversely, those points that are incorrectly classified are assigned a higher weighting value. You see the problem? Those points categorized correctly in the first wave are subsequently misclassified after the first iteration. This occurs for multiple iterations. Finally, all the models have associated a weight that is dependent on the accuracy. These model results are then aggregated to make one ensemble model with a unique effect. Gradient boosting is appropriate as a seismic feature extraction methodology where we wish to classify stratigraphic or structural traps on a seismic image. We can generate a feature vector that, for example, represents a labeled seismic characteristic from multiple attributes that, when combined uniquely, define the characteristic such as a pinch-out or a subtle facies change.

Gradient Descent

Gradient descent optimization identifies the minima of a functional relationship between dependent variables and the multiple independent variables that act as predictors. Like the theory of gravity evolved by Newton and Einstein, gradient descent is seeking a solution to minimize something. Namely, gravity addresses the potential energy states and gradient descent strives to resolve a loss or error function. Identifying the minimum value(s) of a function can be achieved several ways. One of the more efficient ways, if there are few predictor variables, is to employ differential calculus. This approaches the problem from a logical perspective.

Consider the function:

$$f(x) = x^4 - 5x^2 + 17$$

Equating the first differential of the function to zero:

$$d/dx f(x) = 4x^3 - 10x = 0$$
$$x = +/-2.5^{1/2}$$

Thus, the minima of the function $f(x) = x^4 - 5x^2 + 17 = +/-1.58$.

An iterative methodology to solve for the minima is more appropriate when the number of predictors is large and the functional relationship is more complex. This would be the standard when addressing most business problems seen in the Oil and Gas industry.

$$\breve{y} = M \times X + C \quad \dots \text{ Equation 1}$$

The equation $\breve{y} = M \times X + C$ represents the line that is a linear fit through the bivariate plot of cumulative gas against proppant volume values as expressed in Figure 2.6. Solving the linear equation, we get

$$\breve{y} = 14.16 X - 629.91 \text{ where } \breve{y} = \text{Qg100 and X} = \text{ProppantVol}$$

Applying the gradient descent methodology, we are trying to define the values of the coefficients (M and C). Initially, we must find the loss function for the linear regression model. We turn to the generalized equation for a loss function:

$$\text{Loss Function (LF)} = 1/N \, \Sigma \, (y - \breve{y})^2 \quad \dots \text{ Equation 2}$$

Essentially we are solving the original value of y minus the expected value $\breve{y}$. Substituting Equation 1 into Equation 2, we get:

$$\text{Loss Function (LF)} = 1/N \, \Sigma \, (y - (mX + c))^2 \quad \dots \quad \text{Equation 3}$$

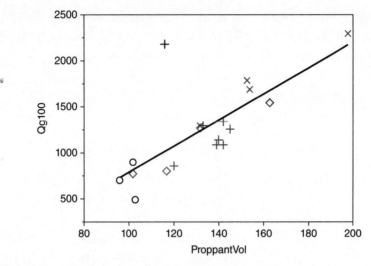

Figure 2.6 Gradient descent solves linear regression

Gradient descent identifies the direction of the downward slope at every point on the loss function on both *m* and *c*. Then, it modifies *m* and *c* to attain the objective through an iterative calculation to arrive at the same values for the coefficients expressed in Equation 1. The values of the coefficients represent the minimum values of loss or error on the Loss Function in Equations 2 and 3.

Factorized Machine Learning

A good example of a general predictor model is the *factorization machine* (FM). It is essentially an SVM characterized by a polynomial kernel. Thus, FMs can model the entire family of possible interactions between the variables by adopting factorized parameters. Using FMs enables geophysicists and petrophysicists to estimate interactions in sparsely populated datasets.

Evolutionary Computing and Genetic Algorithms

Evolutionary computing (EC) methodologies are formulated to emulate the Darwinian theory of evolution through natural selection. Or was it Alfred Russel Wallace? Genetic algorithms (GAs) are a fundamental element of the EC approach. It is understood that most of the GA applications hitherto are designed to perform an essential optimization routine for search engines. EC and GA were first used in health care and epidemiology. There is a rapid adoption of machine learning (ML) and associated deep learning (DL) workflows across multiple engineering schools adopting data-driven and soft computing technologies. This has escalated recent interest in the application of GA, particularly in the unconventional reservoirs in the United States. Why? There are much uncertainty and misunderstanding in the operational parameters used to exploit these resources. This is primarily due to the complexity of the geologic environment where subtle stress fields and geomechanics dilute the strength of traditional interpretation of conventional reservoirs.

We can posit GA as a multipurpose and versatile technique to not only identify parameter learning for artificial neural network implementations but also ascertain membership relationships or rules when applying fuzzy logic workflows.

EC is a blanket term that characterizes systems designed to resolve computer-based problems implementing evolutionary-like models.

These systems all have the Darwinian common denominators:

- Selection
- Mutation
- Reproduction

The Oil and Gas industry has gravitated toward GA from the array of available EC techniques. GA is initialized with a matrix of selected points (seismic attributes, peaks, and troughs of wavelets, petrophysical characteristics, etc.) to enable a search routine to identify a set of maximum or minimum points in parallel. The genetic operator allows the exchange of knowledge across multiple local points to reduce the probability of advancing toward a local minimum and omitting the global minimum. As an optimization methodology, we need to calculate the derivative of the objective function, but unlike most optimization algorithms, GA assesses the objective function, for several differing sets of data points. Thus, there is only one output from the GA workflow that represents the value of the performance metric.

All the transition rules are probabilistic as opposed to deterministic.

A standard GA workflow is made up of several steps that logically adhere to the Darwinian model of natural selection. The method of encoding a solution to an oil and gas problem that strives to isolate the critical seismic attributes and petrophysical properties to represent a stratigraphic or structural feature can be formulated to create a base population. The encoding mechanisms and the evaluation function coalesce to account for the chain of links between the GA and the feature identification problem. The optimal encoding device is binary by nature (Holland, 1975). Ostensibly it is preferable to have a few potential options for multiple bits rather than the inverse: many options for far fewer bits. The evaluation function in a GA workflow essentially emulates the environmental playground where a natural evolution takes place.

ARTIFICIAL INTELLIGENCE: MACHINE AND DEEP LEARNING

Machine learning (ML) encapsulates a methodology for data analysis to automate the building of advanced analytical data-driven models. The algorithms iterate through a learning cycle sourced by different datasets. Ultimately, ML enables computers to surface hidden trends, insights, and patterns with no a priori knowledge programmed into their directives. The iterative nature of ML algorithms allows the models to evolve independently and thus survive as a valid and trustworthy means to discover similar patterns in new data. The array of current ML algorithms allows geophysicists to automatically generate models against bigger, more complex data, delivering faster and more accurate results on a colossal scale of input data. Thomas H. Davenport, an analytics thought leader, wrote in the *Wall Street Journal* (September 2013) that with fast changing and growing volumes of data "you need fast-moving modeling streams to keep up." And you can do that with ML techniques. He says, "Humans can typically create one or two good models a week; machine learning can create thousands of models a week."

Deep learning (DL) has evolved from machine learning (ML) to gather the latter back into the realm of artificial intelligence (AI). DL is underpinned by a stack of algorithms that are designed to model high-level abstractions inherent in datasets. There are several architectural possibilities compatible with DL as we transcribe an observation such as an image into its composite representation as a vector of intensity values for each pixel:

- Deep forward neural networks
- Convolutional deep neural networks
- Recurrent deep neural networks
- Stacked denoising autoencoders

We shall take a deep dive into these four neural network topologies in Chapter 8, where we illustrate not only the architectural nuances but also their applicability across the E&P sectors.

REFERENCES

Breiman, L., "Bagging Predictors," *Machine Learning*, 26 (1996): 123–140.

Friedman, J., T. Hastie, and R. Tibshirani, *The Elements of Statistical Learning*, Springer-Verlag (2001).

Gelman, A., "Exploratory Data Analysis for Complex Models," *Journal of Computational and Graphical Statistics*, 13, no. 4 (2004): 755–779.

Ghaemi, R., Md. N. Sulaiman, H. Ibrahim, and N. Mustapha, "A Survey: Clustering Ensemble Techniques," *World Academy of Science, Engineering & Tech.*, 50 (2009).

Hippel, K. W., and A. I. McLeod, "Time Series Modeling of Water Resources and Environmental Systems," *Developments in Water Sciences*, 45, Elsevier, New York (1994).

Hoaglin, D. C., F. Mosteller, and J. W. Tukey, *Understanding Robust and Exploratory Data Analysis*, John Wiley & Sons, New York (1983).

Holland, J. H., *Adaptation in Natural and Artificial Systems*, University of Michigan Press, Ann Arbor, MI (1975); reissued by MIT Press (1992).

Huang, S. C., and Y. F. Huang, "Bounds on the Number of Hidden Neurons in Multilayer Perceptrons," *IEEE Trans. Neur. Networks* (1991): 2, 47–55.

Hush, D., B. Horne, and J. M. Salas, "Error Surfaces for Multilayer Perceptrons," *IEEE Trans. Systems, Man and Cybernetics* (1992): 22, 1152–1161.

Kosaraju, Raj, "How Machine Learning Affects Everyday Life," https://icrunchdata.com/how-machine-learning-affects-everyday-life/, accessed July 6, 2016.

Romeo, G., "Seismic Signals Detection and Classification Using Artificial Neural Networks," *Annali di Geofisica* (1994): 37, 343–353.

SAS Enterprise Miner 7.1 Extension Nodes: Developer's Guide, http://support.sas.com/documentation/cdl/en/emxndg/64759/HTML/default/viewer.htm#n0npe25scre3jnn1g6z770h3awle.htm, SAS Institute Inc., SAS Campus Drive, Cary, NC USA.

Shahab, D. M., "Recent Developments in Application of Artificial Intelligence in Petroleum Engineering," SPE Paper 89033, JPT (April 2005), p. 86.

Strehl, A., and J. Ghosh, "Cluster Ensembles: A Knowledge Reuse Framework for Combining Partitionings," *American Association of Artificial Intel.* (2002).

Topchy, A., M. Law, A. Jain, and A. Fred, "Analysis of Consensus Partition in Cluster Ensemble," *IEEE Int'l. Conf. Data Mining* (2007): 225–232.

Tukey, J. W., *Exploratory Data Analysis*, Addison-Wesley (1977).

Wang, Yuhong, "Determination of Uncertainty in Reserves Estimate from Analysis of Production Decline Data," thesis submitted to the office of graduate studies of Texas A&M University (May 2006).

CHAPTER 3

Advanced Geophysical and Petrophysical Methodologies

"Data is widely available; what is scarce is the ability to extract wisdom from it."

Hal Varian, chief economist at Google

INTRODUCTION

This chapter illustrates several typical applications of data-driven analytical methodologies, ideally suited for both geophysical and petrophysical datasets. There is an in-depth discussion on the subtle variations of petrophysical data types and how they manifest in an analytical workflow. The important concept is that geophysical and petrophysical data, when integrated into a data-driven study, are no longer siloed. These geosciences cross boundaries to aggregate with both operational and other engineering data types for a complete assessment of a business problem. The important aspect of any study is the multidimensional characteristic.

ADVANCED GEOPHYSICAL METHODOLOGIES

Seismic data can be classified or segmented or clustered from a spatial or temporal perspective. As a geophysicist, you may be focused on a specific stratigraphic formation or set of distinct structures that are characteristic of a potential reservoir. As the depth of the seismic profile increases, the resolution in space and time of the seismic response invariably deteriorates. Increasing the window of interpretation along either axis adds more fuzziness and uncertainty across the attributes under study. Thus, classification becomes more difficult, and so clustering techniques and their implementation become more critical to attaining business value.

A facies segmentation in a soft-computing methodology necessitates an abstraction of seismic attributes, extracting absolute measurements for a variety of attributes such as frequency, amplitude, and geometric measures. The segmentation process classifies each unique box-shaped area of the 3D seismic space or voxel to a finite number of clusters. Each cluster is representative of a seismic facies that in turn may map to some distinct geologic facies.

How Many Clusters?

How do we determine the number of clusters appropriate for the study? This is a question that carries no deterministic outcome, no matter the cluster analysis implemented (Everitt, 1979; Hartigan, J. A., 1985; Bock, 1985). The mere adoption of cluster analysis is to essentially summarize the seismic data with no method of classifying the attributes into meaningful clusters. Invariably, it is sufficient to note the R-square for each attribute and generate plots of R-square against the number of clusters.

When challenging the validity and rigor of the variances among the clusters, it is not unusual to adopt ordinary significance tests such as analysis-of-variance F tests. However, as we are striving to exploit the separation characteristics of the clusters, any norms of the significance tests, be they parametric or nonparametric, are radically disrupted. Let us consider a population of some 100 distinct observations from our seismic attribute dataset and assume a univariate normal distribution. Generating only two clusters, we would notice a p-value of less than 0.0001. Thus, methods that test for clusters against the null hypothesis, stipulating that clusters are randomly assigned objects (such as McClain and Rao, 1975; Klastorin, 1983), are inadequate.

Most practical tests for clusters have inflexible sampling distributions and comprise null hypotheses for which dismissal is vague. When classifying seismic attributes, it is best to adopt clustering methodologies based on distance matrices. A favorite null hypothesis states that all permutations of the values in the distance matrix are equally likely (Ling, 1973; Hubert, 1974). Adopting this null hypothesis, we can perform a rank test or a permutation test. An improvement on the permutation null hypothesis is the multivariate normal null hypothesis. But it is not fitting since there is usually a high probability of elimination if the seismic data is appraised from a distribution with lower kurtosis than a normal distribution, such as a uniform distribution.

A more efficient null hypothesis is that the data is extracted from a uniform distribution (Hartigan, 1978; Arnold, 1979; Sarle, 1983). The uniform null hypothesis inexorably reflects constant error rates when the data is sampled from a strongly unimodal distribution such as the normal.

Sarle (1983) employed a broad range of simulations to mature the Cubic Clustering Criterion (CCC). We can apply CCC for basic hypothesis testing to approximate some population clusters. The CCC assumes that a uniform distribution on a hyper-rectangle will be divided into clusters shaped roughly like hypercubes. We can split large sample datasets into a suitable number of hypercubes to yield very accurate results.

We can run nonparametric tests to determine the number of appropriate clusters and calculate nonparametric density estimates. Adopting this method requires us to sample the observations independently, applying much weaker assumptions compared to mixture models. Mueller and Sawitzki (1991) developed nonparametric methods that necessitated significant computational requirements.

Wong and Schaack (1982) attacked the problem of determining the ideal number of clusters by using a kth-nearest-neighbor density estimate. They applied varying values for the number of clusters. The estimate of the number of modal clusters for each value was calculated across a wide array of values. If there appeared a constant number, then it was deemed as a reliable indicator of the number of modes in the sample population.

There is a less computationally expensive methodology proposed by Sarle and Kuo (1993) to ascertain an ideal number of clusters:

- There are zero distributional assumptions.
- Any smoothing parameter is appropriate.
- The input data may be either coordinates or distances.

Case Study: North Sea Mature Reservoir Synopsis

The reservoir's geologic history predominantly consists of fluvial deposits with alternating sequences of sandstone and shale. The reservoir contains an approximately 1000m-thick pay zone that is tough to interpret with deterministic approaches owing to the individual sandstone and shale formations being relatively thin and thus below current seismic resolution. It is of paramount importance to fully understand the fluid movements and map the drainage patterns in a temporal fashion. Such dynamic changes in the reservoir across different vintages of the 3D data cubes enable identifications of changes in pressure observed on the amplitude and velocity variations relative to time shifts. It is essential to collate those seismic attributes deemed significant for enhanced reservoir characterization. We can enumerate via a sensitivity study all those attributes that provide the most statistical impact on a stated objective function. Some of the addressable business and technical issues are drainage patterns and fluid movements through the reservoir, increased hydrocarbon production, plateau duration, and the reservoir recovery factor.

Production optimization and increased recovery factor are attainable when all critical nonoperational parameters are identified and assessed. These parameters, referred to as key performance indicators (KPIs), must be analyzed and quantified through an exploratory data analysis (EDA) methodology that surfaces hidden patterns and identifies trends and correlations in a multivariate complex system. Hypotheses worth modeling will be enumerated because of the EDA processes.

To garner maximum value from the 4D seismic cubes, the operator has established an interpretation strategy allied with data-driven workflows to promote confidence in the deterministic studies. We used multiple disparate datasets, such as production and injection data, production logging tool (PLT) data, and tracer information. We also developed processes to upscale the 4D seismic into the geological and simulation grid.

Through a suite of data cleansing, transformation, and EDA methodologies, we established scalable and repeatable workflows for identification, selection, diagnosis, and solution finding. The operator benefited by understanding the correlations and trends as well as identifying signatures that propose hypotheses worth modeling. Ultimately the solution improved the drilling surveillance, governance, and control process. It is designed to handle vast amounts of disparate data from a variety of sources to offer a robust analytical solution. In delivering these capabilities, the soft computing techniques efficiently answer questions about a precise business issue and provide strategic decisions to optimize an asset.

Characterizing the reservoirs in a brown field necessitates the analysis of massive datasets aggregated from historical production data, pressure transient analysis (PTA), and rate transient analysis (RTA) datasets as well as core analysis results. Geophysicists map seismic attributes to reservoir properties through some fundamental neural networks, leading to a richer input dataset for reservoir characterization. It is critical to capture the subtler observations inherent in these datasets and to comprehend the structure of the data. Invariably, geostatistical methods can be implemented to quantify heterogeneity accurately, integrate scalable data, and capture the scope of uncertainty. However, between 50 and 70 percent of effort in a reservoir characterization study should be focused on EDA workflows and immersive data-driven visualizations.

In addition to spatial analysis, simulation, and uncertainty quantification, EDA ensures repeatable and scalable integration, aggregation, and overall management of the different datasets under study.

Interpretation of the time-lapse seismic data is essential not simply from a cumulative perspective but from an individual time-lapse period. The 3D seismic static data should also be interpreted from the standpoint of identifying raw differences— time-shifted raw differences as well as the absolute differences. A stepwise methodology is vital that integrates workflows to manage the data, aggregate, transform, and impute the data as well as quality check for robustness before creating data marts for advanced analytical workflows. EDA processes invoking multivariate data insights are very critical to surface the hidden trends and fully comprehend the patterns and correlations in a complex and heterogeneous system such as a North Sea field.

Case Study: Working with Passive Seismic Data

Continuous monitoring of the behavior of the subsurface is a long-established discipline with its origins in the earliest seismological networks. The deployment of acoustic sensors and the subsequent integration of measurements, combined with non-seismic observations such as felt effects, building damage, and water table effects have enabled complex models of the subsurface to be created.

Seismological monitoring is tuned to detecting and characterizing seismic events as stress is released from faults in the crust. Practical application to monitoring intra-formation fracturing is challenged by:

- The scale of such an observation network regarding the energy released in detectable events
- The amount of attenuation and dispersion of the initial wave and the coda of waves that evolve over the typical travel times

Acoustic monitoring is also capable of detecting mechanical energy released by fluid removal or drilling activity.

The purpose of this chapter is to show how measurements from sensors operating passively (i.e., listening continuously) can provide impactful insights that complement their more traditional deployment in active mode. The key technological enablers in this instance are rapid data communications to allow timely processing of the data. The process is usually a linear workflow operating on continuous time series streams that comprise denoising, pattern recognition, and statistical analysis steps.

Typical deployments for continuous subsurface monitoring vary with environment and length scale:

- *Temporary deployment, onshore field:* A microseismic array to cover a few square kilometers that will have a travel time of 1–2 seconds across the area of interest. They are typically deployed for the duration of hydrofracturing and well-stimulation activities.

- *Temporary deployment, offshore field:* Ocean-bottom seismometers are deployed from ships or ROVs and listen continuously for weeks or months. The cost of the equipment and operational constraints mean that only localized surveys can be performed over a few square kilometers. Larger areas result in sparser coverage.

- *Permanent deployment, offshore field:* With the advent of permanent reservoir monitoring (PRM) for frequent, highly repeatable, 4D seismic, it becomes logical to use these arrays in passive mode. Data transfer and storage considerations, as well as a lack of proven value, are inhibiting this at the time of writing.

- *Localized deployment, around/inside a well:* Digital acoustic sensors in commodity optical fiber are sensitive to higher frequency and lower amplitude signals. This makes listening to the sounds of fluid movement and drilling activities a reality.

Seismic sensors themselves have evolved to four-component (4C) low- and high-bandwidth devices at ever lower commoditized price points. The data from both microseismic sensors and optical fibers has very low signal-to-noise ratios. Pattern extraction is challenging and has defeated real-time processing architectures in even the most modest onshore arrays. The practical considerations of bringing a processing capability, specifically a containerized data center, along with the rough roads in the humid and dirty environments of an Eagle Ford or Bakken shale play, have hampered the evolution of a fit-for-purpose real-time processing capability. The other solution is to transfer the data to a remote computing facility. Moore's Law will win out eventually, and this will happen at the well location.

The algorithmic challenge still stands, though. What geophysical insight can be extracted from an array of low signal-to-noise ratio geophones? Building on our thought experiment of listening to a distant flute through background noise, we are now faced with the challenge of listening to a single strike of a drumstick on a snare drum against the same background noise. We don't know where it is coming from, but we have the benefit this time of many listeners who can compare notes with each other whenever any one of them thinks they have heard the drum.

When dealing with microseismic data, the data stream from a receiver—we assume here that each stream is a single component of a 4C receiver—must be stored in an appropriate-length storage buffer. If a pattern or state is detected in one channel or data stream, then it can be searched for across all other incoming data streams. Thus, the source of the acoustic event can be in time and space—simple tomography. This is almost directly equivalent to the data architecture for earthquake seismology.

This can be viewed as a real-time version of the concepts introduced earlier. Statistical techniques can be used to identify events in a crude but effective way. For a buffer of, for instance, 10 seconds of data, the 10-second buffer will be sampled every 2 ms, so each buffer will contain 5000 samples. Four channels (and hence four buffers) per receiver, across an array of thousands of receivers, presents a formidable processing problem if we are looking for patterns across the whole array through time. For each channel, the mean, median, and range will be continuously calculated in the buffer. As familiarity grows with the demographics of the data, a meaningful characterization of events will evolve in terms of metrics such as range thresholds or the extent to which a value is an anomaly. If our window of interest is five seconds for an array of a few kilometers across, then we can afford to push more data into our window every second. Thus, we are constantly looking 2.5 seconds before and after the 5-second window of interest, and we may want to update this every few seconds with a new 10-second chunk. The character of the data is illustrated in Figure 3.1.

This is clearly an architectural and data management issue that is on the edge of what is computationally possible in the field, if not the data center. The main computational challenge is to load all channels into a buffer simultaneously in a time that is much smaller than the time window in the data. With many channels, the potential to profile the data with meaningful metrics is attractive as it allows the rest of the data to be discarded. With a large enough dataset, the data scientist can characterize the data and develop a strategy for extracting meaningful patterns—either time domain aggregate statistics or frequency or wavelet domain metrics such as dominant frequencies. This approach is particularly appropriate where the acoustic source may be continuously variable in nature (fluids, bubble concentration) and source location.

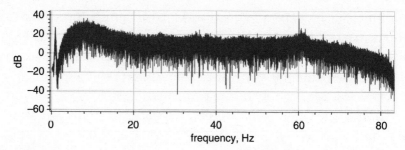

Figure 3.1 A typical spectral window of 4500 samples from a single component channel of passive seismic data lasting 9 seconds from a sea-floor seismic array. The signal to noise ratio is about 1:1. Dominant frequencies include 60 Hz mains AC and its harmonics, and much lower frequencies from nearby drilling.

We hope this gives a flavor of how data science and analytics can be put on a near-real-time footing. The data movements alone make this a challenging area. It is also worth remembering that such monitoring networks often come at an extremely high cost as the value of insight they bring is similarly high. Any analytical insight derived from such an approach must be equally robust if it is being used in such a commercial setting!

ADVANCED PETROPHYSICAL METHODOLOGIES

Well Logging and Petrophysical Data Types

We hope to explain how data-driven insights can be garnered from physical measurements of rock properties (from the Greek: *petra* = rock; *physics* = nature). The petrophysical domain is the bridge between the imaging domain and the physical world of the subsurface. The domain also underpins reservoir characterization and simulation, well planning, drilling, and production optimization. Working with petrophysical data requires a subtle blend of domain insight, data engineering, and some basic statistics but can generate impact and scientific value without too much investment in analytical resources.

It is likely that petrophysical data are utilized across more of the upstream knowledge-based workflows and activities than any other data type. Petrophysical data are used in seismic imaging, seismic interpretation, reservoir characterization and simulation, well planning, drilling, and production optimization. The robust curation and custodianship of petrophysical data are fundamental to all activities that drive reserves estimation, operational effectiveness, and most importantly, safety.

There are many resources for working with well logging data. We recommend Asquith and Krygowski (2004), and it is not our intention to duplicate any of this beyond the basic overview of the domain. Our scope here is to create an intersection between the domains of petrophysics, data engineering, and analytics to enable rapid productivity in what is a very challenging space. Figure 3.2 proposes some possible workflows and the staging areas for the various key components from data integration to implementing artificial intelligence methodologies.

Petrophysical data starts life as sensor-derived measurements collected by drilling and well logging contractors either during or immediately after drilling a borehole. Is it collected to understand the rock formations and the environment of the wellbore? Can we use petrophysical data to formulate an understanding of the reservoir, its hydrocarbon content, and the potential mobility of the hydrocarbons? These are often reduced to two areas of interest—net pay and permeability. These qualities are based on measuring direct and indirect physical properties through spontaneous potential (SP), gamma ray, resistivity, density, and acoustic logs.

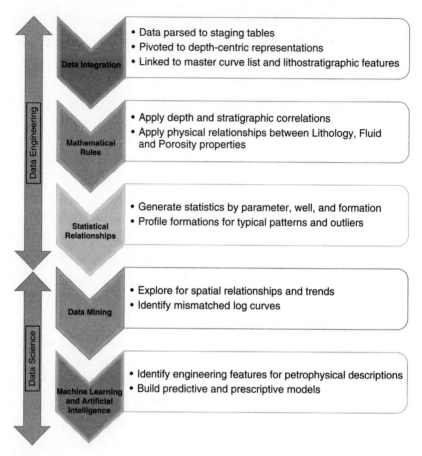

Figure 3.2 Petrophysical business studies in a data science context

Most users of well logging data think of it as a series of raw measurements that are typically interpolated and then validated against ranges of acceptable values and made available for reuse under a strong data governance regime. The management system values custodianship and interoperability but reflects the file-centric approach of days gone by when data was stored and transmitted on tape, and QC'd by eye as plain text. In addition to logged parameters, there is a data ecosystem of well-tops, geologists' reports, and other operational logs to give context and meaning to what is essentially a bunch of (relatively, by today's standards) short time series, with some human-readable header information.

If petrophysical data is so simple to work with and has such an important role in the upstream value chain, why is it not used in a more data-driven model? There are three hurdles to jump:

1. *The format of the data:* Do you work with a suite of individual curves or the interpreted properties?
2. *The storage of the data:* Usually kept in an application database, it is rare for multi-well data to be exposed to numerical analysis.
3. *It is conceptually challenging:* Finely sampled down the borehole and then spatially sparse, statistical analysis is challenged by scales at which each of the different petrophysical properties operates.

Well logs are usually stored by the well location and by parameter curve in a proprietary database. It may also contain information about the borehole trajectory, check shots, and—in larger organizations—petrophysical and geotechnical information. Sometimes it is advisable to store engineering data about the drilled rock formations, the planning and execution of the drilling, and the design and implementation of the well completion strategy. Typically transfer of log data is by ASCII text file in the Log ASCII Standard (LAS) format, and spreadsheets or plain text files for the rest.

Let's begin our data-driven project with some LAS files. Experienced users of well logs are familiar with at least two data types in a LAS file. To a data engineer, it is that most painful of data structures, a multi-structured file. While the archive format is well described, it can be implemented in an infinite variety of ways such that each well in a field will have differing metadata and sets of measurements. Typically, there are blocks in the file structure that contain data about:

- The data type itself—the version information block
- Metadata about the well, the logging contractor, and the logging run—the well information block

- The parameters measured in the logging run—the curve information block
- Metadata about the well—the parameter information block
- The physical measurements themselves

The format specifies that all measurements at a given depth are provided in a single row. Herein lies the root of the data management challenge when working with LAS files. The data must be pivoted out to either a curve-wise or well-wise structure, but there is a many-to-many relationship between wells and curves that varies by well and depth window that until recently defeated the data structures of most programming approaches.

For the data engineer and data scientist, a good way of thinking about the data contained in a LAS file is a group of one-dimensional physical measurements preceded by some spatial and logical context. Note that the depths are usually downhole and need to be corrected for true depth and location using the well trajectory (if it exists).

Data Collection and Data Quality

Even though well logging underpins many activities, we do not fully appreciate the potential for errors hidden in well logging data. Well logs are collected in the time domain by drawing logging tools through a well bore with the velocity of the logging being used to convert the log to a downhole depth. There is room for errors to sneak in through wrongly recorded datum and logging velocities, and subsequent mismatching with logs made by subsequent runs.

Random errors can be introduced by siting of logging equipment, its jerky movement (i.e., pull rate) during logging, and the positioning of the instrumentation of the logging sensors themselves. We are not accusing the logging crews of technical incompetency—the problem is usually a compromise with the design of the borehole and the state of the formations of interest after being drilled.

Similarly, an understanding of the borehole environment regarding depth alignment, borehole size, mud invasion effects, and borehole rugosity (small-scale variations of amplitude in the height of a surface) is vital when interpreting logs and providing a level of error or uncertainty with an interpretation. These factors compound piecemeal problems in interpretation, yielding a result in errors more than +/–100 percent.

Many techniques have been introduced over recent years to mitigate most issues—mainly because of the miniaturization of computing power to allow autocalibration and autocorrection to be performed at the logging tool itself. However, given that some fields contain decades' worth of logging, the existence of numerical errors in old logs should be assumed. It should be noted that different parameters are subject to errors in various ways, arising from the geometry and physics of borehole environment and instrumentation. Furthermore, the combination of suites of measurements from different logging runs and contractors can be subject to mismatches arising from positioning and datum errors.

Once recorded, a logging run will likely undergo correction for any of the above issues. Where logging is undertaken in areas where the geology is well understood, significant errors will be visible. The next challenge before analytical usage is to develop rules to cope with gaps in the data. This is a problem in working with any continuous series of data. LAS files will typically contain a special number (usually –999.99) to indicate a null value—usually because of a bad sensor reading. Fortunately, most mathematical libraries in the R or Python languages contain robust exception handling and will offer a range of options as function parameters to deal with *null* values.

It is rare for the rawest sensor data to be provided from a logging sensor. Some form of correction is applied, if only for instrumental drift during logging. Other approaches may be used that correct for the modification of geophysical parameters by the presence of fluids and muds in the wellbore.

The dynamic range of logged data may come as a surprise when first encountered. Many types of variability exist that will require careful consideration when exposed to the techniques of the data scientist:

- Some properties vary slowly, steadily, and linearly (and hence may need detrending) such as borehole temperature.

- Some sensors record a measurement that varies in a continuous but seemingly erratic way such as borehole diameter.

- Some measurements are highly discontinuous as they reflect a rock property and will change, often dramatically, from one lithology to the next. Moreover, some logged measurements will have a linear relationship with the property being recorded, whereas some will be nonlinear (such as the properties that interrogate the electromagnetic domain).

It will behoove anyone performing analysis on well log data to work in close collaboration with a petrophysicist to ensure that the scientific aspects of the data are respected. There is room for understanding the data demographics efficiently and ensuring that extreme or statistically questionable values are meaningful rather than garbage. This level of curation and understanding is vital for effective analytics. A relatively small population of measurements often represents thin, but critical, lithology.

What Does Well Logging Data Tell Us?

As previously sketched out, the purpose of logging a well is to provide information about the reservoir rocks and the hydrocarbons and other fluids contained therein. The details of this picture are filled in by calculating properties and parameters to describe the rocks being drilled, the fluids included in the pore spaces of the rock, the state of the borehole, and the presence and influence in the borehole environment of materials used in, or created by, drilling.

For the petrophysicist and geologist, this will be second nature. To the data scientist who is meeting well logging data for the first time, it pays to go slowly through this area with your subject matter expert and understand the stages in the maturity of well logs. The raw measurements once cleaned and corrected are then converted to interpretations of physical and mechanical properties.

We should illustrate where a lot of science is abstracted away behind a couple of simpler parameters. For example, there is no direct measurement of basic concepts such as porosity; this property is calculated from well-established relationships between formation density and hydrogen concentration (where the voids are). If you have been paying attention to your data, you will not have spotted these parameters, either: density is inferred from gamma ray bombardment (the gamma log) and hydrogen concentration from the neutron log as detected by radionuclides of hydrogen-3 (the compensated neutron log). Further corrections are often made by the petrophysicist during the data preparation phase using sonic and photoelectric measurements.

Also, combinations of logged measurements infer some properties. The reliability of calculated fluid properties can only be understood if the rugosity and integrity of the borehole are taken into consideration.

These illustrations are the tip of an iceberg that represents a massive body of knowledge based on the sound scientific understanding of well-understood physical relationships. They are included to serve as a caution that unsupervised analysis in the absence of domain expertise can result in spurious or even misleading insights. It also underlines the requirement to ensure that analysis is performed with strong leadership and support from domain experts.

To answer the question, "What does well logging data tell us?," it gives us a multi-physical description of the subsurface down a well bore. It is possible but unlikely that data science techniques will uncover any new insights based on a single well. Typically, correlating well logs with seismic images develops an understanding of the stratigraphy and structure of the subsurface from a spatiotemporal perspective. Good data engineering allows well logging data to be accessed in a more meaningful context to compare wells and logs across formations and basins, something that has been hitherto impossible without such an approach.

Stratigraphic Information

Armed with some pivoted well log data, grouped by well and parameter and ordered by depth, the next step could be to provide some geological context. One of the longest-standing endeavors of geologists has been to name the layers of rock at ever-finer levels of detail from units of rock many kilometers in thickness down to individual layers or horizons of a few millimeters. These types of observations relate to a geological event, such as a volcanic eruption or a lake drying out, or conversely, flooding. Overprinted on the depositional and erosional rock record are physical movements that can fracture and fault brittle rocks if the stresses are sufficient. The rocks could fold if more ductile. Geochemical reactions will modify rocks as their depth exposes them to changes in their temperatures and confining pressures.

This is straying into the territory of geological domains and requires a degree course to do it justice. These simple observations should provide some high-level context to the data scientist who is desperately trying to make sense of a whole new scientific domain, and act as a starting point when drawing deeper domain expertise from a petrophysicist.

Integration with Stratigraphic Data

Whence does stratigraphic data come? The best source of stratigraphic insight is a geological interpretation. It has surprised many colleagues from a computing background that a geologist can look at a lump of rock and describe its visual and physical properties and often go on to assign it a name, type-location, and formation history. If the rock is sedimentary (i.e., made of muds, sand, or carbonate), then there will likely be some fossils, however tiny, that aid greatly in this task. This takes years of training but is no different to a medical consultant identifying symptoms and making a prognosis. There is the same (limited!) scope for error, especially when a geologist has been studying rocks from one area or reservoir for a while (decades in some cases!).

So, in simplest terms, a geologist can look at a rock core retrieved from a borehole and readily identify the layers and hence the boundaries between the layers. There is little margin for error unless the core is damaged or missing, or unless there is an unclear boundary or gradation from one layer to the next. From such a well, a basic understanding of the subsurface is generated. Core retrieval is a costly process in terms of time spent doing it (core extraction on a drilling platform in the North Sea costs tens of thousands of dollars an hour to operate), and there is a geotechnical risk in retrieval, and hence the availability of core logs is limited. Well logs are interpreted by the stratigrapher (the petrophysicist responsible for finding the layers) based on prevailing geological understanding, and possibly cross-checked with the bio-stratigrapher to ensure that the fossil content makes geological sense.

Formation tops are then assigned. These are the downhole depths of the tops of each of the rock formations identified. Confusingly to the non-geologist, the term *formation* is often misused as a generic term for a layer of rock as well as the sense as the primary unit of stratigraphic classification. The International Stratigraphic Commission (ISC) (www.stratigraphy.org) provides many backgrounds, but it suffices to know that the ISC hierarchy is summarized thus:

- Supergroup—several groups and formations with significant commonality
- Group—two or more contiguous formations that together provide a "useful means of simplifying classification"
- Formation—the primary unit of classification
- Member—a lithologically distinct zone of a formation
- Bed—a single stratum in a sedimentary sequence

Typically, the scales that interest the geologist at the reservoir range are groups (such as the Brent Group in the North Sea) and formations (such as the constituent formations that generate the acronym *Brent* group name—Broom, Rannoch, Etive, Ness, and Tarbert). A member is not necessarily present in a whole formation for whatever subtleties of the depositional or erosive processes, and similarly, not all formations are continuously present to a group, and there may be no definite boundary.

Bear these thoughts in mind when trying to interpret a statistically driven study. We present these concepts as much to highlight opportunities where viewing data at scale can be insightful across an area the size of a basin, as to show that there may be reasons why your personal machine learning approach is struggling. Hence, the visual picking of formation tops from a suite of well logs is an expert-driven activity but is open to subjectivity and cognitive bias.

This is the process by which the depth information is created, but this is not integrated geological context to enable data science. First, the data must be extracted from its system of record. This could be a stratigraphic database, and if so, then a well-curated spreadsheet of a unit name (from a limited vocabulary if you're lucky), its type (formation or group), the top and bottom depths, and the well log on which it was picked will all be present *and* correct. If you're less fortunate, then you may need to be creative, or just downright bloody-minded.

Extracting Useful Information from Well Reports

We have experienced a workflow where the second page of every PDF document in a directory of over 200 well reports had to be scrapped and the stratigraphic table compiled by the data management consultancy responsible for the basin scale study extracted and parsed through some basic text analytics. This resulted in a basic spreadsheet of formations, groups, and approximately 20 percent random words, but with the prize of the formation tops numerically intact and with the unit of measure alongside to ensure data integrity (i.e., no digits went astray). A couple of hours of manual cleaning were followed by some equally simple (but tedious) rationalization of unit names. This process introduced a consistent stratigraphic vocabulary that gave a basin scale view that was hitherto unclear to any one of the drilling parties during the 30 years of activity in the basin.

While this approach could have been matched in time by some simple copy-and-paste over the two days of elapsed time, with this simple data cleansing workflow in place the next basin only took a couple of hours. A logical step then would be to apply machine learning to this task and automate the process entirely, asking for expert guidance where there exists no precise action.

As a general comment on working with text representations of a parameter, if this can be reduced to a number (i.e., an index or quantity), then it is computationally more efficient. It is far easier to perform analytics with numerical classifications and representations (e.g., use a unit ID instead of a formation or group name). Character and string handling are a greater computational overhead than working with an integer; working with integer representations of classified data will speed up your complex analyses and simplify workflows.

Integration with Other Well Information

Besides the well logs themselves, well reports can provide vital operational information about how and why a well was drilled, which can in some cases provide many pages of petrophysical and geological context. Well reports provide a bridge to the wider geological domain with the downside (from an analytic perspective) that the preferred data type here is free text. Text mining is beyond the scope of this book, but there have been several successful attempts to generate dictionaries and keyword lists from stratigraphic nomenclature. From these dictionaries and lists of word pairs, triplets, and longer tuples it is possible to apply rich context at the formation level.

This context can be used at a very fundamental level to test the rigor and consistency of geological interpretation—that is, are opposing concepts used to describe similar petrophysical patterns? An example illustrated (Rahman, 2015) where the similar facies descriptions of sandstone-mudstone and siltstone-mudstone were incorrectly applied by pattern matching in the well logs and comparing with the text extracted from the well reports.

Integration with Other Technical Domains at the Well Level

A wealth of information from the life cycle of a well could be integrated for higher value. Some operators have been employing data-driven techniques in some of the areas for several years, but for most of the upstream community, this is still a new field.

Information sources span business domains:

- *Planning information* includes the reservoir target, trajectory planning, casing and integrity planning, infrastructure and facility planning, and the logistics required to support drilling, completion, and subsequent production, operation, and maintenance.

- *Drilling information* specifically contains valuable information about the equipment, techniques, and processes employed, and all the equipment measurements captured during drilling (MWD) and geophysical parameters logged during drilling (LWD).

- *Production information* could include flow rates, oil/gas/ water splits, injection rates, and fluid compositions.

- *Operational information* includes well status, maintenance interventions, and shut-ins.

The technical and functional domains contain data of varying quality and accessibility. Much analytical work has been carried out by operators of unconventional assets, where field development has become highly operationalized, to drive best practices based on insights from these data domains. It has become clear that certain methods of well stimulation (e.g., "the super-frac") have a statistically significant effect in certain reservoir formations, even when no geomechanical hypothesis can be validated. Similarly, an understanding of the likelihood of requiring an accurate bill of materials for well delivery or stimulation based on geological knowledge can make an operator's supply chain much more efficient in supporting business requirements.

Across the industry, the most impactful use of petrophysical data, when combined with other technical data, has been in understanding drilling effectiveness and operational efficiencies and understanding overall best practice in the delivery of wells at the scale driven by unconventional field development.

Fundamental Insights

At the hierarchical level of a significant formation or even relatively homogeneous groups, straightforward profiling can be achieved with aggregated statistics:

- The minimum and maximum to understand the range of values
- Mean, median to understand the "normal" behavior of the data
- The standard deviation to quantify the degree of variance from the mean value

When carried out for each logged parameter, this information is sufficient to provide a statistical profile of the quality of the data contained in logs, as well as an understanding of the variability of the data and hence its likely vertical heterogeneity. On the data quality, the range should ideally be provided in a master curve list, and illegal values can be corrected by developing and applying rules—as is typically carried out in conventional workflows. A richer approach would consider the other aggregate statistics so that anomalous or suspicious data, having a higher standard deviation than would be expected from exact physical measurements, could be flagged up to a petrophysicist.

At the level of a thick (more than several tens of meters) formation (i.e., several thousand data points) there is sufficient information about the demographics of logged data to enable comparison from one well to the next. Particularly insightful are the wells or individual well curves that show extreme behavior on the rest of the population in a formation. In carrying out such studies across a variety of geological settings, it became apparent that the vertical heterogeneity of most formations is sufficient to undermine the value of any statistical information contained in any particular petrophysical parameter. A correlation matrix of Pearson Coefficients from one well to the next will show broadly similar relationships but there is a lack of clarity, and the heterogeneity inhibits quantitative description. It is more useful to present as much of the information in as few dimensions as possible.

Nonparametric dimension reduction methods such as *k*-means clustering and principal component analysis (PCA) have been applied to well log curves over many years such as in prospectivity geotechnical studies and production engineering applications. It has been used successfully to describe and relate formations across wells in a basin scale formation to underpin machine learning techniques.

The first properties that become visible when data is presented regarding its statistical and demographics descriptions at such scale are often the outliers. Where a formation or a complete suite of well logs deviates in character from the wider population it tells us that there is something we can learn from this behavior. If the outlier is a function of poor data governance at some point between acquisition and interpretation, then it can be repaired or disregarded and the overall data quality will improve. Such impacts arise from mismatched well logs, for example, pull rates, datum, missing data, or, as shown in Figure 3.3, a mismatch in units.

If the outlier is at the reservoir or formation level, then the petrophysical parameters embodied in the statistical property of interest should be reviewed and interpreted.

An example could be where, for instance, a gravel channel sequence is drilled in a formation where turbidites are encountered. If the geometry of the channels or the thickness of the formation is below seismic resolution, then the significance of the association through visual correlation may have been lost, particularly in a historical dataset or where the interpretation was performed before a more mature understanding of the formation had emerged. This effect is illustrated in Figure 3.4.

Even in well-curated and well-understood geological localities there is scope for listening to what the data might tell us.

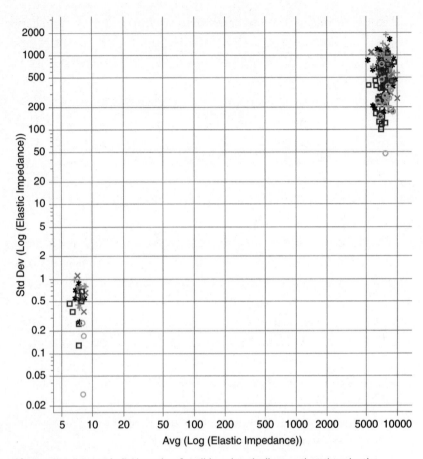

Figure 3.3 A statistical study of well log data indicates that the elastic impedance at the formation level across 180 wells falls into two clusters. Closer inspection of the data revealed that a milli- prefix had persisted for some wells. This is a data governance issue to be addressed before data can be used for analysis.

Untethered by outlier values, it is then worth investigating the degrees of freedom in the data for trends that may lie within. Elementary relationships between burial depth and elastic parameters should be apparent, and detrending for depth is a relatively straightforward step. Trends may exist in other dimensions and, freed of the spatial constraints that are applied in most subsurface modeling software packages, patterns in, for instance,

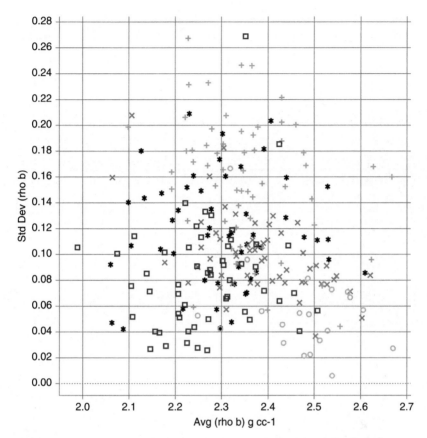

Figure 3.4 Average formation density and its standard deviation for the BRENT group (Broom blue/circle, Rannoch pink/X, Etive brown/square, Ness purple/+, Tarbert red/*). The more heterogeneous Etive formation contrasts with the homogeneous sandstone of the Broom. Of interest are the outlier wells for each group and the diversity in variability across the Tarbert.

geochemical and other non-spatial domains can become apparent. Pre-burial, geochemically induced trends can become apparent. Similarly, radial and other nonlinear geometries will be more evident when explored using a non-spatial approach.

Feature Engineering in Well Logs

Once fundamental statistical descriptions of petrophysical data are established, then feature identification can take place. At the simpler end of the spectrum, this could be along the lines of looking for thermal spikes in the temperature logs. Rahman (2015) used the Symbolic Aggregate Parser (SAX), which maps the numerical values on a statistically derived set of bins. Settling on a handful (5–7 worked optimally) of bins, Rahman assigned a character (e.g., a–e) to the re-binned temperature values. He then used basic regular expression parsing, available in most languages (Unix Shell script, Python, etc.,), to detect such features across hundreds of wells in a matter of seconds.

Building on the concepts of feature engineering introduced in Chapter 1, there is a broad range of properties that can be used across petrophysical data. Before performing a regression or dimension reduction on a suite of log curves to assess overall similarity across wells, it may be useful to search for a pattern in a log. It may be that some facies are a pay zone and the simple geological question is, "Show me something like this in other logs." The variability in most log curves requires approaches such as wavelet or shapelet transformations. These methods capture the key features such as peaks, troughs, relative sizes, and positions and allow them to be encapsulated as a template that can then be offered across a wider dataset for comparison and ranking of similar candidates. A wavelet transform was used by Rahman (2015) to match wavelet properties of interbedded sedimentary units and compare them against the geological interpretations for each borehole to identify different interpretations. The approach yielded powerful insights and rationalized a complex sedimentary model for the basin's development. An example of features defined in one well and found using wavelet techniques are illustrated in Figure 3.5.

At a more gross level, state change descriptions can be applied to support and guide well correlation by identifying discrete states in a log curve with no a priori information about where a formation top may lie. This approach is used in industrial analytics while monitoring the condition and

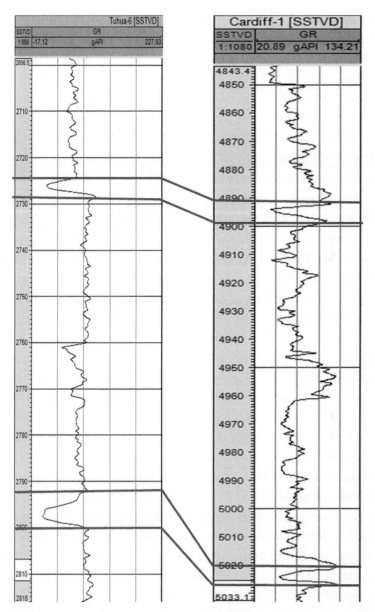

Figure 3.5 Coal measures determined in a borehole in the Taranaki Basin, NE New Zealand, were used to create a wavelet-based template that was applied to the boreholes for the rest of the basin with great success. Rahman (2015) reports occasional false positives pointing to a need to tune the technique further, but also reports many candidate features that had not been interpreted as coal but occurred in interpreted formations that were associated with coal.

performance of complex machinery but has yet to surface in the petrophysical space beyond some initial prototyping.

Toward Machine Learning

At the time of writing, it is not yet sufficiently proven that machine learning (ML) techniques can do a better job than a domain expert of capturing critical information and then using it in a usefully predictive model at the scale of basins or across the complexities of multi-domain workflows such as 4D history matching. This is most likely a function of the maturity of the discipline rather than lack of applicability. It is becoming clear that ML can deliver insights faster and draw the expert's eye to where the data doesn't make sense. The major inhibitor to wider industry uptake of ML in this area has been any visibility of the activity.

Use Cases

The use cases for data-driven studies in the petrophysical domain are few. We anticipate a massive explosion in the use of analytical and data science techniques. We have demonstrated simple approaches for assessing data quality, and we feel that this will be a vital and complementary activity to the current data management community.

Beyond the geological and prospectivity use cases that we introduced earlier, there have been prototype studies in drilling effectiveness using measurement and logging while drilling data, and this could be extended to well delivery and well performance when combined with operational data.

As we become better as a community at understanding the statistical character of our domain data, the application will potentially take in target selection, understanding reservoir behavior, and, eventually, closed-loop activities such as history matching.

Concluding Remarks

Armed with a set of basic tools we can capture information contained in data from geological formations that transcends any single petrophysical property. There is still much work to be performed to ensure that a level of context and subject matter expertise is applied to such data-driven insights, but there is also much that is immediately practicable at the scale of a large dataset.

The approach is efficient and has the potential for extension and reuse far beyond the scope of the general field-scale study. It should become a matter of course to calculate (and regularly recalculate) and store for reuse this encapsulated information as an essential building block to wider analytics. Basic feature engineering techniques should be applied to log curves to build a suite of patterns or features that capture fundamental phenomena in a library of well logs. Such an endeavor could be a critical piece of competitive intellectual property to an operating company. Important reservoir properties may present themselves to extents that are governed by drilling techniques, such as some fluids present during drilling or the damage to the formation and its impact on the ability to log other geophysical properties.

REFERENCES

Abdul-Rahman, Alias, and Morakot Pilouk, *Spatial Data Modelling for 3D GIS*, Springer (2007).

Arnold, S. J., "A Test for Clusters," *Journal of Marketing Research*, 16 (1979): 545–551.

Asquith, G. B., and D. Krygowski, "Basic Well Log Analysis," AAPG Methods in Exploration Series No. 16 (2004): 0891816674.

Bock, H. H., "On Some Significance Tests in Cluster Analysis," *Journal of Classification*, 2 (1985): 77–108.

Cao, Q., R. Banerjee, S. Gupta, J. Li, W. Zhou, and B. Jeyachandra, "Data-Driven Production Forecasting Using Machine Learning,"

Society of Petroleum Engineers (June 1, 2016). DOI: 10.2118/180984-MS.

Chen, J., Z. Li, and B. Bian, "Application of Data Mining in Multi-Geological-Factor Analysis. In: Cai, Z., C. Hu, Z. Kang, and Y. Liu (eds.), *Advances in Computation and Intelligence*, ISICA 2010, *Lecture Notes in Computer Science*, vol. 6382, Springer, Berlin, Heidelberg. DOI: 10.1007/978-3-642-16493-4_41.

Coste, J.-F., J.-P. Valois, Elf. TotalFina, "An Innovative Approach for the Analysis of Production History in Mature Fields: A Key Stage for Field Reengineering," paper SPE 62880 presented at the 2000 SPE Annual Technical Conference and Exhibition, Dallas, Texas (October 1–4).

Everitt, B. S., "Unresolved Problems in Cluster Analysis," *Biometrics*, 35 (1979): 169–181.

Hall, B., "Facies Classification Using Machine Learning," *Leading Edge*, 35, no. 10 (2016): 906–909, http://dx.doi.org/10.1190/tle35100906.1.

Hall, Matt, and Brendon Hall, "Distributed Collaborative Prediction: Results of the Machine Learning Contest," *Leading Edge*, 36, no. 3 (2017): 267–269. DOI: 10.1190/tle36030267.1.

Hartigan, J. A., "Asymptotic Distributions for Clustering Criteria," *Annals of Statistics*, 6 (1978): 117–131.

Hartigan, J. A., "Statistical Theory in Clustering," *Journal of Classification*, 2 (1985): 63–76.

Holdaway, K. R., L. Fabbi, and D. Lozie, "Unconventional Data-Driven Methodologies Forecast Performance in Unconventional Oil and Gas Reservoirs," paper 1910-2015, presented at the 2015 SAS Global Forum, Dallas.

Hubert, L., "Approximate Evaluation Techniques for the Single-Link and Complete-Link Hierarchical Clustering Procedures," *Journal of the American Statistical Association*, 69 (1974): 698–704.

Jochen, V. A., and J. P. Spivey, "Probabilistic Reserves Estimation Using Decline Curve Analysis with the Bootstrap Method," paper SPE 36633 presented at the 1996 SPE Annual Technical Conference and Exhibition, Denver (October 6–9).

Johnston, J., and A. Guichard, "Using Big Data Analysis Tools to Understand Bad Hole Sections on the UK Continental Shelf," Society of Petroleum Engineers (2015). DOI: 10.2118/1015-0060-JPT.

Klastorin, T. D., "Assessing Cluster Analysis Results," *Journal of Marketing Research,* 20 (1983): 92–98.

Ling, R. F., "A Probability Theory of Cluster Analysis," *Journal of the American Statistical Association,* 68 (1973): 159–169.

McClain, J. O. and V. R. Rao, "CLUSTISZ: A Program to Test for the Quality of Clustering of a Set of Objects," *Journal of Marketing Research,* 12 (1975): 456–460.

Mueller, D. W. and Sawitzki, G., "Excess Mass Estimates and Tests for Multimodality," *JASA,* 86 (1991): 738–746.

Patricelli, J. A., and C. L. McMichael, "An Integrated Deterministic/Probabilistic Approach to Reserve Estimations," *JPT* (January 1995).

Rahman, Laique, MSc dissertation: "The Design of a Statistically Driven Classification System for Data Mining and Automated Processing of Well Logs and Associated Data," University of Manchester (2015).

Saenger, E. H. et al., "A Passive Seismic Survey over a Gas Field: Analysis of Low-Frequency Anomalies," *Geophysics,* 74, no. 2 (2009), https://doi.org/10.1190/1.3078402.

Sarle, W. S. *Cubic Clustering Criterion,* SAS Technical Report A-108, Cary, NC: SAS Institute Inc. (1983).

Sarle, W. S., and An-Hsiang Kuo, *The MODECLUS Procedure,* SAS Technical Report P-256, Cary, NC: SAS Institute Inc. (1993).

Schnetzler, Emmanuel, T., and David L. Alumbaugh, "The Use of Predictive Analytics for Hydrocarbon Exploration in the Denver-Julesburg Basin," *Leading Edge,* 36, no. 3 (2017): 227–233. DOI: 10.1190/tle36030227.1.

Thompson, R. S., and J. D. Wright, "The Error in Estimating Reserve Using Decline Curves," paper SPE 16295 presented at the 1987 SPE Hydrocarbon Economics and Evaluation Symposium, Dallas (March 2–3).

Wong, M. A. and Schaack, C. "Using the kth Nearest Neighbor Clustering Procedure to Determine the Number of Subpopulations," *American Statistical Association, Proceedings of the Statistical Computing Section,* 40–48 (1982).

CHAPTER **4**

Continuous Monitoring

"Alice laughed: 'There's no use trying,' she said; 'one can't believe impossible things.'"
"I daresay you haven't had much practice," said the Queen.
"When I was younger, I always did it for half an hour a day. Why, sometimes I've believed as many as six impossible things before breakfast."

Lewis Carroll (*Alice's Adventures in Wonderland*)

INTRODUCTION

Continuous monitoring of multivariate and multidimensional complex systems' physical state is a relatively immature technology in geophysical exploration. There are seismological surveillance solutions for 4D surveys that monitor subtle changes in oil and gas reservoirs. A controlled seismic system, named ACROSS (Accurately Controlled and Routinely Operated Signal System), has been implemented in some of the aging Middle East fields. There are also seismic methods to image individual lithological zones that vary in physical properties over time. Continuous monitoring of the physical state of oil and gas reservoirs can be extended in carbon capture and sequestration (CSS) and aquifer environments. The application of data-driven analytical techniques enables continuous monitoring solutions with event stream processing engines. The intelligent reservoirs equipped with sensors source real-time data to dynamic soft computing models at the edge where data is generated.

Digital oilfields and intelligent wells are instrumented to continuously send data to analytical centers of excellence and remote geoscientific technology hubs for real-time monitoring and decision making. We can report on downhole conditions throughout the entire portfolio of an asset's production wells. Fiber optics and automated analytical workflows implemented on streaming data have combined to increase the importance of monitoring sensors. We shall discuss *distributed temperature sensing* (DTS) and *distributed acoustic sensing* (DAS) data and their evolving importance to manage the life cycles of an oil and gas reservoir. Machine learning (ML) and deep learning (DL) data-driven analytical workflows are influential in generating real-time knowledge from multiple streaming datasets. Let us explore the time series geophysical and petrophysical datasets that can be harnessed to address upstream business problems. We can move beyond the traditional point sampling and deterministic interpretation by aggregating innovative datasets and data-driven cognitive soft computing techniques. The industry has witnessed an evolution from the focus of permanent sensors distributed to monitor downhole well conditions to characterizing the reservoir in its entirety.

CONTINUOUS MONITORING IN THE RESERVOIR

Today we witness instrumented producing wells that continuously relay data that describes the signatures of downhole conditions. Advancements in deployment tactics, fiber optics, and innovative interpretation workflows have coalesced to increase the footprint of permanent monitoring sensors delivering real-time knowledge of the subsurface. Continuous real-time temperature (DTS) and pressure data streams emulate well logs during the production phases. Such datasets address both technical and business problems during interventions and stimulations in tandem with reduction in OPEX and deferred production. Point sampling has been and continues to be an issue in the Oil and Gas industry as we strive to understand the complexities of the subsurface systems. However, we are piecemeal evolving from point sampling to an industry acceptance of continuous measurements via fiber optics. As innovative fiber-optic sensor technology is adopted, we notice the focus of installing permanent sensors that enable reservoir characterization in addition to simple monitoring and surveillance. However, to maximize the value of all the measurements from permanent sensors, we must adopt and implement automated and semi-automated advanced data-driven analytical methodologies. Let us look at some of the applications and benefits of harnessing continuous monitoring data streams to step beyond mere surveillance and enable reservoir characterization. We can then reduce the decision-making cycles as business and technical tactics and strategies are made in real time.

MACHINE LEARNING TECHNIQUES FOR TEMPORAL DATA

Why do we wish to study time series data? Perhaps we want to predict the future based on historical signatures or control more tightly the process generating the temporal datasets. Is it more fundamental to understand the mechanism behind these time series signatures, or do we only want to document the description of the significant features hidden in the data?

Certain measurements are continuously changing, such as temperature and pressure, but invariably a digital recording is collated discretely in time. There is univariate and multivariate time series, but in the seismic signature identification, we can focus on the former where one kind of measurement is repeatedly made.

Dynamical machine learning (DML) is quickly hitting the streets as the *sine qua non* of the artificial intelligence (AI) domain. These workflows necessitate real-time recursive learning algorithms. Implementing these types of algorithms require time-varying data models that continuously learn. There are four benefits to DML:

1. Real-time learning.
2. Machine learning acclimates to aging hardware to attain a new normal state.
3. Fewer false positives owing to meta-models being established by the underlying system states.
4. The ease and efficiency of evolving digital twins enable continuous closed-loop performance enhancements.

SPATIOTEMPORAL PERSPECTIVES

Uncertainty in the subsurface invariably stems from a fuzziness (Aminzadeh, 1991) as opposed to pure chance. There is a much more critical need to model the complexity in the spatial and temporal heterogeneity of the subsurface as fluid flows through a "living" and dynamic reservoir.

We are solving an inverse problem through a suite of calibration steps. Having achieved a calibrated model of the heterogeneity, the well-forecasting and field-depletion strategies are more robust and reliable. There are essentially two paths for model inversion. First, from a computational perspective, we can achieve efficiency by adopting filtering workflows that count on the linearity inherent in the models. Second, to address the more pervasive nonlinear models associated with reservoir characterization we must rely more heavily on pure optimization methodologies.

Spatiotemporal issues necessitate formulation of an inversion problem from the standpoint of a functional mismatch between input observations and the numerical models' output values. All the independent observations are thus functions in space and time. The uncertainty inherent in the data acquisition can also be expressed in the mismatched functional relationship between input and output parameters. We can change the model parameters at each grid node within the reservoir discretization to render an optimal search protocol. Invariably, optimizing the inversion of a model, working with a nonlinear and non-convex objective function, requires multiple time-consuming simulations. To add to this modeling issue are the degrees of freedom that are greater than the number of observations.

We can address these problems by adopting *principal component analysis* (PCA) to reduce the dimension of the input dataset to a smaller space and retain the range of variance across the input observations. The first principal component is the largest possible variance in the spatial geological features under study, and hence accounts for most of the variability in the input dataset. We can trim down the number of optimal solutions by growing the diversity of the observations within the dataset.

TIME SERIES ANALYSIS

Let us from the outset define what a time series is so that we can assign appropriate algorithms to analyze such a series. Essentially it is a sequence of vectors or scalars that are dependent on time. We are studying patterns in a temporal dataset associated with specific points or periods of time. In the Oil and Gas industry we are considering the following examples of time series data that are either discrete or continuous by nature:

- *Discrete data:* individual data points or phases of a time series
- *Continuous data:* data containing any value deemed feasible within a range

Time series data comprises attributes in two distinctive shades:

1. Contextual attributes
2. Behavioral attributes

The first shade is temporal by nature and the second maps to a temporal measurement.

If we dig deeper into the temporal data world, we can identify two groups of distinct classification:

1. We can categorize precise moments in time. Outstanding events can be predicted to occur at specific moments in the time series data streams. We associate labels with the specific times, and then the classification is based on the behavioral attributes for each moment.
2. We can alternatively classify a time window or a complete time series. In such cases, the association of the labels is with windowed temporal samples or the entire time series.

Potential risks associated with strategic decision making in upstream are reduced or even mitigated with intelligent time series forecasting data-driven analytical workflows. ML is expanding the array of data-mining soft computing technologies by enabling computer algorithms to adjust to new data without explicitly being reprogrammed dynamically. From a time series perspective, this ability offered incredible accuracy for continuous monitoring of time series data generated at high frequencies and sampled at sub-second intervals.

In a stationary time series the mean, variance, and auto-correlation properties are constant. The majority of forecasting methodologies are grounded on the supposition that the time series can be *stationarized* by using mathematical transformations. It then becomes easier to predict the time series since the future statistical properties will be the same as the historical values.

We can elicit meaningful sample statistics from a stationarized time series as descriptors of future behavior. Be aware that extrapolating regression models fitted to nonstationary time series data is problematic.

ADVANCED TIME SERIES PREDICTION

It is imperative in the Oil and Gas industry to generate robust and efficient forecasts from the near- and far-term perspectives. The reservoirs are very complex, and an empirical trend analysis of the historical production data provides fundamental decline curve analysis (DCA) and tenuous time series predictions. ML workflows have emerged across multiple vertical businesses to address the uncertainty inherent in traditional forecasting techniques and time series analysis. Essentially, we can put prediction methods into two baskets:

1. Qualitative
2. Quantitative

The first methodology describes those case studies where the Oil and Gas industry relies solely on geoscientific expertise and experience, and *not* on data. The second approach is underpinned by data and classic data-driven time series analytical workflows.

There are several standard time series models available across the industries. Some of the temporal model predictors include:

- ARIMA (autoregressive integrated moving average)
- VAR (vector autoregressive)
- Holt-Winters
- Linear regression
- Nonlinear regression

Most time series models necessitate good-quality data to generate accurate forecasts. Thus, it is imperative to complete a set of data-processing steps to ascertain a robust dataset input to the temporal modeling processes.

It is important to understand that no single forecasting technique is optimum for several geologic environments. There is, for example, a significant difference in fluid flow through conventional and unconventional reservoirs. The traditional ARP's equations are overly optimistic when fitted to unconventional reservoirs' historical production data, owing to the very low permeability and poor porosity values of the reservoir rocks.

Is it feasible to combine multiple data-driven time series forecasting techniques to attain a more robust and reliable workflow to predict events in the Oil and Gas industry?

Let us study the three most important components of any time series data set:

1. Trends and cycles
2. Seasonality
3. Residuals

Trends can be surfaced through identification of a long-term increase or decrease in the data window. And, of course, these trends can alternate between increasing and decreasing directions. The cyclical nature of time series data reflects the highs and lows or ups and downs of the data from a time window or periodicity that is not fixed.

Seasonality refers to patterns that take shape owing to repeated factors impacting the data at fixed and understood time windows, such as when a well is shutting in periodically each month. Remember, seasonal is different from cyclical in that the former has a fixed characteristic associated with periods in a calendar year. Figure 4.1 illustrates an original time series dataset convolved with an additive model, and Figure 4.2 shows the decomposition panels for the inherent trends and seasonality of the temporal signatures.

The decomposition process to extract each of these components from a time series dataset enables the analyst to appreciate the key driving factors that are signatures of past and potentially future events. Is there an increasing or decreasing trend inherent in the data over a time window? How much fluctuation do we see on a weekly or monthly basis? How many outliers are there in the temporal dataset?

Here is a proposed additive model:

$$y_t = T_t + S_t + R_t$$

where the time series data is represented by y_t and the Trends (T_t), Seasonality (S_t), and Residuals (R_t) are the contributing components over a period of time t.

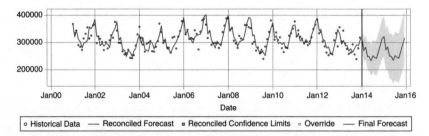

Figure 4.1 Original time series convolved additive model

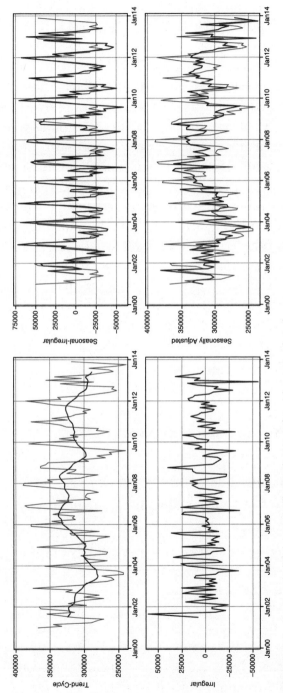

Figure 4.2 Decomposition panels illustrating trends and seasonal cycles

We could also look at the time series data from a multiplicative perspective. Here is a proposed multiplicative model:

$$y_t = T_t \times S_t \times R_t$$

When the size of the seasonal oscillations or the dissimilarity inherent in the trend-cycle does not show variance with the level of the time series, the additive model is more appropriate. However, when the seasonal pattern and trend-cycle variations appear to be about the level of the time series, then it is better to implement a multiplicative model. With seismic time series, additive models are more prevalent.

One of the most important steps in the analytical time series workflow is the first phase of smoothing the data. There are again multiple approaches:

Best Non-Seasonal Smoothing Models:

- Damped trend exponential smoothing
- Linear (Holt) exponential smoothing
- Simple exponential smoothing
- Double (Brown) exponential smoothing

Best Seasonal Smoothing Models:

- Winters (additive) method
- Winters (multiplicative) method
- Additive seasonal exponential smoothing

Post-smoothing, we need to identify any seasonality inherent in the time series data across the window of study.

Production Gap Analysis

Production of hydrocarbons throughout the life cycle of a mature field can be erratic or even exponentially decline at a gradual pace. Well tests and EOR stimulations compartmentalize periods of continuous production. We also implement secondary and tertiary artificial lift methods to mitigate non-production times (NPT). Oil and gas companies strive to sustain a rate of production to minimize the gap between the ideally forecasted level and that level at the point of sale, further downstream from upstream activities. The gap increases as inefficiencies creep into the multitude of workflows and processes across the various systems, namely, reservoir, wells, and surface facilities.

The accuracy of production rate forecasts is critical to preempt unnecessary costs and mitigate risks associated with CAPEX and OPEX on field redevelopment activities. Ideally, we would like to deliver an enterprise solution that enables a probabilistic set of data-driven methodologies married to a suite of deterministic interpretations based on first principles and the geoscientists' experience. It is important to evolve the solution by integrating a scalable and repeatable set of steps as detailed in the SEMMA process (see Chapter 6, "Seismic Attribute Analysis"). Data quality and enrichment steps precede exploratory data analysis (EDA) visualization. EDA is implemented to identify trends and patterns in the multivariate and multidimensional datasets.

After applying factor analysis and transformation workflows, we can establish some soft computing techniques to generate a probabilistic set of models. The assessment step in SEMMA delivers the optimal model based on the input data and the statistical influence of the independent variables on the target parameter. We can then operationalize this model in the existing architecture to search for patterns and signatures in the new data as it streams through the predictive model to address the production gap under study.

Figure 4.3 illustrates a few of the trends a temporal data-driven analytical workflow is likely to identify.

Two time series analytical models used in a gap analysis are *auto-regressive integrated moving average* (ARIMA) and *unobserved components model* (UCM).

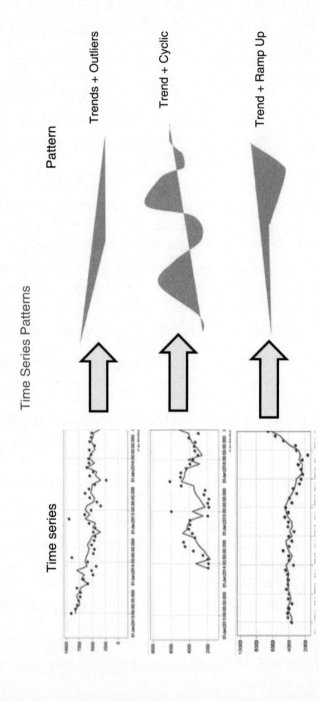

Figure 4.3 Time series patterns enable a hydrocarbon production gap analysis

ARIMA:

■ Forecasts evenly spaced and univariate time series data

■ Predicts a value as a linear combination of previous values in the same time series and current and historical values of other temporal datasets (ARIMAX model)

■ Breaks analysis into three stages: identification, estimation, and diagnostic forecasting

UCM:

■ Decomposes temporal data into trends, cycles, and regression effects

■ Delivers an array of diagnostic workflows to score the strength of a fitted model

■ Provides a succinct analysis of all underlying mechanisms inherent in the time series

■ Encapsulates the versatility of ARIMA and benefits of all smoothing models

The predictive advantages of a time series data-driven analysis are illustrated in Figure 4.4. The traditional DCA workflow, using the empirical ARP's equations, shows a remarkable decline in the forecast from January 2006. The actual production is very close to the UCM model. The shaded area represents reconciled 95 percent confidence limits that depict the uncertainty in the forecast with upper and lower bounds of production prediction.

Applying ARIMA and UCM soft computing models to forecast hydrocarbons production provides business value over the traditional DCA workflows. We can capture the patterns and trends in the field's production. We are better placed to adopt more accurate forecasts to improve resource utilization and mitigate NPT and lower deferments that adversely impact performance.

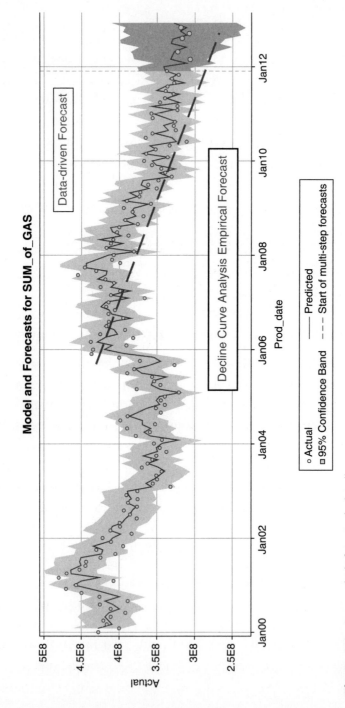

Figure 4.4 Gap analysis for a typical well

DIGITAL SIGNAL PROCESSING THEORY

When we examine a time series process, *P*, directed by linear dynamics, we are moving into the area of *digital signal processing* (DSP). Invariably we are modeling a specific time series process to predict future inputs that bear signatures with a priori significance.

DSP theory can be segregated into four the following four soft computing models: potential groups of linear models:

1. Autoregressive (AR[p])
2. Moving average (MA[q])
3. Autoregressive moving average (ARMA[p, q])
4. Autoregressive integrated moving average (ARIMA[p, i, q])

Most software packages that perform time series analysis and hence forecasting capabilities stipulate certain data criteria:

- The dataset has one variable for each dependent variable.
- There is a time identification variable that reflects a periodicity for each row of data. Invariably it is necessary to sort on this variable to ensure a linear temporal progression of observations for the data under study.
- The data points are equally set apart such that successive observations adhere to a fixed time interval. This enables a characteristic periodicity such as hourly or monthly.

HYDRAULIC FRACTURE MONITORING AND MAPPING

The monitoring and subsequent mapping of the fracture network generated by a hydraulic fracture strategy enable engineers to optimize hydrocarbon production. It is critical to identify the optimum completion tactics for a given reservoir to maximize the cumulative production of hydrocarbons and to enhance water management strategies. Engineers can use production logging tool (PLT) data to discover which stage in a multilayer reservoir is generating the individual rates of production for oil, gas, and water. With this knowledge, it is plausible to target an optimum number of stages and their locations along a given wellbore. Appreciating the fracture network is key to driving the design of the operational parameters to exploit maximum reserves. We can mitigate risk factors through analytical workflows that implement soft computing techniques during real-time monitoring of the hydraulic fracture. Where is the fluid movement? Can we discover fracture progression and connectivity across the reservoir? Are the fracture fluids and proppant in our zonal target? The stimulation operating parameters are dynamic even from the same part of the reservoir. We need insightful observations, and microseismic data provides answers to improve well spacing and completion strategy.

Microseismic data aggregated with geologic, petrophysical, and active seismic datasets extends the business benefits by providing in-depth geological and geomechanical analysis. The fracture modeling enables us, through monitoring and mapping, to estimate stimulated rock volume (SRV), the propped half-length, and properties of the fracture network that impact the recovery factor and rates of production.

COMPLETIONS EVALUATION

A simple data-integration and data-mining suite of supervised and unsupervised workflows were implemented by an operator in the compound anticlinal structure in the Pinedale asset in Wyoming. The database included general well information, operational stimulation parameters, and PLT data. Other datasets aggregated into the analytical data mart included some formation physical properties, such as sums and averages of the petrophysical data for the sands and various lithologies across the anticline. Production gas rates and flow-back regimes completed the study data mart for analytical purposes. The operator assessed both univariate and multivariate analytical workflows (Huckabee and Minquan et al., 2010) and determined a bivariate and multivariate hybrid methodology provided far greater accuracy, owing to the commingled and heterogeneous nature of the reservoir.

A fast feed-forward neural network after a cluster analysis enabled the geoscientists to understand the subtle differences in fluid production as it relates to the completion strategy of each well under surveillance. This is an example of an effective ensemble methodology for data-driven analytics. The study initially focused on identifying which stages produced most of the water and ascertained maximum flow-back regimes and proppant amount to not only reduce OPEX but also increase gas production. The study has a plausible extension. We could analyze the geological parameters, implemented to characterize stage location, such as the slope of the anticline (first derivative), curvature (second derivative), and distance from the global maximum at the peak of the structure. This analysis could determine the completion strategy to maximize location of subsequent wellbores across the reservoir structure.

RESERVOIR MONITORING: REAL-TIME DATA QUALITY

Quality assurance (QA) of real-time data is essential to maximize the intrinsic value in exploration work processes. On a high level, the real-time data consists of time series with tag information (a tag describes a data collection point) and measures (pressure, temperature, flow, etc.).

A lot of resources are used to monitor normal state when the desired situation is to manage deviations. We must ensure the robustness of the data to automate the QA processes and enable more sophisticated exploitation of the raw data.

We must aspire to some basic requirements in a data QA platform. The requirement areas must address:

- Identification of data not received within expected timeframe
- Imputation of missing data
- Documentation of data deemed outside of predefined thresholds
- Violation of QA rules
- Exploration of trends and correlations across dependent and independent variables
- Aggregation and integration workflows for a spatiotemporal database
- Manipulation and transformation operations
- Management of all predefined data quality rules
- Communication of alerts caused by rule violations and abnormalities

A combination of real-time data, near-real-time data, and batch data are received from different sources and in different formats. The data should be used for different purposes:

- Near-real-time for monitoring and alerting
- Analytical workflow and process support

Real-time data must be checked against a simple set of rules ("Level 1 Rules") before populating a real-time data mart in near real time.

Real-time, near-real-time, and batch data should be substantiated against a more complex set of rules, as depicted in Figure 4.5. Those rules might consist of sophisticated time series analysis, other analytical functions, comparison with historical data, and other complex rules. To be fed into the Process Support/Decision Support, data must be filtered, aggregated, and integrated. The accepted latency in the dataflow should be investigated, but the complexity will not allow for accurate real-time execution.

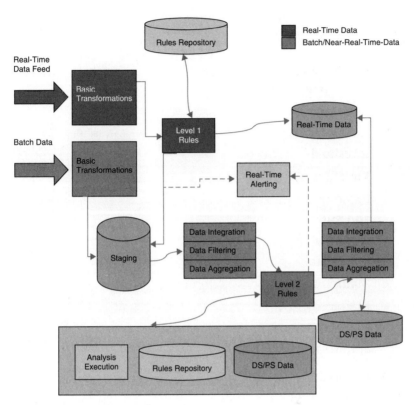

Figure 4.5 Data QC workflows

For both Level 1 and Level 2 rules, appropriate alarms must be triggered.

High-level platform architecture describes the services necessary for an overall data QC solution. At a high level, a potential solution, as depicted in Figure 4.6, necessitates the following services:

- Data acquisition services for both real-time and batch/near-real-time data
- Data quality services with rules execution services
- Data integration services for both real-time and batch/near-real-time data
- Data storage services

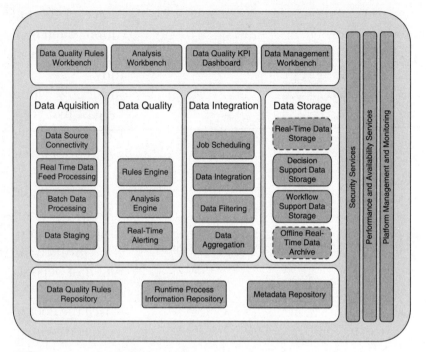

Figure 4.6 Data QC solution platform

- Repository and metadata services for both design time and runtime
- Client tools
- Platform services

DISTRIBUTED ACOUSTIC SENSING

Distributed acoustic sensing (DAS) systems take advantage of the fiber-optic cables that consist of one or several optical fibers used to transmit light. It is an emerging technology that finds its roots across the department of defense. A laser pulse propagates along an optical fiber that features scattering locations, resulting in discretely distributed interferometers that have a pulse length comparable to the gauge length. A temporal function is established that measures the intensity of the reflected light over time after the laser pulse transmission. Another pulse is sent along the fiber once the previous pulse has traveled the full length of the fiber and returned to its initial location. Sequential pulses are compared to note any fluctuations in the intensity of the reflected light from the same area under study.

We can apply DAS workflow analysis to monitor flow within a system. Interesting literature published in the past five years has tended to concentrate on the vertical and horizontal wells drilled in the tight gas reservoirs across North American assets (Van der Horst et al., 2013).

The collated DAS datasets are ideal for understanding liquid production flows across different zonal regions. We can monitor inter-zonal reservoir flow and hence optimize artificial lift strategies as we observe in near real time the fluid flows through the wellbores, noting any leaks or significant accretion of deposits in the well. Success in pipeline integrity monitoring with DAS (Williams, 2012), initiated several years ago, opened the door to DAS moving into the realm of downhole applications (Koelman et al., 2012).

Applying DAS as a surveillance tool supersedes traditional monitoring techniques. The fiber-optic technology is ideally suited for time-lapse or continuous monitoring. DAS provides high spatial resolution at sample periods as high as 20 kHz along the entire length of a horizontal wellbore. It is thus feasible to create a permanent real-time surveillance and monitoring system for a broad range of well operations at a low OPEX.

Enhanced oil recovery (EOR) techniques are evolving with the onset of innovative digital technologies. It is necessary to adopt a data-driven set of workflows that analyze fiber-optic datasets to improve both secondary and tertiary recovery solutions.

DISTRIBUTED TEMPERATURE SENSING

Distributed temperature sensing (DTS) systems enable downhole temperature measurements to be collected at multiple points simultaneously by way of fiber optics. It is understood that wellbore temperature, as measured along the entire interval of the fiber extent, is strictly correlated to contemporaneous flow conditions in the localized reservoir. DTS measurements are critical to validate production surveillance.

Let us examine a case study where we interpret the significance of the formation properties and flow rate inherent in the DTS data. It is an inverse problem. Sui et al. (2008) adopted the least-square methodology to determine formation properties using DTS data. Zhuoyi et al. (2010) developed a soft computing model to measure both pressure and temperature distributions along a horizontal well. They implemented a Markov Chain Monte Carlo workflow to ascertain flow rates from the DTS data.

Goals:

- Continuous downhole monitoring of temperature measurements along a horizontal wellbore
- Optimization of hydraulic fracture completion strategy
- Reservoir performance monitoring
- Catastrophic completion failure

We used data provided from several wellbores drilled in an unconventional tight gas reservoir in the Barnett field. There were 29 measurements taken at 86-second measuring intervals that generated 220,000 temperature records at a maximum depth of 12,445 feet.

Considering the close surface proximity and the temperature distribution, the temperature "turbulence" can be attributed to effects of cold-water jets (at 1000 m depth). Similar effects could be observed during the well stimulation in fracking. It is worth remarking on the fact that the visual effect of temperature turbulence is significantly reduced when the temperature aggregation is done over smaller depth ranges.

When it comes to DTS data, where data points represent samples from a common data surface, a special fast rendering

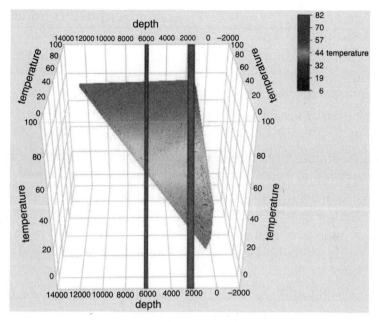

Figure 4.7 Surface plot of temperature DTS data

algorithm was developed to allow smoothing over the gaps between datasets, giving a "clean" terrain look (Figure 4.7).

Figure 4.7 illustrates the DTS data with temperature decreases corresponding to distinct reservoir layers. The fiber-optic DTS data reflects the temperature changes as gas inflows are cooled by the Joule-Thomson effect at two different depths that map to the two-tiered reservoir. We observe the temperature decreases in the reservoir layer at the shallower depth (2000 ft.) are greater than those witnessed at the greater depth (6000 ft.). Figure 4.7 illustrates this by the mapping of the thickness of the line indicating the two reservoir layers. This behavior is indicative of the drawdown being less at 2000 ft. than at 6000 ft. DTS data enables geoscientists to monitor the gas/oil ratio (GOR) since any increase in GOR results in the reservoir fluid viscosity to decrease and the flow rate to alter. Thus, there is an apparent drop in temperature.

The currently provided DTS data, which features variables such as Time × Depth → Temperature, can be enhanced with other properties commonly available from the fiber sensors, for example, pressure and the speed of flow, and combined with seismic and drilling data. The visualizations of such data could include dynamic layered models of multiple simultaneous properties measured across the reservoir, for example, distribution of temperature across the reservoir at the different depths, changes of gas or liquid pressure at various areas over time, and level of equipment deterioration.

With the development of several novel methods for installing optical fibers in oil and gas wells for DTS, the search is on for gaining the considerable value offered from this remarkable technology.

An extremely cost-efficient and accurate method of determining steam breakthrough in producing wells has been developed that takes advantage of the power of DTS technology.

Various studies have been undertaken that implement the DTS technology to identify steam breakthrough intervals. It is critical to determine precise entry points of different fluids and particularly the emergence of steam within the wellbore based on temperature transients that are activated by water injection. DTS technology provides an almost instantaneous understanding of the temperature profiles throughout the entire length of the wellbore. This is obviously advantageous over snapshots of the temperature changes post–water injection. It is critical for reservoir management to understand the breakthrough in space and time of all injected fluids across all production wells included in an EOR technique. By extension, robust and practical steam management relies on steam breakthrough understanding at the production wells. To identify which zones are generating steam is key to an economically viable steam-flood process. Of course, reservoir geology underpins the mechanism that drives the steam progression across the zones impacting the production wells. To mitigate a dramatic decrease in oil production, the steam breakthrough identification methodologies necessitate a data-driven workflow tied with an empirical reservoir management interpretation. Well temperature profiles and pulsed neutron logs provide critical data.

DTS technology expands and enhances the breakthrough identification techniques, delivering real-time surveillance and monitoring via fiber optics.

Figure 4.8 shows DTS data applicability to optimize a hydraulic fracture strategy in the unconventional reservoirs where tight rocks and low permeability require the breaking of the rocks to initiate the flow of the hydrocarbons to producing wells.

We can quickly identify temperature profiles across the entire horizontal wellbore and use this knowledge to evaluate fracture origination depth, vertical exposure, and the number of fractures generated by the fracture fluid. We can also note the flow-back regimes in greater detail to assess the efficacy of the stimulation process.

The DTS data can be challenging to interpret. Using a sophisticated mathematical set of models, we can simplify the interpretation of both the heat and mass transfer throughout the hydraulic fracture strategy. Thermal models can be built to simulate the temperature gradients along the entire wellbore, accounting for the impact of both conduction and convection. Figure 4.8 is a surface plot that demonstrates changes in temperature, ranging from blue, representing cooler temperatures, to red, indicative of the highest temperatures across the wellbore during the fracturing stimulation process. Blue zones are symptomatic of poorly perforated stages. The independent parameters on the right-hand side of the surface plot can be toggled to different values, and associated measurements are then visualized in the 3D cube. This enables the engineers to identify the best and worst stages across the wellbore as the fluids flow through the producing wellbore. We can see the

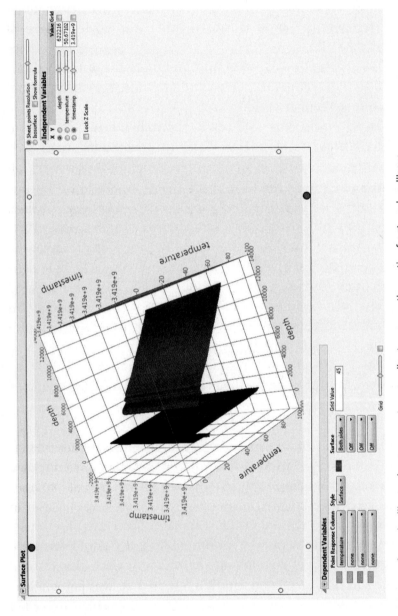

Figure 4.8 Surface plot illustrating temperature gradients across the entire fractured wellbore

blue peak at a depth of about 2000 feet, reflecting an isolation problem with the hydraulic fracture strategy carried out on this wellbore. With this type of knowledge, we can design more accurate fracture models and estimate, to a higher degree of fidelity, the conductivity across the fracture geometry. Perhaps we need to address the number and location of perforations and which stages to close in for following fracture strategies in adjacent wellbores?

Several viable diagnostic methodologies have evolved to improve the interpretation of the fracturing networks generated by the hydraulic fracture strategies. Microseismic plays an important role as well as tilt meters and radioactive tracers, logs of temperature gradients, and even borehole images. Often production data analysis and pressure transient analysis (PTA) are employed from an empirical perspective. The advent of fiber-optic adoption in the industry is enabling a complementary and efficient technology to interpret the temperature and acoustic properties that can be associated to fracture growth and networks based on both visualization determinism and a data-driven soft computing methodology.

CASE STUDY: TIME SERIES TO OPTIMIZE HYDRAULIC FRACTURE STRATEGY

Let us consider the analytical methods that underpin the integration of both seismic and microseismic data with engineering data to maximize a hydraulic fracture suite of operational parameters in the Eagle Ford shale field in the Western Gulf Basin in South Texas.

Historically the wells drilled in the Eagle Ford play were developed based on a geometric spacing to maximize the acreage coverage such that the wells' azimuth was perpendicular to regional stress direction. Many of the wells have exceeded expectations, but the performance range has been somewhat broad when measured by daily production.

Here are some characteristics from the seismic data collected in the Eagle Ford field:

- TOC
- Porosity
- Brittle/ductile quality (LMR–MuR)
- Young's Modulus
- Bulk Modulus
- Poisson's Ratio
- Differential stress
- Stress field orientation
- Azimuthal anisotropy
- Pore pressure
- Facies (rock type, clay content)
- Qg100: Cumulative gas production 100 days after PLT data was initiated

Dataset—Seismic

- PSTM (isotropic)
- Velocity model
- Depth converted volume
- Azimuthal anisotropy
- Acoustic impedance
- Brittle/ductile
- Lambda rho, mu rho
- Poisson's Ratio
- Young's Modulus
- TOC
- Seismic facies
- Coherency
- Curvature
- Spectral decomposition

Performance Metric = Maximum Monthly Cumulative Gas
Production

Potential indicators: 36 seismic attributes and three engineering characteristics. It is important to include engineering and geological parameters as well as seismic attributes in this initial assessment of potential performance indicators.

Five Primary Performance Indicators Selected:

1. *Lateral length*—intersect more productive rock
2. *Brittle/ductile elastic inversion*—"fracability"
3. *10 Hz spectral decomposition*—presence of gas
4. *32 Hz spectral decomposition*—Eagle Ford thickness
5. *Azimuthal seismic anisotropy*—differential stress

Reservoir Characterization and Tukey Diagrams

The suite of visualizations used to perform reservoir characterization for any E&P business problem is best implemented via a Tukey set of diagrams, harnessed by several EDA workflows.

John Tukey developed interactive graphical techniques with PRIM-9 in 1972. It opened a window into the world of multivariate data to be seen from multiple perspectives. These insightful and intuitive plots and graphs surfaced hidden structures and trends in the datasets under study.

We can take advantage of the array of visualizations to explore the petrophysical and geophysical datasets to identify the correlations and relationships between the dependent and independent parameters deemed critical from the first-principle point of view.

One such visualization is depicted in Figure 4.9 and is named after Captain Matthew Henry Sankey, who adopted this kind of diagram to show the energy efficiency of a steam engine in 1898. The width of the arrows is proportional in size to the quantity of the flow under study. Figure 4.9 details the relationships

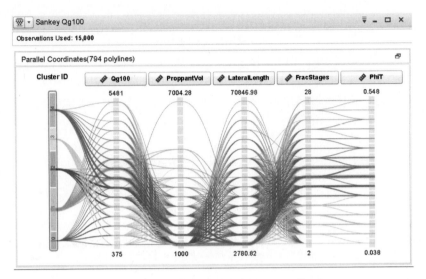

Figure 4.9 Sankey diagram for the cumulative gas production

between clusters of varying operational parameters that have been deemed statistically sensitive to the dependent variable, cumulative gas production 100 days out from when PLT data was first collected. We note the flow lines that not only reflect the correlations of the independent variables between clusters but also demonstrate ranges of values for each parameter that can be implemented as coefficients to a functional relationship that optimizes cumulative gas production.

Sankey diagrams are utilized to visualize energy or material transfers between processes. Interpretation of the Sankey diagram in Figure 4.9 enables the geoscientists to focus on clusters 1 and 4. The cumulative gas production is highest in cluster 1. As we trace the flow lines from cluster 1, we see an optimum range of values for some of the operational parameters: proppant volume, lateral length, and the number of stages used in the fracture strategy. Conversely, the Sankey diagram illustrates not only the best practices but also the worst practices. Figure 4.9 clearly shows little impact on cumulative gas production at the very long lateral lengths that are characteristic of cluster 0.

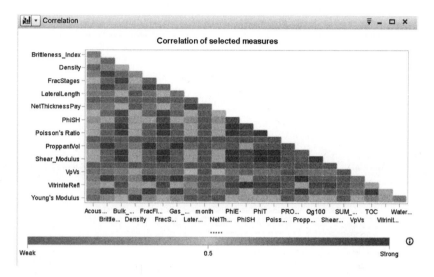

Figure 4.10   Correlation matrix

The correlation matrix depicted in Figure 4.10 is noteworthy for its internal and intuitive representation of the strength of the relationship between the main parameters in the hydraulic fracture strategy study. The color bar explains the weak to the strong correlation between the dependent and independent parameters. The identification of critical parameters becomes apparent as we glance across the matrix. Pinpoint the target variable Qg100 and enumerate those operational parameters and important geophysical and petrophysical attributes that are key drivers for maximum gas production. We can reduce the input space and begin to formulate a functional relationship to develop and evolve a soft computing model as a solution to a business problem. The business problem could be: How do I optimize the hydraulic completion strategy to maximize gas production?

The bubble plot shown in Figure 4.11 is a very traditional Tukey-style visualization as we can depict several dimensions of the data in one picture. It has the bonus of enabling a temporal dimension, as the dynamic display is ideally suited by way of

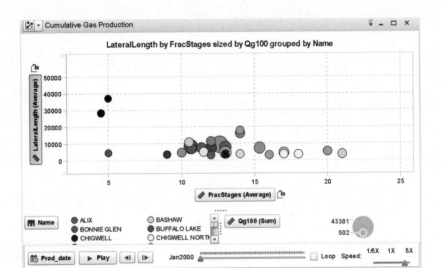

Figure 4.11 Bubble plot

"The Dance of the Bubbles" bringing to life the subtle changes in the correlations over a time window.

Figure 4.11 depicts the average lateral length along the Y-axis and the number of fracture stages along the X-axis. The cumulative gas production is reflected by the size of the bubble. We are looking for the larger size bubbles to determine optimum ranges of values for both operational parameters: lateral length and number of fracture stages. The largest bubble noted in January 2000, the beginning of the production data, illustrates the ideal number of stages to be either 12 or 13. The corresponding lateral length is noted to be about 10,000 units. By animating the bubble plot, we can observe the dynamic changes to the two operational parameters vis-à-vis the production data. The different regions add another dimension of information to the Tukey plot.

A network diagram, Figure 4.12, shows the geophysicist and petrophysicist the significant relationships between category values through a sequence of linked nodes. We generated an ungrouped version of the traditional network diagram as opposed to a hierarchical structure using a set of categories.

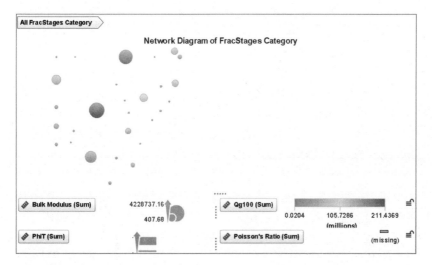

Figure 4.12 Network diagram

The target variable, Qg100, was the focus of the study. We want to understand the relationships and the statistical importance of the independent variables on our target or dependent variable. Figure 4.12 introduces the target variable, Qg100, representing the cumulative gas production. We can also see the statistical impact on gas production by the three reservoir characteristics: bulk modulus, porosity, and Poisson's Ratio. The network diagram links this knowledge together under the category of fracture stages.

The SOM maplets depicted in Figures 4.13–4.16 are ideal vehicles to visualize the dynamic correlations of the critical parameters and their associated values.

Kohonen Self-Organizing Feature Maps (SOMs), are fascinating beasts. Teuvo Kohonen, a professor of the Academy of Finland, invented them. We can represent multidimensional data in one or two dimensions. There is a data compression methodology known as vector quantization that decreases the dimensionality of vectors. Also, the Kohonen technique generates a connected network to store knowledge so that any topological relationships are established and persisted.

A typical example used to help teach the principles behind SOMs is the mapping of reservoir properties from the three-dimensional perspectives into two dimensions. One of the most interesting aspects of SOMs is that they learn to classify data without supervision. You may already be aware of supervised training techniques such as back-propagation where the training data consists of vector pairs: an input vector and a target vector. With this approach, an input vector is presented to the network (typically a multilayer feed-forward network) and the output is linked to the target vector. Any differences suggest altering the weights of the network to decrease the error in the output. This process is iterated multiple times with several sets of vector pairs so as to achieve a likely and acceptable result.

Figures 4.13–4.16 detail the 10 × 10 maplets for each of the four parameters under study:

1. Qg100 (cumulative gas production 100 days after PLT data is collected)
2. Bulk modulus
3. Fracture stages
4. Proppant volume

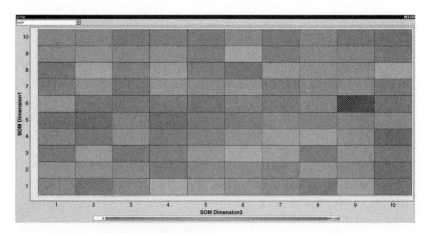

Figure 4.13   SOM diagram—Qg100

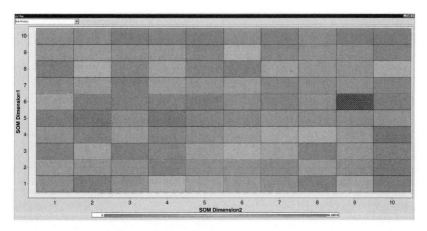

Figure 4.14 SOM diagram—Bulk modulus

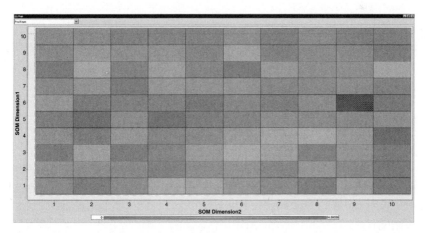

Figure 4.15 SOM diagram—Fracture stages

Let us quickly illustrate the visual power of these SOM outputs. Figure 4.13 represents the cumulative gas production. The highest production is noted in rectangle [9,6]. We can then glance at the maplets of the other parameters, focusing on the same rectangle [9,6]. Figures 4.14 and 4.15 reflect the bulk modulus and number of fracture stages respectively. Note that rectangle [9,6] for each of these parameters shows a high value based on the color scheme and sliding value of the measurements. However, Figure 4.16, representing the

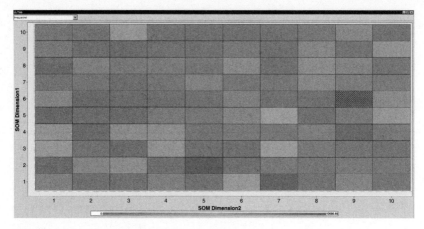

Figure 4.16 SOM diagram—Proppant volume

proppant volume, tells another story. Rectangle [9,6] reflects a lower value to the measurement of proppant poundage that will generate the highest gas production. We can see those rectangles that illustrate the higher ranges of proppant volume do not correlate with the highest gas production in Figure 4.13.

Visualizing the data using Tukey techniques is an efficient methodology to grasp the relationships and trends of the data under study. We can answer both technical and business questions as well as stimulate more insight from a data-driven perspective to complement the traditional workflows of determinism based on first principles.

REFERENCES

Aminzadeh, F., "Where Are We Now and Where Are We Going?" In: *Expert Systems in Exploration* (eds. F. Aminzadeh and M. Simaan), Tulsa, OK, SEG (1991), pp. 3–32.

Echeverria, D., and T. Mukerji, "A Robust Scheme for Spatio-Temporal Inverse Modeling of Oil Reservoirs," Department of Energy Resources Engineering, Stanford University, 367 Panama St., Stanford, CA 94305-2220, 18th World IMACS/MODSIM Congress, Cairns, Australia, July 13–17, 2009.

Hoaglin, D. C., F. Mosteller, and J. W. Tukey, *Understanding Robust and Exploratory Data Analysis*, John Wiley & Sons, New York (1983).

Huckabee, P. T., and Jin Minquan et al., "Tight Gas Well-Performance Evaluation with Neural Network Analysis for Hydraulic Propped Fracture Treatment Optimization," SPE Annual Technical Conference and Exhibition, Florence, Italy, September 19–22, 2010.

Koelman, J., J. L. Lopez, and J. Potters, "Optical Fibers: The Neurons for Future Intelligent Wells," Paper SPE 150203, presented at the 2012 SPE Intelligent Energy International, Utrecht, The Netherlands, March 27–29, 2012 .

Mohaghegh, S. D. et al., "Design Optimum Frac Jobs Using Virtual Intelligence Techniques," *Computers and Geosciences*, 26, no. 8 (October 2000): 927–939, Elsevier Science Publications, Amsterdam, Holland.

Montgomery, Douglas C., *Design and Analysis of Experiment*, John Wiley & Sons, 2004, ISBN: 047148735X.

Sui, W., D. Zhu, A. D. Hill, and C. A. Ehlig-Economides, "Model for Transient Temperature and Pressure Behavior in Commingled Vertical Wells," SPE 115200-MS, paper presented at the SPE Russian Oil and Gas Technical Conference and Exhibition, Moscow, October 28–30, 2008.

Tukey, J. W., *Exploratory Data Analysis*, Addison-Wesley (1977).

Van der Horst, J., H. den Boer, P. Panhuis, R. Kusters, D. Roy, A. Ridge, and A. Godfrey, "Fiber Optic Sensing for Improved Wellbore Surveillance," International Petroleum Technology Conference, 2013.

Williams, J., "Distributed Acoustic Sensing for Pipeline Monitoring," *Pipeline and Gas Journal*, 239, no. 7 (July 2012).

Zafari, M., and A. C. Reynolds, A.C., "Assessing the Uncertainty in Reservoir Description and Performance Prediction with the Ensemble Kalman Filter," SPE 95750, 2005 SPE Annual Technical Conference and Exhibition, Dallas, October 9–12, 2005.

Zhuoyi, Li, "Predicting Flow Profile of Horizontal Well by Downhole Pressure and Distributed Temperature Data for Water Drive Reservoir," SPE Production and Operations, 25, no. 3 (August 2010): 296–304.

CHAPTER **5**

Seismic Reservoir Characterization

"People who wish to analyze nature without using mathematics must settle for a reduced understanding."

Richard Feynman

INTRODUCTION

How do 3D seismic data volumes map to production, petrology, geology, lithology, and well logs? The current literature of reservoir characterization relates several machine learning (ML) techniques that provide insights, extrapolating reservoir properties away from localized well control. Geostatistical approaches are methodologies that take seismic inversions and correlate them to a statistical simulation of the rock properties (M. Bosch et al., 2010). Neural networks are often implemented to map rock properties, calculated from cores and well logs to seismic attributes (Haykin, 1999). Fancy names such as *adaptive neuro-fuzzy logic systems* (J. Jang, 1993) and *type-2 fuzzy logic systems* (S. O. Olatunji et al., 2011) have shown gradations in the successful application for reservoir characterization.

SEISMIC RESERVOIR CHARACTERIZATION: KEY PARAMETERS

Reservoir characterization relies on an array of different exploration and production (E&P) data collated from all the geoscientific silos. We are striving toward a probabilistic range of acceptable outcomes based on a multivariant, multidimensional, multivariate, and stochastic analysis of the aggregated data. This perspective is fundamental to transforming raw data into actionable knowledge that inexorably leads to more sound strategic and tactical decision making to address E&P business issues.

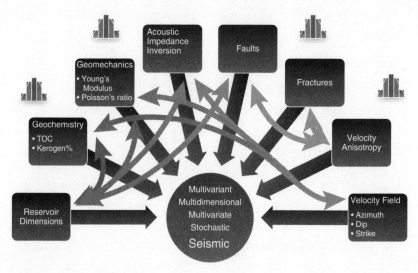

Figure 5.1 Multivariate, multivariant, multidimensional, and stochastic seismic characteristics

Let us define some of these relevant terms as depicted in Figure 5.1:

Multivariant: Multiple independent variables that affect the outcome of a singularity.

Multidimensional: Dimensions that affect independent variables. For example, reservoir compartmentalization can be interpreted by sub-seismic faults that themselves are characterized by both pre- and post-stack derived attributes. It refers to an input space where several exploratory variables may epitomize the property of collinearity where the values demonstrate an exact or approximate linear relationship. Anisotropy, inherent in some rock properties such as permeability, increases the dimensionality of the input space since it is directionally dependent.

Multivariate: Multiple dependent variables that must be predicted to reach an objective on a singularity. These are typically variables that have interdependencies that can impact the outcome of the singularity.

Stochastic: Variability and erratic behavior of independent variables.

Let us enumerate some of the key parameters that provide essential features in a typical unconventional reservoir:

- Reservoir geology:
  - Thickness and lateral extent
  - Mineralogy
  - Porosity and permeability
- Geochemistry:
  - Total organic content (TOC)
  - Maturity and kerogen richness
- Geomechanics:
  - Acoustic impedance
  - Young's Modulus
  - Poisson's Ratio (Vp/Vs)
- Faults, fractures, and stress regimes:
  - Fracture maps
  - Fault volumes
  - Stress maps

The first step in a traditional seismic interpretation workflow produces a large-scale structural perspective of the field of study. The geophysicist generates a suite of horizons and integrates a network of faults and pinch-outs. The horizons are seismic reflectors that can be traced across contiguous wavelets. Appropriate wells are tied to the time series seismic data to provide local control. The second step identifies fault locations representing reflector discontinuities. Fault characteristics can often be determined by visual inspection of the seismic traces. Rapid vertical displacement of seismic sequences is indicative of the fault plane, as illustrated in Figure 5.2.

Seismic interpretation generates multiple plots detailing the structure across the oil and gas field. The structural description

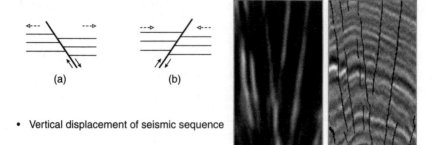

- Vertical displacement of seismic sequence

(a)   (b)

Figure 5.2 Traditional seismic fault interpretation

consists of identifying horizons and fault planes. Horizons are surfaces that the interpreter selects as reflectors based on well ties and extrapolating them over the entire 3D volume. The 3D seismic volume consists of a series of inlines and orthogonal crosslines. The manual detection of faults involves two steps. First, the geophysicist finds the fault location through deterministic visualization, noting reflector discontinuities. Second, the fault is inspected more closely to estimate the fault parameters. This is done by matching seismic sequences from both sides of the fault. In seismic images, faults are recognized by angular vertical displacement of seismic sequences along some plane (i.e., the fault plane), as illustrated in Figure 5.2.

Seismic reservoir characterization invariably adopts a suite of workflows or methodologies that incorporate the seismic attributes derived from a 3D seismic cube. Figure 5.3 illustrates such a method that executes the following steps:

- Data integration and quality control
- Exploratory data analysis
- Principal component analysis
- Self-organizing maps
- Basin characterization

Both conventional and unconventional reservoirs can be addressed by the data-driven methodology to answer questions

Figure 5.3 Seismic reservoir characterization data-driven methodology

on flow assurance, drilling performance, well categorization for field compartmentalization, optimization for additional strategies, and tactics in mature fields as well as reservoir characterization.

Principal Component Analysis

This multivariate technique examines the relationships among multiple quantitative variables, such as seismic attributes, to identify the respective contribution of the data. A *principal component analysis* (PCA) workflow (Figure 5.4) is used to summarize or factor data and detect linear relationships, thus reducing the dimensionality of the input data space.

Self-Organizing Maps

Self-organizing maps (SOMs) can be implemented as a clustering technique, providing immersive visualization and abstraction of the input data. They fall into the unsupervised, competitive learning family of neural networks. The SOM categorizes the multidimensional data space into an array of clusters. The organizational aspect of the SOM algorithm builds a suite of maplets designed on the relative distances between

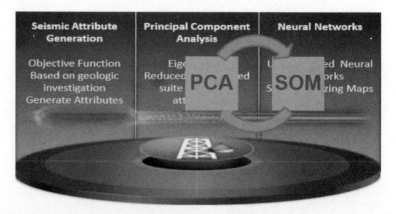

Figure 5.4 Principal component analysis workflow

the generated clusters. The algorithm establishes a natural cluster of attributes mapped to a point in space as a neuron. Neural training classifies those attributes in a seismic volume deemed essential by PCA to assign each input data sample to an optimized fitting neuron. The resulting two-dimensional map correlates to how the attributes cluster in n dimensions. This map enables geoscientists to discriminate between geologic and stratigraphic features as well as to identify direct hydrocarbon indicators (DHIs).

Integration between the PCA and SOM processes reveals a greater understanding of the geology and stratigraphy of the prospect. Offering a complementary insight into the seismic volume, traditionally achieved by conventional interpretation, diminishes the risk.

Figure 5.4 illustrates how PCA-SOM proceeds recursively to surface results that accentuate different aspects of the input space.

- Identify most important attributes for a given objective function.
- Quantify relative contribution of each attribute.
- Emphasize data aspects:
  - Fluid contacts
  - Flat spots
- Discriminate hydrocarbon locations.

MODULAR ARTIFICIAL NEURAL NETWORKS

On account of the heterogeneous nature of a reservoir and the complex interrelationships of a multivariate set of reservoir properties, the use of single artificial neural networks (ANNs) has fallen short of rigor and successful business application. Thus, a hybrid suite of ANNs or modular artificial neural networks (MANNs) has gathered traction (P. Tahmasebi, 2012). This technique is ideal to address a multivariate, multidimensional, and multivariant system or suite of connected systems as represented by reservoirs and wells. The expression "Divide and conquer" was coined in the early 1600s, based on a Latin maxim—*Divide et impera*—and underscored the policy of gaining and retaining power by splitting expansive power structures into smaller strategic power units. In computer science, a MANN is an algorithm that adheres to the paradigm: breaking a problem into sub-problems with similar traits and characteristics as the original problem. The ANN modules solve the simpler sub-problems individually and then the resulting combination achieves the overarching solution to the original business problem: how to characterize a reservoir efficiently under uncertainty from a spatial and temporal perspective. The modularity aspect is accomplished via other soft-computing techniques such as cluster and classification techniques. Seismic attributes and well logs provide sufficient data to serve as the input dimension in reservoir characterization studies. However, there are limitations to this methodology. Seismic attributes are independent variables and not dependent variables in MANNs. What does this mean? We can only use a MANN to predict petrophysical properties from seismic attributes and not the inverse. This may be a limitation, but it still provides sufficient validation as a technique to establish a more robust characterization of the reservoir away from localized well control. When exploring for hydrocarbons, we deal with various lithological groups and zonal focal clusters vis-à-vis well tops and horizons. Well logs shed light initially on the identification of both well tops and horizons of interest. This knowledge is subsequently ingested by the interpreted seismic data across the same geographical extent.

WAVELET ANALYSIS

Wavelets provide an active device to understand and analyze time series data. Wavelet analysis has critical applications in nonparametric modeling, pattern recognition, and seismic feature identification. The wavelets enable geophysicists to localize knowledge across an array of scales and mathematical loci. Traditionally, geophysicists focus on the amplitude differences and variations in the velocity field that are reflected in time shifts across seismic 3D data cubes in a temporal dimension. Any amplitude dimming or brightening is invariably correlated with an increase in water and gas saturation respectively. Additionally, a positive time shift reflects a decrease in pressure and, conversely, a negative time shift infers an increase in pressure. Geophysicists play with wavelets, studying their fundamental mathematical components, to better appreciate the time series seismic data owing to the versatility of wavelet analysis. Wavelets offer the potential to improve nonparametric models, identify hidden patterns, determine seismic features, and improve the resolution of seismic profiles for better stratigraphic and structural understanding. The petrophysicist has access to localized data of high resolution from cores and well logs; geophysicists use wavelet analysis to provide a detailed narrative of the seismic data that substantially restricts the knowledge across an array of scales and spatial locations. Also, the scales and spatial locations can be calculated efficiently via an innate and well-designed mathematical theory.

As a mathematical approach, wavelet analysis embodies both data and their functional relationships. The functions consist of mathematical properties. We can detect different scales and resolutions. Through wavelet analysis, we can accommodate spikes and discontinuities more efficiently than implementing a traditional *fast Fourier transform* (FFT). Traditional applications of wavelet analysis have focused on image compression. Fourier explains that a signal is a synthesis of sinusoidal waves of varying amplitudes, frequencies, and phases. The following example illustrates a seismic wavelet analysis applied to a Fourier transform of the trace data from the *time-offset* (temporal frequency of a wave) domain to the *frequency-wavenumber* (spatial frequency of a wave) domain. The spectrum is expressed

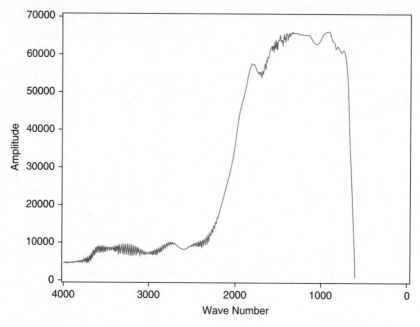

Figure 5.5 Line plot showing seismic trace data post F-K transform

as an amplitude value for each of the wavenumbers. Figure 5.5 is an illustration of the line plot for the data under study. Wavelets can be computed proficiently and provide an intuitive and sophisticated mathematical theory to escort the geophysicist through the maze of subtle signatures. The seismic data used in this study represents a mapping of a stratigraphic trap in a carbonate reservoir in the Middle-East. Widess (1973) developed a wedge model that illustrated maximum constructive interference occurs when there is equality between the wedge and tuning thickness. Subsequently, Laughlin et al. (2002) demonstrated that the channels at a greater depth are defined by stronger amplitudes at the lower frequencies, simultaneously showing that the amplitudes of the flanks at shallower depths are stronger at higher frequencies.

The seismic data is represented at two discrete scales, namely a low-frequency curve overlaid with a high-frequency oscillation that varies across several different bands. The wavelet analytical workflow enables geophysicists to classify the frequencies in the seismic amplitude data as the wavenumber varies. Amplitude is the dependent variable in this wavelet analysis and is sampled at regular intervals across the independent variable, a wavenumber that takes on the role of time.

We read the amplitude variable values into a vector before implementing the wavelet analysis. The third member of the Daubechies wavelet family was identified, and the boundaries were controlled by lengthening the signal as a linear polynomial at each endpoint. The subsequent analytical step initiated the wavelet decomposition workflow and diagnostic plots.

The output generated from the wavelet decomposition workflow and displayed in Figure 5.6 is of limited analytical and business value. A graphical visualization provides greater insight. However, the noise level depicted at the bottom of Figure 5.6 is a relevant and useful value that quantifies the

Decomposition Summary	
Decomposition Name	decomp
Wavelet Family	Daubechies Extremal Phase
Family Member	3
Boundary Treatment	Recursive Linear Extension
Number of Data Points	850
Start Level	0

Wavelet Detail Coefficients for decomp				
Translate	Level 1	Level 2	Level 3	Level 4
0	-1.70985E-9	1.31649E-10	-8.6402E-12	5.10454E-11
1	1340085.30	-128245.70	191.084707	4501.36
2		62636.70	6160.27	-1358.23
3		-238445.36	-54836.56	-797.724143
4			39866.95	676.034389
5			-28836.85	-5166.59
6			223421.00	-6088.99
7				-5794.67
8				30144.74
9				-3903.53
10				638.063264
11				-10803.45
12				33616.35
13				-50790.30

Noise Scale
169.18717

Figure 5.6 Summary of the decomposition analysis illustrating the wavelet coefficients

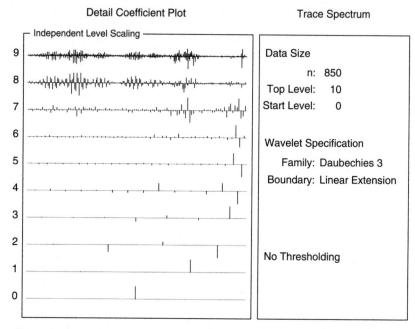

Figure 5.7 Detail coefficient plot for all levels with independent scaling

standard deviation of the highest-level detail coefficients. One of the more powerful diagnostic visualization plots is seen in Figure 5.7. It describes the coefficients prescribed by level.

In Figure 5.7, the detail coefficients for the different levels are scaled independently. We note that the oscillations in the amplitude data are expressed in the detail coefficient plot at certain levels, namely 7, 8, and 9.

We then generated a coefficient plot of only these three levels that are scaled uniformly (Figure 5.8). Noise in the data is represented in the detail coefficient plot, especially in the small coefficients at the higher levels of the data decomposition. When we zero or decrease these coefficients, we get smoother restorations of the input seismic data. By specifying a threshold value for each level of detail coefficients, we can zero or decrease all the detail coefficients below this threshold value.

Figure 5.9 depicts the detail coefficient plot with the thresholding algorithm of Donoho and Johnstone (1995). You can

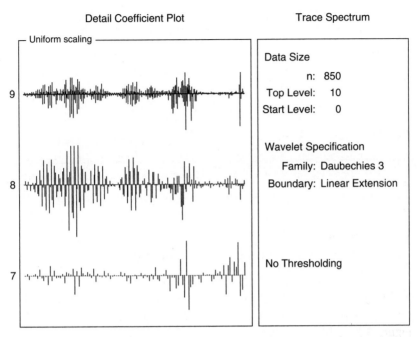

Figure 5.8 Detail coefficient plot with the top three levels scaled uniformly

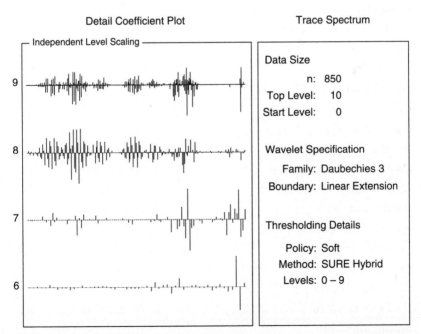

Figure 5.9 Detail coefficient plot using the Donoho and Johnstone algorithm

see the thresholding has zeroed some of the detail coefficients at the higher levels. The larger coefficients that identify the oscillation in the seismic trace data are still apparent. Thus, restorations of the input signal adopting the *thresholded* detail coefficients encapsulate the essential seismic features of the data but are smoother since most of the very fine scale detail has been removed.

A multiresolution approximation plot illustrates the restorations or reconstructions, as seen in Figure 5.10. We can delineate the reconstructions of the input seismic data by level. At a particular level, the reconstruction uses only the detail and scaling coefficients defined beneath that level.

Even at level 3, the underlying form of the input seismic signal has been defined. We have already noted that the oscillations present in the amplitude data are captured in the detail coefficients greater than level 7. Notice that at level 7 and below the

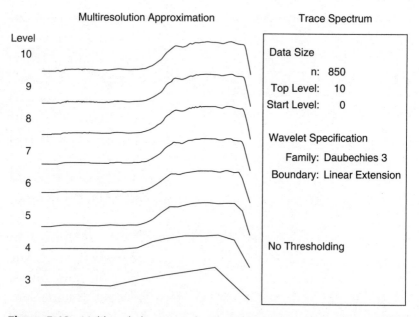

Figure 5.10   Multiresolution approximation plot showing restorations of the input signal

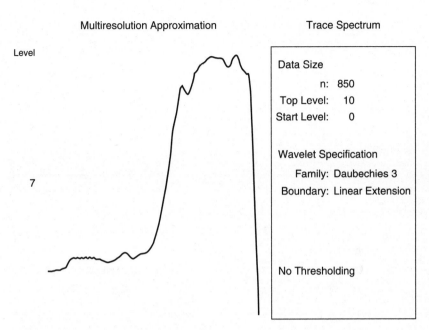

Figure 5.11 Multiresolution approximation plot of a particular level

reconstructions are mostly free of oscillation as they do not use any of the higher detail coefficients. This observation can be confirmed by plotting only this level in the multiresolution analysis as depicted in Figure 5.11.

We can plot any level for the multiresolution approximations obtained with thresholded detail coefficients. Figure 5.12 plots the top-level reconstruction obtained by using the "Sure" hybrid threshold.

The high-frequency oscillation is ever-present in the reconstruction despite the application of the "Sure" hybrid thresholding algorithm.

The multiresolution decomposition plot, as shown in Figure 5.13, depicts the detail coefficients for every level. The plot includes both the starting-level reconstruction at the lowest level and the reconstruction at the highest level. Adding suitably scaled versions of all the detail levels to the starting-level reconstruction recovers the final reconstruction.

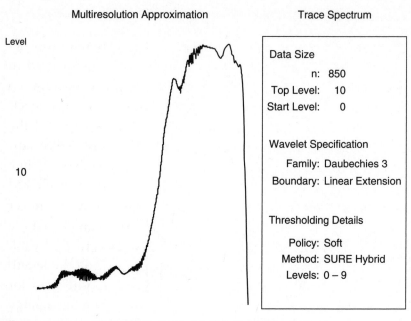

Figure 5.12 Multiresolution approximation plot for level 10

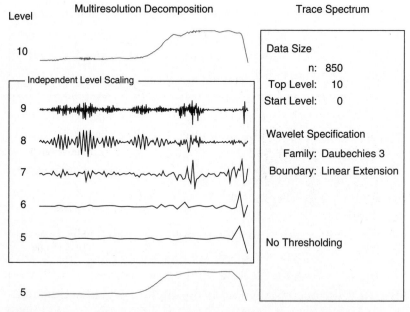

Figure 5.13 Multiresolution decomposition plot for the seismic data

Wavelet Scalograms

Wavelet scalograms are analogous to the discrete wavelet transformation (DWT) of the prevalent periodogram used in time series spectral analysis. Geophysicists use scalograms to decompose the seismic energy into appropriate energy levels and validate the time-frequency localization properties of the DWT. Figure 5.14 plots the detail coefficients as colored rectangles mapping to the size of the coefficient. The coefficient's time interval and frequency range determine location and dimensions of each rectangle depicted in the scalogram. At the lower energy scales, we note that the coefficients are rectangles whose width and length are larger and smaller respectively. The width reflects a wide time interval in the seismic data, and the length defines a limited array of frequencies. The opposite goes for those rectangles indicating coefficients of the higher energy

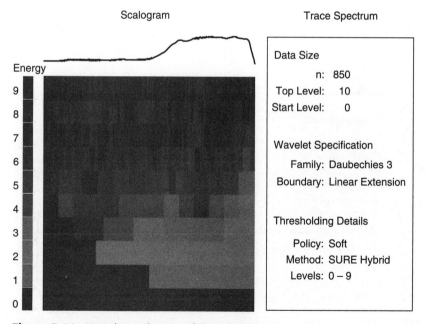

Figure 5.14   Wavelet scalogram of the seismic trace

levels. We note thinner and taller rectangles that are indicative of smaller time ranges and larger frequency ranges.

Figure 5.14 illustrates a scalogram plot of all levels with "Sure" hybrid thresholding applied. The horizontal axis reflects the time component, and the vertical axis represents the energy scale. The third dimension is the color that characterizes the logarithm of the squared modulus of the wavelet coefficients.

The overall energy of each level for the seismic trace is represented by the colored bar to the left of the scalogram plot. We sum the squares of the detail coefficients at every level to define the energy level. It is apparent that the higher energies are observed at the lower levels where the coefficients reflect the major features of the data. The geophysicists looking to interpret the finer-scale features within the seismic are directed to the higher levels. Levels above five are shown in Figure 5.15. There is no logarithmic scale applied to the rectangle heights in

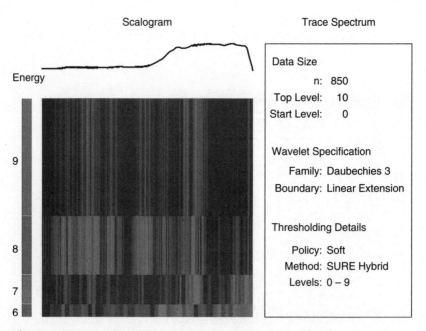

Figure 5.15 Wavelet scalogram showing most energy at level 8

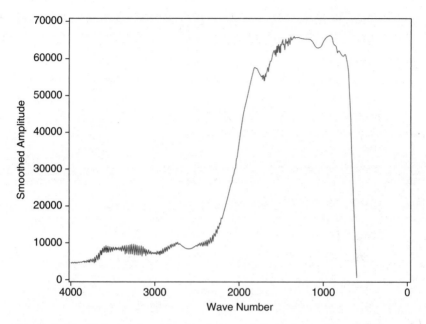

Figure 5.16   Line plot showing seismic trace data post wavelet smoothing

Figure 5.15 where the energy of the oscillation is focused in the detail coefficients at the eighth level.

When we compare Figure 5.5 and Figure 5.16, it is apparent that the wavelet smoothing of the seismic data has conserved the very critical features.

SPECTRAL DECOMPOSITION

Spectral decomposition is a powerful analysis tool that has seen significant success in delineating channels, fans, over-bank deposits, and other relatively thin architectural elements of clastic and carbonate depositional environments.

Fagan, van Wijk, and Rutledge (2013) note that "identifying individual subsurface faults in a larger fault system is important to characterize and understand the relationship between micro-seismicity and subsurface processes." The authors provided a methodology to clearly identify evidence of closely spaced overlapping faults from a suite of events originally designated in the time-offset domain. They noted that the frequency domain expression accentuated any subtle differences between events:

> Power spectra based on the Fourier transform of the time-domain autocorrelation function were used, as this formulation results in statistically independent intensities and is supported by a full body of the statistical theory upon which decision frameworks can be developed.

The following tools are demonstrated:

1. A data-mining tool with visualization brushing techniques
2. Principal component analysis on SEG-Y data
3. Wavelet trace decomposition
4. Fast Fourier transform (FFT) on trace data
5. Discussion on how seismic data can be statistically analyzed
6. Statistical models to find/group attributes comprising the most exciting features

FIRST ARRIVALS

Seismic acquisition and processing in the petroleum industry analyze P-waves (compressional) and S-waves (shear). The first arrivals of both types of waves are recorded and studied to garner critical information about the subsurface. It is essential to ensure that the first arrival data is associated not with noise, be it intrinsically random or linear, but with a real seismic event. The 3D seismic datasets are made up of thousands of shot-points, and the receiver arrays generate thousands of records. Thus, the manual analysis of all shot- and receiver-oriented records is too voluminous to interpret individually. One of the earliest applications of an artificial neural network (ANN) in the siloed world of geophysics was to address the interpretation of the first arrivals. Extant and most recent literature detailing this approach can be found written by McCormack (1990) and Veezhinathan et al. (1991).

Essentially the ANN is a pattern recognition methodology. So the binary logic dictates that the first arrival is either seismically generated or born out of noise trains. We can window the time series seismic data for each record and create several Hilbert attributes. Taner et al. (1979) introduced an array of Hilbert attributes derived from windowed seismic data.

Some of the key Hilbert transform seismic attributes for a plausible first arrival study include:

1. Amplitude (maximum)
2. Power level (mean)
3. Power ratios
4. Envelop slope peak

The data-driven analytical workflow to identify first arrivals analyzes three adjacent peaks across contiguous traces. The first binary rule based on a pattern recognition soft-computing model determines if the middle peak is the first arrival. We used a back-propagation neural network with seven hidden layers of neurons.

NOISE SUPPRESSION

First arrivals are associated with another issue: editing noise from the seismic record. In contrast to identifying events of seismic origin, we are focused on suppressing events of non-seismic origin. To increase the signal-to-noise (S/N) ratio, the geophysicist can employ a data-driven analytical workflow that is based on pattern recognition soft computing models. Artificial neural networks (ANNs) are appropriate as candidate modeling techniques for the noise elimination process.

Zhang and Li (1995) edited the entire noisy trace. The learning process for the ANN is based on reading multiple seismic shot records. We can then appreciate the wavelet properties of the noise characterized by high amplitudes, or by the low frequency with a linear and coherent behavior.

We can enhance the learning phase via a set of unsupervised cluster analyses that distinguish "good" from "bad" traces. It is ideal to set rules representing thresholds of acceptance for certain seismic trace characteristics. As new seismic records are fed into the network, it will identify noise and throw those traces into the "edit" bucket.

Another workflow to attenuate noise is based on the predictive separation of coherent noise in a pre-stack shot record. The methodology strives to nondestructively separate hyperbolic ground roll from primary reflections.

Let us consider the acquisition of seismic in the field. Is it feasible to attenuate coherent and random noise in real time based on a predictive model? We must identify signatures of seismic noise trains across the localized geologic model.

Traditionally, expensive data acquisition with low S/N ratio encumbers both marine and land seismic collection. Ground roll, consisting of direct arrivals and energy scattered off near-surface unconformities, contributes to the low S/N ratio.

In (t, x, y) space, the ground roll falls nearly within a cone centered at the shot location. It is critical to adopt agile seismic processing techniques to identify and filter out the ground roll. However, ground roll can take on multiple characteristic traits owing to the unpredictability of the unconsolidated near-surface geologic strata. Hence, it's hard to standardize on a common and universally accepted workflow to process ground roll.

Often ground roll occupies a much lower frequency band than the primary reflections, in which case the ground roll is easily removable by (w, x) mute, at the expense of the low-frequency component of the signal, which is crucial for acoustic impedance inversion.

F-K filtering is one method adopted to eliminate linear events. However, aliasing is a problem as the ground roll is invariably aliased at regular receiver spacing. The aliasing becomes even more pronounced in 3D since acquisition costs usually prevent adequate sampling in the crossline direction.

Strong, dispersive, aliased ground roll with hyperbolic move-out contaminates the lower portion of the seismic image. The signal-to-noise ratio is quite low.

Given a dataset, we can estimate a prediction error filter (PEF) and see the Gaussian noise components of the data in the null-space of the estimation. It is a known (Claerbout, 1976) that the frequency response of a PEF approximates the inverse spectrum of the data from which the PEF was estimated. By computing a PEF ($f - x$ domain) from the noise-contaminated data, this approach obtains an "in situ" estimate of the signal power spectrum. Application of Wiener reconstruction (Castleman, 1996) then yields an optimal (least squares) estimate of the signal.

Ground roll is highly dispersive, and thus nonstationary, and so it seems plausible to choose a time-offset method utilizing nonstationary PEFs. Ground roll is usually a potpourri of different wave trains, all with different dispersion rates, actively violating this temporal stationarity assumption. The nonstationary time-offset domain technique has no such limitation.

An effective, general method for ground roll removal in 3D may have profound effects on the future of seismic acquisition. If severe ground roll necessitates the recording of extremely long offsets or the use of large receiver arrays, the ability to remove the ground roll robustly from single-sensor data will cut acquisition costs considerably.

Let us look at a method to do S/N ratio separation, and not merely noise removal. The output estimated noise might contain useful information, such as shear wave velocities. Multicomponent seismology is a promising specialty which would certainly benefit from any additional constraints provided by a robust "noise" extraction.

Considerable effort is currently expended in pursuit of the perfect noise model, particularly in multiple suppression. However, the results presented here show that predictive S/N ratio separation produces good results with an imperfect noise model. An open question remains: Might more primitive methods of obtaining multiple models suffice if passed to a predictive S/N ratio separation algorithm?

Our approach is based on a two-step data-driven methodology, without first principles, to identify patterns in the amplitude and frequency content of the time series data. This tactic is intended to identify events and discriminate between noise, both coherent and random, from the primaries and signal energy that represents geologic strata.

Removal of coherent and random noise from seismic data acquisition creates two datasets:

1. The seismic signal that displays either the earth's reflectivity series or those stationary components that correspond with the localized reflectors

2. Coherent and dispersive noise trains with aliasing qualities in the F-K domain, and ambient random noise

We adopted a data-driven methodology to ascertain key attributes of the ground roll and random noise to set it apart from the primary signal. This approach is intended to reduce the high acquisition costs by producing data with an improved S/N ratio in the field. Chief among the low S/N ratio is ground roll, which consists of direct arrival, and scattered energy from shot-generated Rayleigh waves.

Identifying the signatures of the ground roll in some geologic regions will enable a predictive model to be built to address the issue of dominant noise trains. To attenuate said noise, the hyperbolic move-out can be determined through data analysis of the seismic traces.

The intent is to break the amplitude signal into its uniquely elemental components utilizing PCA, a statistical technique adopted to analyze and transform multivariate datasets. This approach assumes a set of N-dimensional vectors as inputs that will represent the entire volume of a shot record. The process ranks the principal components (PCs) by their contribution to the total variance of the seismic traces in the whole dataset. The PCs are deemed fully independent and as such are appropriate for further advanced analytical processes.

Decision tree analysis will also be considered, given the nature of continuous events inherent in the seismic trace attributes. A decision tree is a logical model that illustrates the value of a target variable's predictive qualities.

The ground roll study is conducive to multiple periodic pattern identification problems found in nature. It demonstrated periodicity at many levels with piecemeal changes over time and space. We applied generalized multiple linear regression methodologies (ARIMA) with the following criteria:

- Time-varying intercept and slope (variety of trend patterns)
- Time-varying periodic patterns
- Nonlinear regression effects through spline regressors
- Correlated noise

The study then created an unobserved components model (UCM) that is essentially a structured model in the temporal domain. It analyzes and subsequently forecasts equally spaced univariate time series data. The UCM model breaks down the seismic response time series into constituent components such as trend, cycles, and any regression effects that are due to predictor series. These components enable geophysicists to identify salient features of the series, beneficial to interpretation and forecasting the typical behavior of the coherent noise trains such as ground roll. UCMs provide the versatility inherent in the ARIMA models while extending the ability to interpret the smoothing models. Dynamic models are very similar to UCMs and find favorability in the Bayesian time series literature. We developed an algorithm to forecast the values of the response series and the component series in the model.

Let us write some pseudo-code for a prediction algorithm applicable for seismic coherent noise trains across 30 contiguous traces:

Suppose, for $1 <= t, x <= 30$,

$$g(t, x) = 5 + 6^* \sin(2^* \text{pi}^* t/35) \text{ (Figure 5.17)}$$
$$+ \cos(2^* \pi^* \exp(x/35))$$
$$+ 2^* \sin(2^* \pi^* t/35)^* \cos(2^* \pi^* \exp(x/35))$$

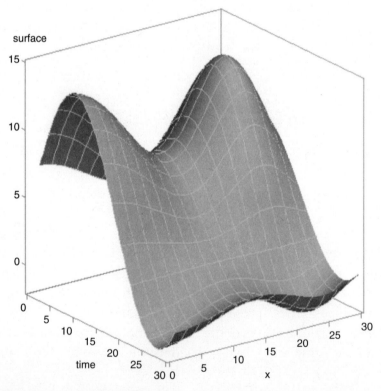

Figure 5.17 True surface $g(t, x)$

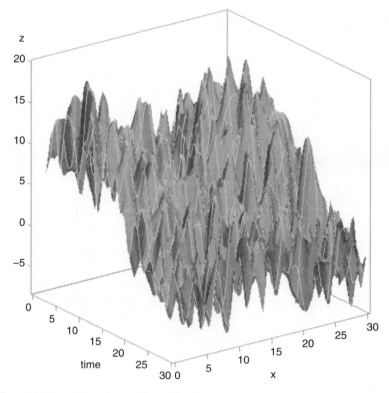

Figure 5.18 Noisy observations $Z(t, x)$

We observe a noisy version of $g(t, x)$ (Figure 5.18):

$$Z(t,x) = g(t,x) + \varepsilon \qquad \varepsilon \sim N(0; 9)$$

We can assume that, for a given t, the functional relationship $g(t, x)$ is represented as a cubic spline in x with four evenly spread knots in the x range (1:30). Then, for a 7-dimensional spline variable vector $\text{Spl}(x)$ and the regression coefficient βt, we establish the relationship:

$$Z(t,x) = \text{Spl}(x)\beta t + \varepsilon t$$

Also, suppose that βt changes in the t direction as follows:

$$\beta t + 1 = T\beta t + \eta t + 1$$

for some "transition" matrix T and covariance of disturbances ηt and εt.

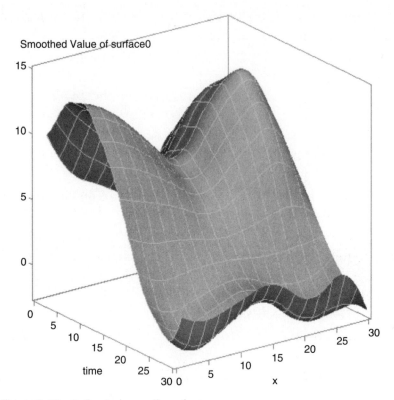

Figure 5.19 Estimated smooth surface

We obtained a *denoised* version of the input seismic record. Any missing or bad traces in the shot record were interpolated by generating the missing values of the response series from the historical period (i.e., the previous shot record). Figure 5.19 represents the full sample of the traces for the shot record, which are *smoothed* estimates of the component series in the UCM model.

It is suggested by Lendzionowski, Walden, and White that the maximum number of important independent attributes that can comprehensively describe a seismic trace segment is a quantity 2BT, where B = Bandwidth (Hz) and T = Trace segment length (Seconds). This assumption leads to the conclusion that there is inherent ambiguity or partial redundancy in some of the common attributes garnered from seismic traces, lending complexity to noise attenuation from shot records.

To limit the potential for ambiguous results, it is our assertion that we should derive significant seismic attributes in a single transformation. The intent is to break the amplitude signal into its most uniquely elemental components. To that end, we propose implementing PCA, a statistical technique adopted to analyze and transform multivariate datasets. It is intended to take as input a set of N-dimensional vectors that will represent the entire volume of a shot record. The sampling window size constrains the dimensionality of each vector. PCA outputs N linearly transformed eigenvectors known statistically as principal components (PCs). The process ranks the principal components by their contribution to the total variance of the seismic traces in the entire dataset. The PCs are deemed fully independent and as such are appropriate for further advanced analytical processes.

Clustering of the PCs reduces the relevant information about seismic noise into a single categorical property. Decision tree analysis may be another approach, given the nature of continuous events inherent in the seismic trace attributes. We applied the data-driven analytical workflow to predict ground roll noise trains to a raw shot record as depicted in Figure 5.20.

After applying the sequence of steps that implemented the noise suppression algorithm to the raw shot record, we generated the output shot record in Figure 5.21. There are still remnants of the coherent noise trains across the traces. We determined that the learning aspect of the algorithm required more data from contiguous shot records. By subtracting the entire shot record data captured in Figure 5.21 from the raw data depicted in Figure 5.20, we could see the results of the denoising algorithm in Figure 5.22. Note the suppression of the ground roll coherent noise across the traces. More detailed finesse is required to optimize the workflow. An iterative approach with more shot records is recommended to finalize the data-driven analytical methodology.

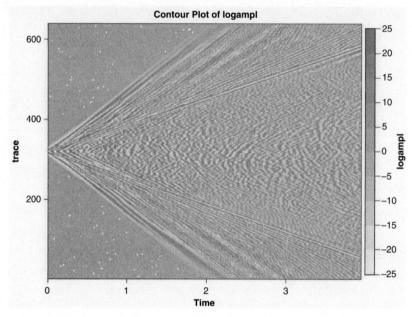

Figure 5.20 Shot record with ground roll before applying noise suppression algorithm

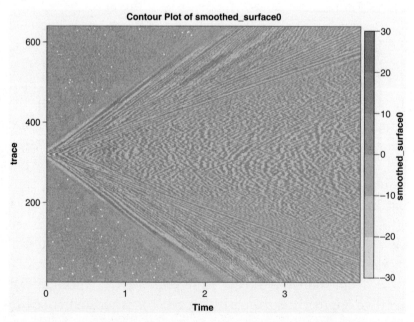

Figure 5.21 Shot record after applying noise suppression algorithm

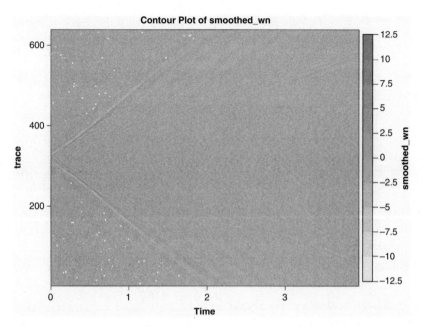

Figure 5.22 The attenuated noise

REFERENCES

Atmospheric Radiation Measurement Program, "ARM Archive," http://ncvweb.archive.arm.gov/, accessed February 1, 2016.

Bengio, Y., A. Courville, and P. Vincent, "Representation Learning: A Review and New Perspectives," *IEEE Transactions on Pattern Analysis and Machine Intelligence*, 35 (2013): 1798–1828.

Bosch, M., T. Mukerji, and E. F. Gonzalez, "Seismic Inversion for Reservoir Properties Combining Statistical Rock Physics and Geostatistics: A Review," *Geophysics*, 75, no. 5 (September 2010): 75A165–75A176.

Castleman, K. R., *Digital Image Processing*. Prentice-Hall, Upper Saddle River, NJ, 1996.

Claerbout, J. F., *Fundamentals of Geophysical Data Processing*. Blackwell, 1976.

Donoho, D. L. and I. M. Johnstone, "Minimax Estimation via Wavelet Shrinkage," submitted to *The Annals of Statistics*, 1995.

Doyen, P. M., "Porosity from Seismic Data: A Geostatistical Approach," *Geophysics*, 53, no. 10 (1998): 1263–1276.

Fagan, D., K. van Wijk, and J. Rutledge, "Clustering Revisited: A Spectral Analysis of Microseismic Events," *Geophysics*, 78, no. 2 (March 2013): KS41–KS49.

Hall, P., J. Dean, I. K. Kabul, and J. Silva, "An Overview of Machine Learning with SAS Enterprise Miner." In: *Proceedings of the SAS Global Forum 2014 Conference*, SAS Institute, Cary, North Carolina (2014), https://support.sas.com/resources/papers/proceedings14/SAS313-2014.pdf.

Hall, Patrick, Jared Dean, Ilknur Kaynar Kabul, and Jorge Silva, "An Overview of Machine Learning with SAS® Enterprise Miner™," paper SAS313-2014, SAS Institute Inc., 2014.

Haykin, S., *Neural Networks: A Comprehensive Foundation*, Prentice-Hall, New Jersey (1999).

Hinton, G. E., and R. R. Salakhutdinov, "Reducing the Dimensionality of Data with Neural Networks," *Science*, 313, no. 504 (July 28, 2006). DOI: 10.1126/science.1127647.

Holdaway, Keith R., *Harness Oil and Gas Big Data with Analytics: Optimize Exploration and Production with Data-Driven Models*, John Wiley & Sons, Hoboken, NJ (May 2014).

Jang, J., "ANFIS: Adaptive-Network-Based Fuzzy Inference System," *IEEE Trans. Syst. Man Cybern.*, 23, no. 3 (1993): 665–685.

Kreutz-Delgado, K., J. F. Murray, B. D. Rao, K. Engan, T.-W. Lee, and T. J. Sejnowski, "Dictionary Learning Algorithms for Sparse Representation," *Neural Computation*, 15 (2003): 349–396.

Krizhevsky, A., I. Sutskever, and G. E. Hinton, "ImageNet Classification with Deep Convolutional Neural Networks." In: *Advances in Neural Information Processing Systems 25* (NIPS 2012), *Proceedings of the Annual Conference on Neural Information Processing Systems* (2012), pp. 1097–1105.

Laughlin, K., P. Garossino, and G. Partyka, "Spectral Decomposition Applied to 3D," *AAPGExplorer*, 23, no. 5 (2002): 28–31.

Lee, H., A. Battle, R. Raina, and A. Y. Ng, "Efficient Sparse Coding Algorithms." In: *Advances in Neural Information Processing Systems 19* (NIPS 2006), *Proceedings of the Annual Conference on Neural Information Processing Systems* (2006), pp. 801–808.

McCormack, M. D., "Neural Computing in Geophysics," *Geophys., The Leading Edge Explor.*, Chapter 10, pp. 11–15 (1990).

Olatunji, S. O., A. Selamat, and A. Abdulraheem, "Modeling the Permeability of Carbonate Reservoir Using Type-2 Fuzzy Logic Systems," *Comput. Ind.*, 62, no. 2 (February 2011): 147–163.

Tahmasebi, P., and A. Hezarkhani, "A Fast and Independent Architecture of an Artificial Neural Network for Permeability Prediction," *J. Pet. Sci. Eng.*, 86–87 (May 2012): 118–126.

Taner, M. T., F. Koehler, F., and R. E. Sherrif, "Complex Seismic Trace Analysis," *Geophysics*, 44 (1979): 1196–1212.

Vapnik, V. N., *Statistical Learning Theory*, 41, no. 4, John Wiley & Sons, New York (1998).

Veezhinathan, J., and D. Wagner, "First Break Picking Using Neural Network," *Expert Systems in Exploration*. SEG, Tulsa, OK, 1991, pp. 179–202.

Widess, M. B., "How Thin Is a Thin Bed?" *Geophysics*, 38 (1973), 1176–1180.

Zhang, X. and Y. Li, "The Application of Artificial Neural Network with SOM: A Neural Network Approach." SEG 65th Annual Meeting, Houston (Oct. 1995).

CHAPTER **6**

Seismic Attribute Analysis

INTRODUCTION

Seismic reflection and refraction data is traditionally the domain of the geophysicists and mathematicians. It is incumbent upon these scientists to identify potential reservoirs based on deterministic interpretation of the seismic traces that have bounced off the subsurface rocks and been detected by surface geophones and water hydrophones. The principles of seismology are entrenched in the mathematical functions and axioms of physics that shed light on the seismic wave perturbations that have traveled through the subsurface. Wave energy interaction at rock interfaces generates an array of acoustic impedances (the product of wave velocity and density) that are signatures resulting from energy being either reflected or refracted. Like other geophysical methodologies (microgravity, frequency and time domain electromagnetics, and electrical resistivity studies), we can approach reflection seismology as an inverse problem. And as such, the resultant model is invariably deterministic by nature and intrinsically not unique. Geophysicists provide an abstract model of a complex physical system, governed by laws written throughout the ages by mathematicians and physicists. As geoscientists, we are constrained somewhat not only by the first principles but also by the uncertainty and sensitivity to relatively small errors in seismic data acquisition, processing, and interpretation. With the confluence of large 3D seismic datasets and petrophysical sources of measurements, it is necessary to adopt not only the traditionally interpreted models but also a data-driven suite of methodologies. One source of seismic data that is ideal as an input domain for the data-driven soft-computing workflows is the rich attributes generated from the seismic traces. Pre-stack and post-stack seismic attributes have evolved as an important source. The array of seismic attributes and the knowledge garnered from their analysis, when married to the stratigraphic and structural interpretation, direct a powerful light on the reservoir characteristics essential for successful hydrocarbon exploitation.

TYPES OF SEISMIC ATTRIBUTES

Seismic attributes are inherently either quantitative, measuring a property reflecting a geologic feature, or qualitative, identifying spatial patterns such as faults or facies changes. Being quantitative by nature, a seismic attribute can represent a target or dependent feature measurement that accounts for a key performance indicator or hotspot. Tables 6.1 and 6.2 list some of the primary seismic attributes that have a geometric and wavelet characteristic.

From a mathematical perspective, a seismic trace is a complex functional representation of the earth's response. The recorded seismic signature is the real part of a complex

Table 6.1 Curvature Attributes

Primary Outputs	Geometric	High Resolution	Shapes	Semblance
Min. Curvature	Dip Azimuth	Dip Curvature	Dome	Cross Correlation of Real vs. Imaginary
Max. Curvature	Dip Magnitude	Gaussian Curvature	Ridge	Derivative of Total Energy
Most Positive Curvature	Inline Apparent Dip	Strike Curvature	Saddle	Outer Product
Most Negative Curvature	Crossline Apparent Dip	Angular Unconformity	Bowl	

Table 6.2 Rock Solid Attributes

Instantaneous Attributes	Wavelet Attributes	Geometrical Attributes
Real Part of Complex Trace	Wavelet Phase	Event Continuity
Imaginary Part of Complex Trace	Wavelet Frequency	Sand/Shale Ratio
Trace Envelope	Wavelet Q Factor	Dip Variance
Instantaneous Phase	Dominant Frequency	Instantaneous Dip
Instantaneous Q Factor	Apparent Polarity of Wavelet	Dip Azimuth

function and the quadrature the imaginary part. The quadrature is a 90° phase-shifted description of the real part. We can compute the instantaneous attributes (amplitude, phase, and frequency) from the complex trace just described. Why are they "instantaneous"? They are concise. They represent quantitative descriptions of the seismic character at any given point along the waveform. The instantaneous attributes feature as critically independent parameters in the seismic facies characterization study later in this chapter. The instantaneous amplitude is a measurement of the reflectivity strength. The instantaneous phase is a representation of the continuity of a seismic event across adjacent traces and the instantaneous frequency measures the rate of change of the instantaneous phase function from a time perspective.

Seismic attributes are commonly classified as:

- *Physical attributes:* Directly correlated to wave propagation and lithology from either a pre- or post-stack perspective. Two sub-classes are by definition instantaneous and wavelet. The former are determined sample by sample and are indicative of the continuous change in both the space and temporal dimensions. The latter define wavelet characteristics and amplitude spectrum.
- *Geometrical attributes:* These include dip, azimuth, and discontinuity.

We can derive post-stack attributes from stacked data after the effects of *normal moveout* have been addressed by applying a suite of velocity models across the spatial extent of the seismic data. In 1979, Tanner first described the "complex trace."

It is defined as:

$$CT(t) = T(t) + H(t)$$

Where:

$CT(t)$ = Complex trace

$T(t)$ = Seismic trace

$H(t)$ = Hilbert transform of $T(t)$

Seismic traces consist of both a real and an imaginary part. The real part is the actual recorded seismic signal. The imaginary part is the quadrature that is the 90° phase-shifted version (Hilbert transform) of the real part. It is a simple process to compute the instantaneous attributes of the seismic signal once the complex seismic trace is established.

Instantaneous amplitude measures the reflectivity strength that is proportional to the square root of the total energy of the seismic signal at a particular instant in time. Its advantage over the amplitude of the real trace is that it is phase independent; however, amplitude sign information is lost. The continuity of the events on a seismic profile is a measure reflected by instantaneous phase, and the temporal rate of change of the instantaneous phase is represented as the instantaneous frequency. Notice that this is not the same frequency typically encountered in spectral analysis.

The amplitude envelope (E) is ascertained from the complex trace:

$$E(t) = \{T(t) + H(t)\}\ 1/2$$

Some of the interpretation benefits garnered from the amplitude envelope include:

- Bright spots
- Gas accumulation
- Changes in depositional environments
- Thin-bed tuning effects
- Unconformities
- Changes in lithology
- Faulting at a localized level
- Spatial correlation with rock properties such as porosity

The instantaneous amplitude that shows the reflectivity strength is a good indicator of bright and dim spots. The instantaneous phase attribute is often a robust delineator of pinch-outs, faults, and on-laps, whereas the instantaneous frequency attribute relates to the centroid of the power spectrum of the seismic wavelet, responding to depositional characteristics.

Geophysicists implement traditional workflows to attenuate multiples and random noise. Instantaneous attributes can be subsequently generated across a 3D seismic cube. It is feasible to run an EDA set of workflows to surface hidden patterns and correlations using the seismic attributes as the input space. The objective function could be to identify all potential stratigraphic pinch-outs that are not easily seen on a low-to-medium-resolution seismic section with poor signal–noise ratio. Those independent variables, represented by the generated seismic attributes, can be statistically correlated to the objective function to classify the most influential parameters to identify features such as pinch-outs.

Coherence or discontinuity is a geometrical attribute that measures the lateral relations in the seismic data. Used to focus attention on the discontinuous events such as faults, we can correlate high amplitudes to discontinuities and low amplitudes to continuous features.

This attribute is useful in comprehending and assessing:

- Values at maximum and minimum coherency direction
- Event terminations
- Picked seismic horizons
- Fault detection
- Zones of parallel and chaotic bedding
- Nonreflecting zones
- Converging and diverging bedding patterns and unconformities

Spectral decomposition attributes allow us to highlight the structures with different frequency bands to deliver higher resolution. Moving the seismic data from the time-offset domain to the frequency-wavenumber domain by applying a discrete

Fourier transform enables geophysicists to identify and quantify thin-bed interferences and subtle discontinuities effectively.

In conclusion, some of the most commonly used attributes are:

- *Envelope:* Presence of gas (bright spots), thin-bed tuning effects, and lithology changes
- *Phase:* Lateral reflector continuity and bedding configurations
- *Frequency:* Presence of hydrocarbons and fracture zones
- *Spectral decomposition:* Bed thickness
- *Coherence:* Faults, fractures, and lateral stratigraphic discontinuities

SEISMIC ATTRIBUTE WORKFLOWS

Analyzing seismic attributes from a data-driven perspective necessitates a scalable and repeatable set of workflows formulated by drawing upon an established process or methodology. What is the difference between a process and a methodology?

- A *process* is defined as a systematic series of continuous actions or operations that occur in a fixed way.
- A *methodology* represents a suite of underlying principles constrained by rules to regulate a discipline such as geosciences.

We are looking for a process for our soft-computing workflows. It typically enables us to address an ongoing and repeatable set of tasks that invariably has no definitive conclusion. It is more conducive to provide a dependable, repeatable, and competent way to apply data-driven analysis.

Let us describe a process appropriate for data-driven analytical studies in the seismic attribute analytical domain. It goes under the acronym *SEMMA*: *S*ample, *E*xplore, *M*odify, *M*odel, and *A*ssess.

SEMMA Process

These workflows are based on a sample-explore-modify-model-assess (SEMMA) process (Figure 6.1). The method implements logical workflows at each stage to ensure a natural progression from data management, exploration, transformation, and analysis. The product is a set of predictive soft-computing models that are then statistically scored to identify the best model. The criteria of scoring take into account the dataset and the objective function that represents the business problem to be addressed.

It is advantageous to implement an integrated product that provides an end-to-end business solution for data mining and one that incorporates a graphical user interface (GUI) that acts as a user-friendly front-end to a SEMMA data mining process:

- *Sample* the data by extracting and preparing a population of the data for model building, implementing one or more data tables. The sampling step provides a window into the dataset. We can subset the observations and reduce the dimensionality of the input space. Invariably the complete dataset, anticipated to address the business problem, is passed to the next step, where exploratory data analysis is performed.

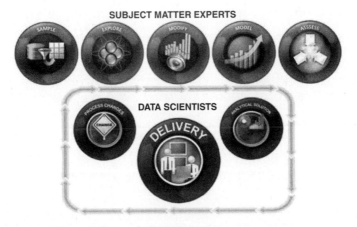

Figure 6.1 SEMMA process for data-driven analysis

■ *Explore* the data by surfacing hidden patterns and trends within the data. We are seeking relationships that are indicative of correlated cause and effect. This step provides a suite of hypotheses worth modeling as opposed to a single deterministic model.

■ *Modify* the data by creating and selecting variables after any transformation that is considered germane to the data mining effort to solve a business problem. The modification can be a distribution analysis to determine if specific variables fall into a Gaussian or non-normal distribution. It is at this step that outliers and skewed values can be edited. Imputation techniques to replace errant or missing values can be exercised in the modification workflow.

■ *Model* the data by using an array of analytical techniques to search for a combination of the data that reliably predicts a desired outcome.

■ *Assess* the predictive models. We can evaluate the worth and reliability of the output soft-computing models statistically. By scoring the models, we can ascertain an excellent array of probabilistic results and the value of each model as measured by the applicability to the business problem under study.

It is essential to initiate any data-driven analytical study with an exploratory data analysis (EDA) suite of workflows. EDA provides, via intuitive visualizations, the ability to surface hidden patterns, correlations, and trends in the underlying datasets. In the case of seismic attribute analysis, you could aggregate multiple attributes from a pre- or post-stack perspective dependent on the objective function or business problem under study. Production optimization or effectiveness of an enhanced oil recovery (EOR) technique such as *water-alternating-gas* (WAG) are two examples of business value propositions that can be translated into a SEMMA data analytical workflow. The data-driven process supplements the traditional interpretation of 3D immersive visualization workflows.

SEISMIC FACIES CLASSIFICATION

What is seismic facies? Essentially it is a seismic unit in three-dimensional space that consists of a set of wavelet reflections. The distinguishing factors between distinct seismic facies units are the different measurements of varying parameters garnered from wavelet analysis and seismic attribute analysis. The seismic facies classification workflow is a suite of cluster data mining techniques, some supervised and others unsupervised, to group seismic parameters within third-order sequences. The result is a quantified description of varying lateral lithofacies and variance in spatial fluid types. Figure 6.2 identifies the critical analytical steps for a seismic facies classification workflow.

Reflection pattern geometries are conceivably the most valuable for tuning to lithofacies, traditionally interpreted from cores and well logs.

Here is a traditional sequence of deterministic steps:

1. Segregate all depositional sequences into distinct seismic facies.
2. Delineate the internal reflection configuration of all seismic facies units.
3. Map all seismic facies from seismic profiles to a shot-point map for each sequence.
4. Aggregate bed thickness and seismic facies distribution.

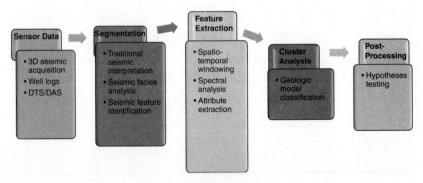

Figure 6.2 Classification in a seismic facies interpretation iterative cycle

5. Map all diagnostic parameters' distribution.

6. Assimilate outcrop and well log data with the seismic facies distribution.

7. Apply deterministic analytical processes to the seismic facies maps.

8. Identify depositional environments: marine or non-marine, basin position, water depth, transport direction, or any other depositional features.

9. Evaluate lithology from all the interpretive results.

Since the onset of big data in the world of seismic exploration, we have witnessed a continuous application of classification soft-computing techniques. These data-driven unsupervised and supervised segmentation methodologies enable geophysicists to establish a more robust framework for traditional interpretation. Geophysicists can marry their intuition and deterministic knowledge based on first principles with the pattern-matching trends garnered from a cluster workflow. Such a marriage makes it more feasible to ascertain actionable knowledge from the large 3D seismic cubes of data as well as the evolving and the increasing number of seismic attributes, both pre- and post-stack.

Calculating the number of seismic facies is difficult since the temporal and spatial resolution is adversely impacted as we go deeper into a seismic profile. Essentially, seismic facies are non-stationary in nature, and diverse depositional environments add to the complexity in classifying seismic facies.

The dataset for a seismic facies study falls into one of two categories, influenced by the lithological variables and their distribution across the spatial and temporal domain. Either the seismic facies dataset is *balanced* or *unbalanced*. One example of this categorization of the datasets surfaces when we look at a fraction of sand within the rock. It ranges from zero to unity and is thus deemed balanced, whereas the liquid saturations are skewed at either zero or unity, rendering an unbalanced dataset.

Having ascertained this characteristic of the dataset, we need to identify which family of soft-computing models is more appropriate to analyze the seismic facies data: *supervised* or *unsupervised*. The former classifiers are invariably chosen owing to the complexities inherent in the study. This is probably true of the majority of upstream E&P data-driven analytical problems. The supervised techniques add an onus to the rigor and sensitivity of the values in the input domain. A balanced dataset is conducive to supervised workflows, and unsupervised cluster algorithms better analyze the unbalanced dataset.

Some of the standard classification algorithms that can be applied to categorize seismic facies across hydrocarbon reservoirs are:

Unsupervised:

1. Hierarchical clustering
2. k-means clustering
3. Self-organizing maps (SOMs)
4. Normal mixtures
5. Latent class analysis

Supervised:

1. Principal component analysis (PCA)
2. Support vector machines (SVMs)
3. Artificial neural networks (ANNs)

Pattern recognition data-driven techniques are ideal tools to detect subtle changes in the 3D multicomponent seismic time-lapse volumes currently acquired. The old-school workflows that included cross-equalized difference detection techniques between 3D time-lapse volumes have borne relative business value from low-resolution images. However, more advanced multicomponent seismic surveys that generate not only higher resolution images but also more robust attributes lend themselves to advanced data-driven machine learning workflows.

Geophysicists are tasked to find, through valid interpretation, features such as channels and mass transport networks, wading through the vast number of wiggle traces. Using 3D immersive visualization techniques, an experienced interpreter examines the characteristics of seismic waveforms, associated frequency, phase, and amplitude as well as the geometric alignment. Seismic facies maps were once manually contoured, but now we can adopt quantitative and automated data-driven workflows to discern patterns in the seismic response and identify characteristics of seismic facies.

Clustering is a multivariate technique that groups together observations that share similar values across some variables. Typically, observations are not scattered evenly in n-dimensional space, but rather they form clumps or clusters. Identifying these clusters provides you with a deeper understanding of your data.

Figure 6.3 depicts an alternative workflow that is key to classifying seismic facies as defined by Duda et al. (2001). The "acquisition" process includes not only the seismic volumes but also well logs and completion tactics and strategies. Production data from brownfields enriches the input data dimension. As we walk through the workflow, it is important to stress the hybrid perspective. Geophysicists focus on "traditional interpretation." It is not uncommon to concentrate on a target stratigraphic unit or set of homogeneous formations as the interpreter identifies geologic strata with characteristic features such as geometric delineations, fault-blocks, and floodplains. During the "feature abstraction" process we are striving to enumerate key seismic attributes, be they quantitative or qualitative in nature. Extracting the key features reduces the seismic characterization into a manageable dimension for input to a data-driven analytical workflow. The "data-driven classification" process adopts one of the soft-computing classification techniques, invariably unsupervised, to complement a more traditional

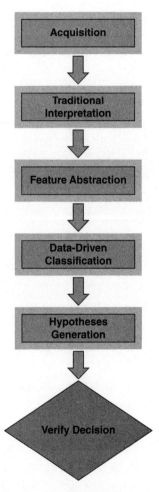

Figure 6.3 Seismic facies classification workflow

experienced-driven classification interpreting the static geologic models. The penultimate process, "hypotheses generation," is an evaluation step that probabilistically ascertains hypotheses worth modeling. The decision step validates the results and determines whether we should modify the input space by generating different attributes to address the business problem under study.

Let us discuss some of the benefits of implementing segmentation soft-computing techniques to classify seismic facies.

Seismic Facies Dataset

There are seven useful reflection parameters:

1. Configuration (reflection geometry)
2. Continuity
3. Amplitude (instantaneous)
4. Frequency (instantaneous)
5. Phase (instantaneous)
6. Interval velocity
7. Acoustic impedance

Bright and dim spots hidden within the seismic profiles are identifiable from the instantaneous amplitude measurements. We can delineate stratigraphic traps, faults, pinch-outs, and on-laps from specific instantaneous phase measurements. The instantaneous frequency attribute is useful as a facies descriptor in condensate reservoirs where high frequencies tend to be filtered out.

The first analytical step after any data aggregation processes is to implement several EDA visualizations to identify trends and correlations. What are the statistical relationships between the dependent and independent variables? Are there outliers? Can we reduce the input space to a range of variables and perhaps window those variables by a range of values?

The seismic facies classification study is a business problem converted into a data mining problem. The objective function enables the supervised or unsupervised clustering of varying facies types across the window of interest in the seismic volumes. As well as classification techniques to cluster facies of similar characteristics, we can, through correlation to the objective function, identify the most critical variables and their attendant range of values. Table 6.3 details some of the critical seismic facies classification measurements of key variables.

Table 6.3 Seismic Facies Classification Measurements

Parameter	Geologic Interpretation
Continuity	▪ Lateral/Spatial Geologic Strata ▪ Depositional Processes
Configuration	▪ Horizon/Bedding Patterns ▪ Fluid Contacts ▪ Depositional Properties
Amplitude	▪ Horizon/Bed Spacing ▪ Horizon/Bed Thickness ▪ Velocity and Density Contrasts: Acoustic Impedance
Instantaneous Amplitude	▪ Reflectivity Strength at Specific Points
Frequency	▪ Fluid Content ▪ Horizon/Bed Thickness
Instantaneous Frequency	▪ Rate of Change of the Instantaneous Phase
Instantaneous Phase	▪ Continuity of Seismic Event
Interval Velocity	▪ Lithofacies Identifications ▪ Porosity Measurements ▪ Fluid Content

Sediment source, depositional environment, and lithofacies can be interpreted by grouping and mapping these parameters into three-dimensional seismic facies clusters.

Seismic Facies Study: Preprocessing

This study proposes a preprocessing workflow to enable accurate predictions of lithological properties based on an array of seismic attributes. Machine learning (ML) methodologies are implemented. The preprocessing platform consists of reconstructing seismic signals, normalizing the input data, and standardizing the target signals. These regularization steps are critical to profile the dependent lithological properties characterized by a high-resolution definition. Such steps to generate ML ready datasets include:

- Fourier transform
- Wavelet decomposition
- Empirical mode decomposition

A seismic acquisition/processing strategy is carried out over a spatial area of geologic interest to understand the subsurface layers and identify potential hydrocarbon reservoirs, be they structural or stratigraphic in nature. The mechanical energy generated by surface sources such as a vibroseis is converted into electrical energy by the array of geophones that record the upcoming reflections and refractions of the waveforms. The signatures of these waveforms are characterized by the seismic attributes associated with the geologic rock properties of each layer, such as velocity and density. The product of these two rock properties (velocity and density) constitutes the acoustic impedance. Instantaneous frequency represents the rate of change of the phase of seismic amplitude and can be used as a predictor or independent parameter in our study.

Hierarchical Clustering

The hierarchical algorithm initiates the clustering process by treating each observation in its cluster. The algorithm computes Euclidean distances between every pair of clusters. It then iterates through a "coalescing" stage where two clusters, characterized by Euclidean distance as being closest, are joined to yield a single cluster. This stepwise process eventually produces a single cluster for all the original groups that initially contained a single variable, hence its synonym: *agglomerative clustering*.

The algorithm finally generates a dendrogram as depicted in Figure 6.4. It is useful to implement this clustering approach to establish a good estimate of the number of appropriate clusters

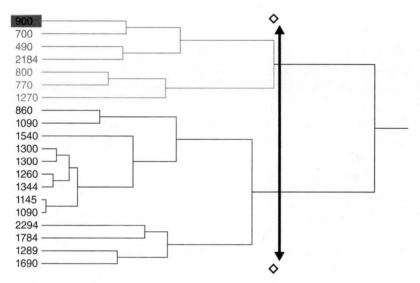

The vertical line connecting the two diamonds is indicative of the cluster number that is appropriate for this dataset: 3

Figure 6.4 Dendrogram generated by a hierarchical clustering algorithm

for a specific business problem. Hence, an interpretation of the dendrogram by a geophysicist is critical.

The hierarchical clustering technique is most appropriate for small datasets not exceeding about 10,000 observations. Character data types are permitted. The reason is that the time to execute increases rapidly as the dataset expands beyond this ceiling. As described later in this section, cluster k-means and normal mixtures are more suited if your dataset is vast.

If we read the dendrogram from left to right, we see the hierarchical clustering process combine the two closest clusters into one cluster. The relative distances separating the clusters are represented by the horizontal gaps between the vertical lines connecting the clusters.

In Figure 6.4, the clusters are designated or labeled by a nomenclature signifying seismic facies and the independent parameters ingested by the hierarchical clustering algorithm are an array of post-stack seismic attributes generated by a 3D seismic data volume. Noting the relatively small differences in clusters up to the line indicating three, it is plausible to suggest three is the ideal starting point for other classification algorithms that require a cluster number, k.

Figure 6.5 depicts a visualization known as a *constellation plot*. The plot arranges the facies labels as endpoints and each cluster connection as a different point. The lines reflect cluster membership and the distance of the line between each cluster estimates the distance between joined clusters.

If we interpret the constellation plot seen in Figure 6.5, it is apparent that the clusters that contain seismic facies (1270, 770, 800) and (900, 700, 490, 2184) are equally distant from the cluster of remaining seismic facies in the upper part of the plot.

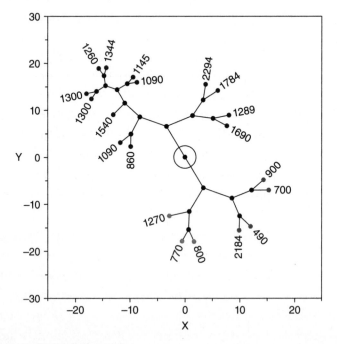

Figure 6.5 Constellation plot

k-means Clustering

The *k*-means algorithm (MacQueen, 1967) is a commonly used unsupervised technique to cluster data. What does the "*k*" mean? It refers to a fixed number of clusters implemented in the algorithm. It is a user-defined value. This poses a potential problem to the geophysicist since it is an a priori value that optimizes the *k*-means clustering algorithm. It constructs several clusters implementing an iterative algorithm to segment the data observations. The goal is to determine k points that represent stable cluster centroids and hence define the clusters such that each observation is assigned to a cluster defined by its nearest cluster centroid. The optimum assignment of cluster centroids is the one that minimizes the sum of the distance from every point to its nearest cluster centroid. The *k*-means algorithm initially establishes a suite of n points termed as cluster seeds that represent first guesses for the mean values of the clusters. The initial clusters are formulated by allocating each data point to the closest seed. The algorithm then iterates through two steps: the *assignment* and the *update* step. The seismic attributes are partitioned into clusters using this two-step process to minimize distances to the cluster centroids.

Another complexity is the different units of measurements inherent in the seismic attributes used to populate the clusters. We may be dealing with frequency (Hz), RMS amplitude (mV), or reflection phase (degrees). It is possible to scale the data using an inverse of the covariance matrix, yielding the "Mahalanobis distance." This avoids the problem of one variable dominating the clustering process.

Figure 6.6 illustrates a typical *k*-means cluster display. The clusters that are the most disjointed from the other clusters based on the first two principal components are those numbered 3, 10, and 11. The cluster centers are encircled, with the size of each circle representing the observation count in a cluster. The shaded portion of the figure reflects the 50 percent density contour around the mean value or centroid. It indicates where

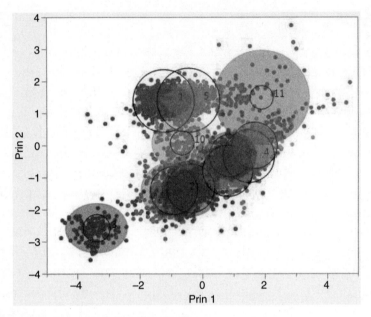

Figure 6.6 *k*-means cluster visualization

50 percent of all the observations in a specific cluster would fall (Mardia et al., 1980). The eigenvalues are depicted in decreasing order.

The *k*-means classification workflow is favorable for million-row datasets but only permits numerical data. Having conjectured the number of clusters, *k*, to run the algorithm, it is initially a guessing game as to the cluster seed points. The algorithm then iteratively assigns points to clusters and calculates cluster centroids.

Self-Organizing Maps (SOMs)

SOM is an unsupervised neural network methodology. Studies have been made using this technique to observe distinct clustering of data (Vesanto and Alhoniemi, 2000). Wavelet transform provides a means to identify the seismic trace singularities, mathematical expressions of each seismic trace (Hoekstra, 1996), across all 3D time-lapse seismic volumes. Classifying the seismic singularities with SOMs develops insightful observations as to an optimized number of clusters or classifications to be applied in the estimation of the number of seismic facies (Matos et al., 2003).

The SOM methodology was initiated by Teuvo Kohonen (1990). The key objective addressed by the SOM algorithm is to formulate clusters in a particular grid such that the observations are nearby not only in the SOM grid but also in the multivariate high-dimensional input space. The arbitrary structure inherent in the classical k-means workflow differs from the grid-based structure characterized by the SOM technique.

Normal Mixtures

If clusters incline to overlap, the k-means algorithm tends to break down, opening the door to the normal mixtures methodology as it is based on cluster membership probabilities as opposed to arbitrary classification assignments founded on limits. The normal mixtures technique is iterative in nature and is centered on the hypothesis that the joint probability distribution of all the data points under study is estimated using a blend of multivariate normal distributions. The blends are representing different clusters. Each cluster is characterized by multivariate normal distributions.

Figure 6.7 depicts contours for the normal densities that are suitable for the clusters. One cluster seems to be noticeably disjointed from the other clusters based on the first three principal components.

If you have data characterized by multivariate, overlapping normal distributions that are numerical, then normal mixture techniques are an appropriate choice for classification. However, if there is an abundance of multivariate outliers, then it is essential to perform an outlier cluster with an assumed uniform distribution. And invariably the "robust normal mixtures" algorithm is an alternative extension to normal mixtures with uniform outlier clustering.

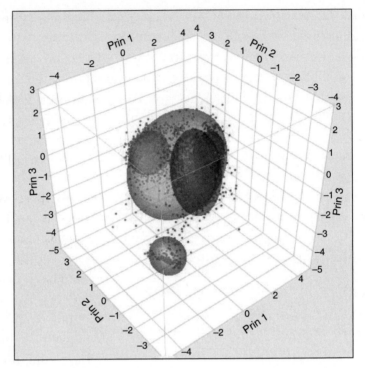

Figure 6.7 Clusters depicted with contours for the normal densities

As in the k-means cluster technique, you need to ascertain an appropriate number of clusters a priori. We adopted a maximum likelihood method to approximate the mean, standard deviation, and correlations simultaneously. Thus, each data point has ascribed a probability of being a member of each group.

Latent Class Analysis

If most of the variables in a facies classification workflow are categorical, then the optimum technique is *latent class analysis* (LCA). Again, the number of appropriate clusters is required to execute the algorithm. We are striving to fit a model that assumes that the distribution is a multinominal mixture. Each observation is classified into a distinct group based on its largest probability of membership, and a maximum likelihood estimate determines this.

This technique allows you to discover clusters or classifications of all the variables into categorical observations. We establish a latent variable as an unobservable classification variable and nominate a latent class for every layer of the latent variable. The algorithm fits a latent class model and calculates the most appropriate cluster or latent class for each seismic attribute observation.

This technique invariably necessitates a domain expert, such as a geophysicist, to interpret the results of a latent class analysis so as to construct definitions for all the latent classes based on the inherent characteristics of the class.

The model is a multinominal mixture model that has two sets of parameters: the y parameters and the p parameters. The former reflects the overall probabilities of cluster membership. The latter represents the probabilities of observing a given response based on cluster membership. A pattern of these conditional probabilities characterizes a latent class.

Figure 6.8 depicts a ternary plot representing the cluster probabilities for each row in the seismic facies dataset. The three vertices seen in Figure 6.8 illustrate a tendency for the cluster membership probabilities to align in these areas. This could mean that the membership probabilities reflect high values for one particular cluster and lower values for the other two clusters. There are a few points collated and scattered in the middle of the plot, indicating that these observations in the seismic facies dataset do not reflect a high probability of membership to any of the clusters. Perhaps we need to focus on these points as such behavior could be indicative of more plausible clusters being appropriate to represent the dataset.

The LCA algorithm is ideally suited to a dataset that is primarily categorical in nature. It is important to ascertain a priori

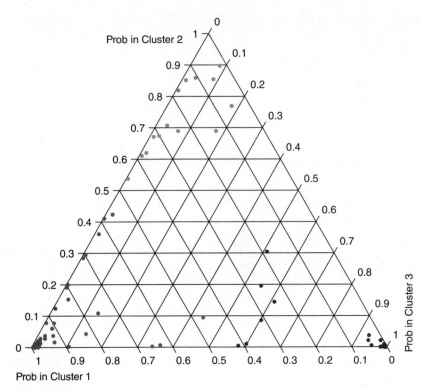

Figure 6.8 Ternary plot explaining the cluster probabilities for each seismic observation

the number of clusters that are plausible to address the business issue. The geophysicist can interpret the array of seismic attributes and other salient input parameters and determine a good starting number, k. The algorithm assumes a multinominal mixture distribution and attempts to estimate the maximum likelihood for each observation to ascertain cluster membership. The largest probability determines the membership.

Principal Component Analysis (PCA)

Principal component analysis (PCA) develops a concise number of independent variables called principal components (PCs). PCA performs an orthogonal transformation of the input observations that may have correlated trends to output a set of linearly uncorrelated PCs. The intent is to encapsulate the variability across the data space in a smaller, more succinct dimension. Hence, it is one methodology to reduce the dimensionality of the data space. In the study to ascertain a seismic facies classification, PCA also performs an EDA of all the different seismic parameters.

If your dataset is sparse by nature, consisting of many variables with a zero value, PCA executes a sparse methodology to calculate a user-defined and hence fixed number of PCs. There are also possibilities for PCA to support factor analysis by performing an orthogonal or oblique rotation to enable interpretation of the resulting PCs.

Classification of seismic facies invariably involves many variables that result in a high-dimensional input space. PCA is an ideal methodology to constrain the redundancy and excess across the seismic attributes. We accept that much of the desired signal is present in the first few PCs (eigenvectors) with the S/N ratio deteriorating the later PCs with uncorrelated noise. The first eigenvector optimally represents the patterns we are seeking in the seismic attributes that are input into the seismic facies classification workflow.

The iterative flow of the PCA algorithm can be reflected in these steps:

1. Generate the first eigenvector, the vector in N-dimensional seismic attribute space that best reflects the patterns.

2. Cross-correlate the N-dimensional input data with the vector output from step 1 at each voxel or value in 3-dimensional space, resulting in the first PC data volume.

3. Scale the first eigenvector by the first PC and subtract it from the original N-dimensional attribute vector; we then generate a residual data vector.

4. Generate the next eigenvector, the vector that best reflects the seismic attribute patterns in the residual data vector.

5. Cross-correlate the next eigenvector against the original data or residual data to create the next principal component volume.

6. Iterate through steps 4 and 5 for all N-dimensions to generate N eigenvectors and N PCs.

Figure 6.9 summarizes the variation of the specified seismic attribute variables with principal components. The report details how the PCs engage the change in the seismic attribute data. The PC points are derived from the eigenvector linear combination of the seismic attribute variables.

Figure 6.9 shows the eigenvalues, and a bar chart of the percent of the variation accounted for by each PC. There are two more plots: a *score plot* and a *loadings plot*. The eigenvalues indicate the total number of components mined, grounded on the extent of variance added by each component.

The score plot displays each element's estimated values about the other, correcting each value for the mean and standard deviation. The loadings plot charts the un-rotated loading matrix between the variables and the components. The nearer the value is to unity, the greater the influence of the element on the variable.

Statistical Assessment

Table 6.4 represents the constraints and best practices for each supervised and unsupervised method used in the seismic facies study.

The results of the seismic facies classification analysis are illustrated in Figure 6.10. We can clearly note the different characteristics for each of the three major clusters that represent the three seismic facies: blue, red, and green.

We implemented a set of fit statistical workflows to differentiate the models. Bayesian Information Criterion (BIC) and Akaike's Information Criterion (AIC) techniques were applied to see which values, invariably the smaller values

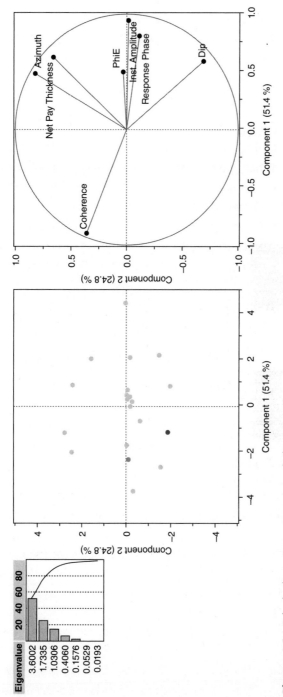

Figure 6.9 Principal components on correlations report

Table 6.4 Statistical Comparison between the Different Data-Driven Methods

Method	Data Type	Data Size	Number of Clusters
Hierarchical	Any	Up to 5000 rows	No
***k*-means**	Numeric	Up to millions of rows	Yes
Normal Mixtures	Numeric	Any size	Yes
Latent Class Analysis	Nominal or ordinal	Any size	Yes

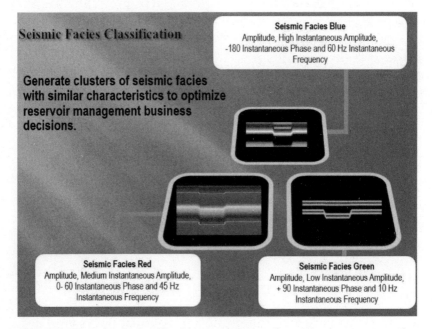

Figure 6.10 Seismic classification set of clusters from a business perspective

indicated, provided the better fit. The corrected AICc and BICc are information-based conditions that evaluate model fit. They are each based on –2LogLikelihood.

AICc is defined as follows:

$$\text{AICc} = -2\text{LogLikelihood} + 2k + 2k(k+1)/(n-k-1)$$

where k quantifies the number of projected parameters in the model and n reflects the number of rows or observations under study. The AICc value varies across different models created by the same dataset. The smallest value often defines the best-fitting model.

BICc is defined as follows:

$$\text{BICc} = -2\text{LogLikelihood} + k\ln(n)$$

There is a parallel interpretation of the resultant values for BICc as there is for AICc. The former tends to discipline those models with a greater number of parameters, preferring the latter statistical assessment.

We also looked at the root mean square (RMS) or quadratic mean. This is a pervasive statistical measure that quantifies the magnitude of variation across our dataset. In the seismic facies classification study, some values ranged into the negative domain from the positive domain. This behavior is typical of seismic traces. RMS underlines the variations, for example, in acoustic impedance within a chosen spatiotemporal window. We noted that invariably the higher the acoustic impedance variations of the stacked lithologies were, the RMS value correlated to a higher value. As an example, a high RMS in a channel is the result of an acoustic impedance contrast of channel fill with the surrounding lithology.

The variance (the opposite of coherency) attribute is measured in three dimensions and represents the trace-to-trace variability over a particular sample interval. Similar traces yield low variance coefficients. On the other hand, discontinuities have high coefficients. Faults and channels invariably produce discontinuities in nearby lithologies.

The seismic facies classification workflow provides an in-depth and intuitive methodology for clustering the various facies and characterizing each facies by the attributes under study. Do not limit yourself to either the number of seismic attributes or the number of clusters ideally suited for the varying classification method. Different results are obtained when implementing each clustering method, but note the guidelines detailed in Table 6.4. You may wish to run several segmentation techniques with varying attributes, and even different numbers of observations, and then compare the cluster profiles for common denominators. The seismic facies classification sequence is both scalable and repeatable.

REFERENCES

Bracewell, R. N., *The Fourier Transform and Its Applications*, McGraw-Hill, New York (1965).

Chawathe, A., "Interwell Property Mapping Using Crosswell Seismic Attributes," SPE 38747, paper presented at the 1997 SPE Annual Technical Conference and Exhibition, San Antonio (October 5–8, 1997).

Doyen, P., "Porosity from Seismic Data: A Geostatistical Approach," *Geophysics*, 53 (1988): 1263.

Duda, R. O., P. E. Hart, and D. G. Stork, *Pattern Classification*, 2nd ed., John Wiley & Sons, New York (2001).

Eren, H., C. C. Fung, and K. W. Wong, "Modular Artificial Neural Network for Prediction of Petrophysical Properties from Well Log Data," *IEEE Trans. Instrum. Meas.*, 46, no. 6 (December 1997): 1295–1299.

Fournier, F., and J. Derain, "A Statistical Methodology for Deriving Reservoir Properties from Seismic Data," *Geophysics*, 60, no. 5 (1995): 1437.

Hoekstra, E. V., "Multiscale Analysis of Seismic Data by the Wavelet Transform," MS thesis, Delft University of Technology (1996).

Holdaway, Keith R., *Harness Oil and Gas Big Data with Analytics: Optimize Exploration and Production with Data-Driven Models*, Wiley, Hoboken (May 2014).

Kohonen, T. The Self-Organizing Map. *Proceedings of the IEEE*, 9 (1990), pp. 1464–1479.

MacQueen, J., "Some Methods for Classification and Analysis of Multivariate Observations." In: Le Cam, L. M., and J. Neyman (eds.), *Proceedings of the Fifth Berkeley Symposium on Mathematical Statistics and Probability*, University of California Press (1967), pp. 281–297.

Mardia, K., J. Kent, and J. Bibby, *Multivariate Analysis*. Academic Press (1980).

Mathieu, P. G., and G. W. Rice, "Multivariate Analysis Used in the Detection of Stratigraphic Anomalies from Seismic Data," *Geophysics*, 34, no. 4 (1969): 507.

Matos, M. C., P. L. M. Osorio, and P. R. S. Johann, "Using Wavelet Transform and Self-Organizing Maps for Seismic Reservoir Characterization of a Deep-Water Field, Campos Basin, Offshore Brazil," 73rd Annual International Meeting, SEG, Expanded Abstracts (2003), pp. 1458–1461.

Nakayama, Kazuo, and Jianyong Hou, "Soft Computing for Reservoir Characterization and Modeling: Prediction of Reservoir Properties by Monte Carlo Simulation and Artificial Neural Network in the Exploration Stage," Springer (2002), pp. 15–33.

Neidell, Norman S., "Stratigraphic Modeling and Interpretation," AAPG Department of Education (1979).

Pairazian, K., "Modelization 3D des reservoirs petroliers par l'integration des donnees sismiques et geologiques: Approches quantitaives multivariable," doctoral thesis, Ecole Nationale Superieur de Geologie: Institut National Polytechnique de Loraine, Nancy, France (December 1998).

Taner, M. T., F. Koehler, and R. E. Sherrif, "Complex Seismic Trace Analysis," *Geophysics*, 44 (1979): 1196–1212.

Vesanto, J., and E. Alhoniemi, "Clustering of the Self-Organizing Map," *IEEE Transactions on Neural Networks*, 11, no. 3 (2000): 586–600.

CHAPTER 7

Geostatistics: Integrating Seismic and Petrophysical Data

"It could be said,
As in The Emperor of the Moon,
That all is everywhere and always like here,
Up to a degree of magnitude and perfection."

G. W. Leibniz

INTRODUCTION

The mining industry is the birthplace of modern *geostatistics* as it evolves as a branch of mathematics that can be applied to address business problems in natural resources exploration. In the early 1950s, the first array of statistical techniques labeled *geostatistics* strived to estimate ore reserves. Earth sciences, across many siloed engineering groups, took the reins of these methodologies to quantify uncertainty in their geoscientific parameters from a spatial and a temporal perspective. We shall detail issues prominent in the spatiotemporal datasets conducive to the application of geostatistics, and particularly in the field of seismic data that is integrated to build earth models for hydrocarbon exploration.

The industry engages the notions of space and time in processing geophysical and petrophysical data natively. Spatial location of a reservoir is critical in engineering decision making, whereas multiple methods stimulate our interest when performing surveillance in time. Thus, another data-driven analytical methodology is adopted with this kind of information. It relies heavily on techniques that use spatially referenced data for attribute interpolation and simulation within a predefined window of interest and is known as geostatistics.

The E&P sectors are made up of many activities that are underpinned by scientific and technological principles. As a result, it is not unusual to work with multiple hard measurements made at specific spatial and temporal locations. So then we have to ask ourselves, what are the values of said measurements away from the sampled points? We have detailed localized well measurements, but inter-well values are extrapolated or interpolated guesses based on statistical hypotheses. It is a commonplace to develop a regular course grid for all unsampled locations across an oil and gas field. The predicted values are then used to generate surface plots and contour maps for the measured parameters under study.

The predicted spatial values for all measurements away from localized well control carry uncertainties that must be quantified to attain any rigor to make sound business decisions. Invariably, frameworks and methodologies based on stochastic analysis formulate the processes that determine and quantify the uncertainties.

One traditional spatial prediction technique is known as kriging. Ordinary kriging generates predicted values for the parameters as well as any related standard errors. We also require a comprehensive specification of the spatial dependency that underpins the space process. Thus, all models that represent the spatial dependence are detailed as expressions of distance between two adjacent locations in the spatial field under study. A covariance or semivariance function makes up these models.

In short, six steps constitute a spatial prediction:

1. Model the covariance or semivariance of the spatial process.
2. Compute an empirical estimate.
3. Ascertain the mathematical form.
4. Determine the parameter values for a theoretical version of the dependence model.
5. Resolve the kriging system at a suite of spatial locations using the dependency models
6. Generate predicted values and associated standard errors.

Data Description

We have to keep in mind that the problems to be resolved across an oil and gas reservoir are multivariate in nature. There is also the issue of multidimensional, multivariant, and stochastic facets to any exploration data deemed requisite for robust reservoir characterization. Before I continue, let me describe each of these labels applied to drilling parameters impacted by rock properties that we may include in our data-driven analytical workflows:

Multidimensional: Dimensions that affect independent variables. For example, vibrations can be axial, tangential, and lateral. It refers to an input space where several exploratory variables may epitomize the property of collinearity where the values demonstrate an exact or approximate linear relationship. Anisotropy is inherent in some rock properties, such as permeability. Anisotropy increases the dimensionality of the input space as it is directionally dependent.

Multivariant: Multiple independent variables that affect the outcome of a singularity.

Multivariate: Multiple dependent variables that must be predicted to reach an objective on a singularity. These are typically variables that have interdependencies that can impact the outcome of the singularity. Torque affects RPM, weight affects torque and RPM, and all three change rate of penetration (the outcome).

Stochastic: Variability and erratic behavior of independent variables. For example, the performance of the bit will vary depending on time, rock strength, and flow rates.

The data must be studied through exploratory data analysis (EDA) in both space and time dimensions as well as the multivariate perspective. Any outliers need to be identified as they disguise structure. The EDA steps enable linked visualizations such that we can surface hidden patterns and correlations and trends in the associated data. Such displays include histograms, correlation matrices, and variogram clouds.

Interpretation

We take the hard data measurements from cores and well logs at discrete locations across a reservoir and through graphical methodologies and EDA workflows we visually interpret the numerical data. Experience plays a major role in the interpretation of the results. First principles and self-evident propositions drive our understanding when assigning the value to the measurements of the hard data. We generate, because of the analysis, soft data in both a spatial and temporal domain. Mostly, we are moving beyond the sampled knowledge measured at remote spatial and time locations as we model the reservoir in both a spatial and time continuum.

Estimation

With the model reflecting the variation in a spatial and time continuum, we can estimate values for those reservoir properties at varying scales and spatial locations away from the local hard data sampled across the reservoir. The methodologies supporting this estimation are founded on least squares and must be adjusted to a varied array of different models determined by first principles and engineering concepts.

The subject of geostatistics can be broken down into four discrete divisions:

1. Linear stationary geostatistics
2. Nonlinear geostatistics
3. Nonstationary geostatistics
4. Geostatistical simulation

Geostatistics plays an essential role during the integration of geophysical and petrophysical data to develop a static earth model for reservoir management activities. Figure 7.1 illustrates an example suite of workflows to attain a static earth model

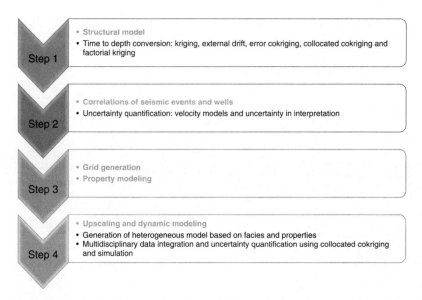

Figure 7.1 Geostatistics and earth modeling

before evolving the dynamic earth model to understand fluid movement through the target reservoir.

THE COVARIANCE AND THE VARIOGRAM

The fundamental measuring technique for the relationship between two random variables is the covariance. We can develop the kriging functions from the relationship derived from the evolution of the variance of the sum of two random variables as a function of the covariance.

$$\text{Cov}(X, Y) = \text{E}\{[X - E(X)][Y - E(Y)]\}$$

This is the basis for all mathematics behind kriging:

$$\text{Var}(X + Y) = \text{Var}(X) + \text{Var}(Y) + 2\,\text{Cov}(X, Y)$$
$$\text{Cov}(X, Y) = 0 \text{ if } X \text{ and } Y \text{ are uncorrelated}$$

We all understand as geoscientists that Mother Nature acts in ways that defy logic or plausible appreciation. Therefore we strive to build geologic models of our reservoirs based on a few wells and active seismic surveys, realizing that these models are simple descriptions of a complex and heterogeneous set of subsurface systems. This seems orthogonal to a deterministic and robust understanding of a hydrocarbon reservoir that enables E&P professionals to develop strategies and tactics to exploit these reserves. The earth models at least reduce the complexity inherent in the multidimensional and multivariate systems to the estimation of a few critical parameters.

The first mathematical assumption that underpins the geo-statistical approach is represented in Figure 7.2.

If (x) can be considered a point in a one-dimensional space, then (x, y) is a two-dimensional space and (x, y, z) is a three-dimensional space. The geological or seismic variable $Z(x)$ will be modeled as a random function reflecting a mathematical object as a random variable at all locations x. We then develop a geostatistical model that takes $Z(x)$ as the sum of a polynomial trend $m(x)$ and a residual random function $R(x)$. The function $m(x)$ is invariably a constant, linear, or parabolic trend in the coordinates of x. As a constant, we are looking at a stationary model of mean equal to m. And as either linear or parabolic, we are looking at a trend surface analysis as depicted in Figure 7.3.

Trend surface analysis is similar in its formalism to linear regression. The intention is to predict one variable, no matter

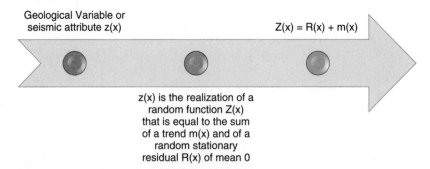

Geological Variable or
seismic attribute z(x)

$Z(x) = R(x) + m(x)$

z(x) is the realization of a
random function Z(x)
that is equal to the sum
of a trend m(x) and of a
random stationary
residual R(x) of mean 0

Figure 7.2 Basic assumption of geostatistics

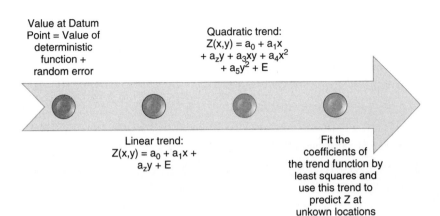

Value at Datum Point = Value of deterministic function + random error

Quadratic trend:
$Z(x,y) = a_0 + a_1x + a_2y + a_3xy + a_4x^2 + a_5y^2 + E$

Linear trend:
$Z(x,y) = a_0 + a_1x + a_2y + E$

Fit the coefficients of the trend function by least squares and use this trend to predict Z at unkown locations

Figure 7.3 Trend surface analysis

whether defined in one or two dimensions. The methodology is least squares and we calculate the coefficients to minimize the average squared error. Note that this falls short of a proper interpolation technique since it does not honor the data points and assumes that the residuals are uncorrelated in a spatial domain.

How do we calculate a variogram? First, we must classify pairs of points by distances, and then we calculate the mean squared difference between pairs corresponding to each distance. A variogram describes the spatial continuity of the data under study. It defines the variance of the difference between observed parameter values measured in the field at two different locations across realizations of the field (Cressie, 1993).

The secret source behind fitting a model for the space–time correlation of an observed event is the variogram. There are two variograms described in the current literature:

- *Experimental variogram:* Visualization of potential space–time correlation
- *Variogram model:* Definition of the weights for the kriging functions

The first variogram represents an empirical estimate of the covariance of a Gaussian process. Thus, it may not be most beneficial for kriging if we do not apply further constraints or processing. This characteristic of inadequacy reduces the number of available variogram models that are beneficial. The linear, spherical, Gaussian, and exponential models are most commonplace.

CASE STUDY: SPATIALLY PREDICTED MODEL OF ANISOTROPIC PERMEABILITY

What Is Anisotropy?

Anisotropy is a characteristic of spatial continuity that is directionally dependent. The implication is that at a particular point in the space domain you can measure different physical or mechanical values along different axes. Permeability is an anisotropic rock property. The value is dependent on the vertical or horizontal axis of measurement.

This example shows how to examine data for nonrandom surface trends and anisotropy. We use simulated data where the variable is relative permeability values measured in Darcy units (DU). The offsets from a point in the southwest corner represent the coordinates of the reservoir to the east and north distances in units of meters (m).

First, we explore the dataset by inspecting the spatial data distribution. Figure 7.4 shows a scatter plot of the observed data. The scatter plot proposes a uniform dispersion of the measured data across the extent of the area to be predicted. There is no unambiguous inference to be ascertained about the presence of a surface trend in the data. However, the apparent stratification of permeability values in the northeast–southwest direction might indicate a nonrandom trend.

The important step now is to investigate the presence of trends in the measurement. We shall suggest how to remove surface trends from the data and then continue the semi-variogram analysis with the detrended data. We can further

Semivariogram in Anisotropic Case with Trend Removal Example
The VARIOGRAM Procedure
Dependent Variable: Permeabilty

Number of Observations Read	300
Number of Observations Used	300

Spatial Distribution of Permeabilty Observations

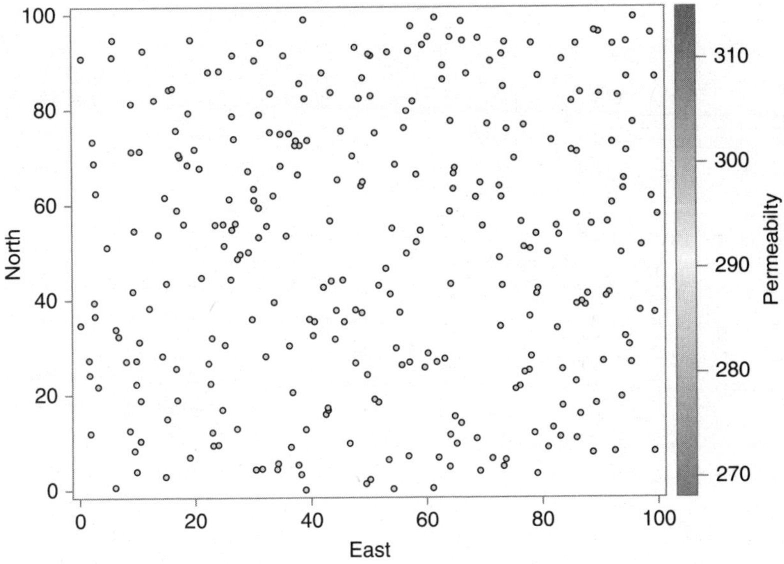

Figure 7.4 Scatter plot of permeability observations at discrete locations across the reservoir

experiment with smaller lag sizes to obtain more points in our sample semivariogram (see Figure 7.4).

Analysis with Surface Trend Removal

We used a predictive modeling procedure to extract surface patterns from the original data. If the goal is a spatial prediction, we can continue processing the detrended data for the prediction tasks, and at the end we can reinstate the trend at the projection locations to report the analysis results.

In general, the exact form of the trend is unknown, and in this case the spatial distribution of the measurements shown in

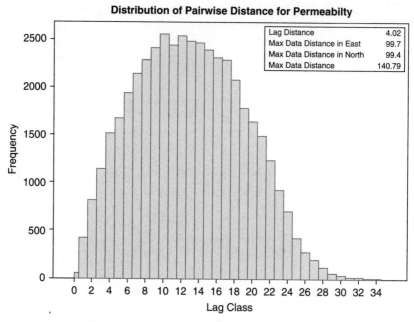

Figure 7.5 Histogram detailing lag classes and the trends in the measurement

Figure 7.5 suggests that we can use a quadratic model to describe the surface trend like the one that follows:

$$T(\text{East, North}) = f_0 + f_1 [\text{East}] + f_2 [\text{East}]^2$$
$$+ f_3 [\text{North}] + f_4 [\text{North}]^2$$

The detrending process leaves us with a dataset that contains the *residual permeability* data residuals. This time we run a variogram again to inspect the detrended residuals, and with a request only for the observations plot, as depicted in Figure 7.6.

Before we proceed with the empirical semivariogram computation and model fitting, let us examine our data for anisotropy. If there is any anisotropy, it manifests itself as different ranges or sills or both for the empirical semivariograms in various directions.

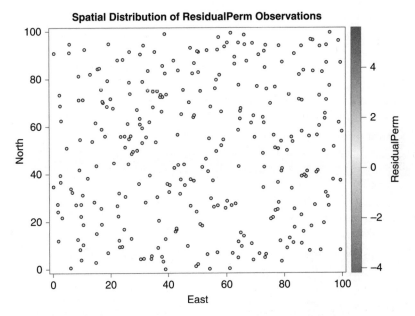

Figure 7.6   Scatter plot of permeability data detrended residuals

We want detail in our analysis, so we set the empirical semivariance in 12 directions. Empirical semivariograms are produced in increments of the base angle $\theta = 180°/12 = 15°$.

It is critical also to be conscious of the angle of tolerance that specifies a range of angles determined by the number of angle classes used in computing the continuity measures. The perpendicular distance cutoff is also an important consideration to determine the angle type for the points under consideration. The distance classes explain a sequence of cylindrically shaped areas while the angle classes radially cut these cylindrically shaped areas.

A different choice of values produces different empirical semivariograms because these options can regulate the number of pairs that are included in a class. Avoid assigning values that are too small to these parameters so that you can allow for an adequate number of point pairs per class. At the same time, the higher the values of these parameters are the more data pairs that come from closely neighboring directions are included in each lag. Therefore, values for these options that are too high pose a risk of losing information along the direction. The side effect occurs because we may incorporate data pairs from a broader spectrum of angles; thus, we potentially amplify weaker anisotropy or weaken stronger anisotropy.

We displayed only the semivariogram plots in the specified number of directions. Default in panels places multiple empirical semivariograms:

The panels shown in Figures 7.7, 7.8, and 7.9 suggest that in some of the directions, such as for θ = 0°, the directional plots tend to exhibit a somewhat noisy structure. This behavior

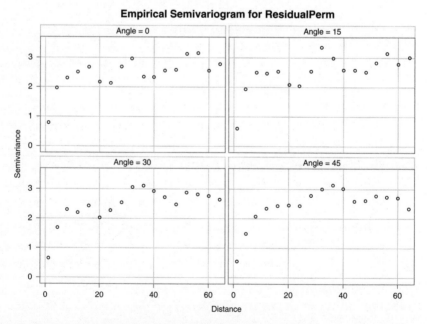

Figure 7.7 Semivariograms for varying angles θ = 0° to 45°

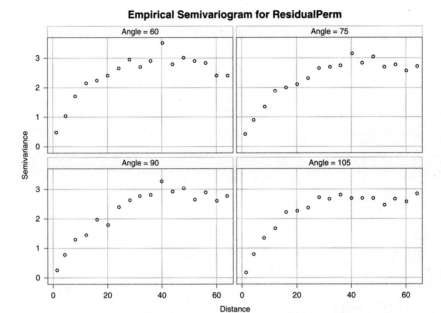

Figure 7.8 Semivariograms for changing angles θ = 60° to 105°

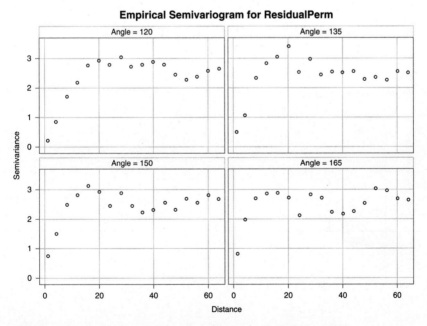

Figure 7.9 Semivariograms for changing angles θ = 120° to 165°

can be due to the pairs distribution across the particular direction. Specifically, based on the lag distance choice there might be insufficient pairs present in a class. Also, depending on the angle tolerance and the bandwidth selected, there might be too many pairs under consideration from neighboring angles that potentially follow a modified structure. These are factors that can increase the variability in the semivariance estimate. A different explanation might lie in the existence of outliers in the dataset. This aspect can be furthered explored in a box plot of the square root difference cloud, as depicted in Figure 7.10.

Figure 7.10 suggests that outliers, if any, do not appear to be adversely affecting the empirical semivariogram in the N–S direction for the petrophysical dataset describing permeability. The effect of the isolated outliers in lag classes 6 and 10–12 is demonstrated as the divergence between the classical and robust empirical semivariance estimates in the higher distances. The difference in these estimates comes from the definition

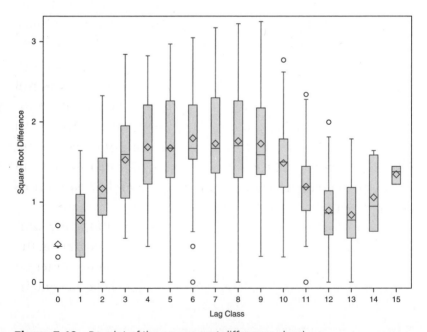

Figure 7.10 Boxplot of the square root difference cloud

of the solid semivariance estimator $\bar{y}_z(h)$, which imposes a smoothing effect on the outlier influence.

This behavior is relatively mild here and should not obstruct your goal to study anisotropy in your data. You can also perform accurate computations in any direction. By doing so, you can fine-tune the calculation parameters. We can also obtain smoother estimates of the sample semivariance.

Further, in this study, the directional plots in Figures 7.7, 7.8, and 7.9 suggest that during shifting from $\theta = 0°$ to $\theta = 90°$, the empirical semivariogram range increases. Beyond the angle $\theta = 90°$, the range starts decreasing again until the whole circle is traversed at $180°$ and small field values are encountered around the N–S direction at $\theta = 0°$. The sill seems to remain overall the same. This analysis suggests the presence of anisotropy in the permeability values, with the major axis oriented at about $\theta = 90°$ and the minor axis situated perpendicular to the major axis at $\theta = 0°$.

The multidirectional analysis requires that for a given lag distance we should also specify a maximum delay value. Since the permeability correlation range is unknown away from the well locations, we can apply the rule of thumb that suggests the use of the half-extreme data distance in the direction of interest. Following the information displayed in Figure 7.5 for different directions, this distance varies between $99.4/2 = 49.7$ m and $140/2 = 70.4$ m. In turn, the pairwise distances table in Table 7.1 indicates that within this range of distances you can specify the maximum lag value between 12 and 17 lags. Let us define it as 16.

At this point, we are ready to continue with fitting theoretical semivariogram models to the empirical semivariogram in the selected directions of $\theta = 0°$ to $\theta = 90°$. By trying out different models, we see that an exponential one is suitable for the empirical data:

$$\bar{y}_z(h) = c_0[1 - \exp(-h/a_0)]$$

Table 7.1 Pairwise Distance Intervals Tabulated for Each Lag Class

Pairwise Distance Intervals				
Lag Class	Bounds		Number of Pairs	Percentage of Pairs
0	0.00	2.01	52	0.12%
1	2.01	6.03	420	0.94%
2	6.03	10.06	815	1.82%
3	10.06	14.08	1143	2.55%
4	14.08	18.10	1518	3.38%
5	18.10	22.12	1680	3.75%
6	22.12	26.15	1931	4.31%
7	26.15	30.17	2135	4.76%
8	30.17	34.19	2285	5.09%
9	34.19	38.21	2408	5.37%
10	38.21	42.24	2551	5.69%
11	42.24	46.26	2444	5.45%
12	46.26	50.28	2535	5.65%
13	50.28	54.30	2487	5.55%
14	54.30	58.33	2460	5.48%
15	58.33	62.35	2391	5.33%
16	62.35	66.37	2302	5.13%
17	66.37	70.39	2285	5.09%
18	70.39	74.41	2079	4.64%
19	74.41	78.44	1786	3.98%
20	78.44	82.46	1640	3.66%
21	82.46	86.48	1493	3.33%
22	86.48	90.50	1243	2.77%
23	90.50	94.53	925	2.06%
24	94.53	98.55	710	1.58%
25	98.55	102.57	421	0.94%
26	102.57	106.59	274	0.61%
27	106.59	110.62	200	0.45%
28	110.62	114.64	120	0.27%
29	114.64	118.66	55	0.12%

Table 7.1 (Continued)

Lag Class	Bounds		Number of Pairs	Percentage of Pairs
		Pairwise Distance Intervals		
30	118.66	122.68	35.	0.08%
31	122.68	126.71	14	0.03%
32	126.71	130.73	11	0.02%
33	130.73	134.75	2	0.00%
34	134.75	138.77	0	0.00%
35	138.77	142.80	0	0.00%

For the purpose of the present example, it is reasonable to assume a constant nugget effect equal to zero, based on the empirical semivariograms shown in Figures 7.7, 7.8, and 7.9. The same output suggests that the model scale is likely to be above 2 and that the range might be relatively small in $\theta = 0°$. We then set initial values for the exponential model parameters and account for these considerations.

We assign an initial value of zero to the nugget effect. Then we request a grid search for the range and scale parameters so that the optimal set of initial values is selected for the parameter estimation in each of the two angles $\theta = 0°$ and $\theta = 90°$. By inspecting the empirical semivariograms in Figures 7.7, 7.8, and 7.9, we specify the value list 2, 2.5, and 3 for the scale and the values from 5 to 25 with a step of 10 for the range. We also set the nugget effect parameter as a constant.

The fitted and empirical semivariograms for the selected directions are displayed in Figure 7.11.

Conclusively, the semivariogram analysis on the detrended permeability data suggests that the permeability SRF exhibits anisotropy in the perpendicular directions of N–S ($\theta = 0°$) and E–W ($\theta = 90°$).

The sills in the two directions of anisotropy are similar in size. By inspecting the empirical semivariograms again in Figures 7.7, 7.8, and 7.9, we could make the reasonable

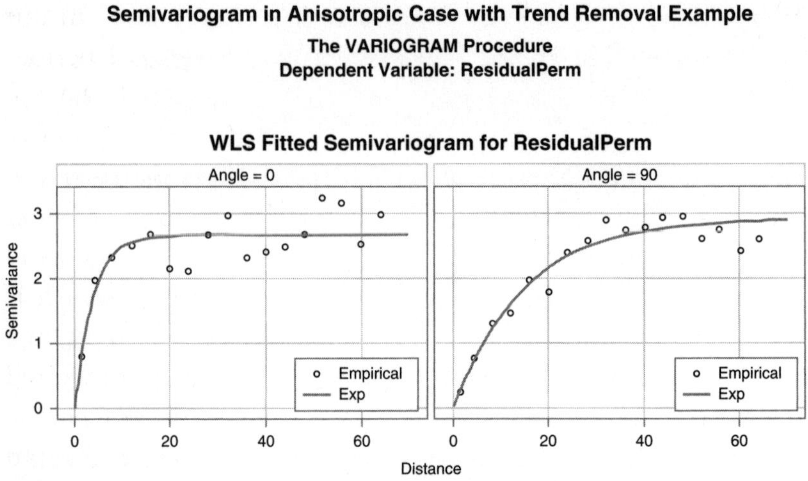

Semivariogram in Anisotropic Case with Trend Removal Example
The VARIOGRAM Procedure
Dependent Variable: ResidualPerm

WLS Fitted Semivariogram for ResidualPerm

Figure 7.11 Semivariograms for angles $\theta = 0°$ and $\theta = 90°$

assumption that we have a case of geometric anisotropy, where the range in the major axis is about 4.5 times larger than the minor axis range. If we would like to use these results for predictions, then we would need to specify a single scale value for the geometric anisotropy sill. In this case, we could choose an arbitrary value for the continuous scale using the narrow interval from the estimated scales in the previous results. As an alternative, we can fit an exponential model to all different angles examined in this example and then select the constant scale value to be the mean of the scales across all directions.

KRIGING AND CO-KRIGING

Kriging is a deterministic technique. By "deterministic" I mean it generates but one solution. Although the model is probabilistic, kriging produces only one solution. As we have illustrated in the petrophysical property case study, permeability is deemed as a variable $Z(x)$ such that it is interpreted as the sum of a polynomial trend, $m(x)$, plus a residual, $R(x)$, of mean zero. Universal kriging (Matheron, 1970) addresses the problem of interpolating a variable by some scattered data points. In our case study, this is an interpolation of layer-averaged permeability from well data, but it could also quite easily be the interpolation of other petrophysical properties such as porosity sampled at discrete space and time locations across the reservoir. Universal kriging is one version of kriging taken in the context of the model in which $Z(x)$ is the sum of a polynomial trend and a residual of mean zero, $R(x)$. What we address in this instance is the estimation of the unknown value, $z(x_0)$, at a location x_0 in a one-, two-, or three-dimensional perspective. We use measured values, $z(x_i)$ obtained at N number of scattered data points; $(x_i).z(x_0)$ is estimated by a weighted average of the measured values $z(x_i)$.

Apparently, the kriging algorithm explains the variogram and the trend model. Any change in either system impacts the kriging weights.

Let us continue the permeability case study by implementing the kriging system on the data. The kriging algorithm first uses the Gaussian-Gaussian model. Table 7.2 shows the saved parameter values of the fitted Gaussian-Gaussian model.

Table 7.2 Parameter Values for the Fitted Gaussian-Gaussian Model

The KRIGE2D Procedure Dependent Variable: Permeability Prediction: Pred1, Model: SelModel	
Covariance Model Information for SelModel	
Nested Structure 1 Type	Gaussian
Nested Structure 1 Sill	1019.3527
Nested Structure 1 Range	369.81059
Nested Structure 1 Effective Range	640.53072
Nested Structure 2 Type	Matern
Nested Structure 2 Sill	1003.9332
Nested Structure 2 Range	190.86061
Nested Structure 2 Smoothness	107.59906
Nugget Effect	2.4574104

The algorithm uses these parameters for the prediction based on the selected model.

Figure 7.12 illustrates the semivariogram of the Gaussian-Gaussian model. The parameters are shown in Table 7.2 that feed into the model.

Figure 7.13 is a map of the kriging prediction of the permeability values across the studied reservoir. The prediction error surface shows a naturally increasing error as you move farther away from the observation locations. Interestingly, kriging predicts an area for greater permeability values located in the northeastern part of the domain. But the trend is gentle.

Next, we implemented the kriging algorithm to perform prediction with the exponential model. The model parameters are shown in Table 7.3.

Figure 7.14 illustrates the semivariogram of the nested exponential model where its parameter values are those shown in Table 7.3.

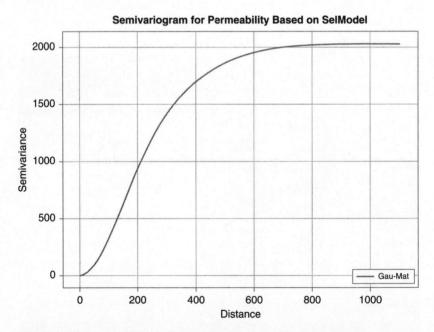

Figure 7.12 Semivariogram for permeability based on the selected Gaussian-Gaussian model

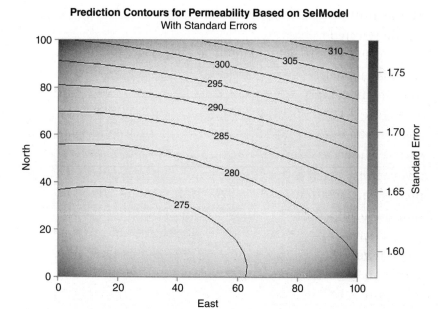

Figure 7.13 Kriging prediction for permeability values across reservoir using selected model

Table 7.3 Parameter Values for the Fitted Exponential Model

The KRIGE2D Procedure Dependent Variable: Permeability Prediction: Pred1, Model: ExpModel	
Covariance Model Information for ExpModel	
Type	Exponential
Sill	26839222
Range	12863919
Effective Range	38591757
Nugget Effect	0

The prediction plot for the exponential model is presented in Figure 7.15. Prediction values and spatial patterns are not too dissimilar overall to those of the Gaussian-Gaussian case with permeability values at around 280 in the southwestern area of the reservoir. Apparently, although both models predict the same essential characteristics of the permeability distribution,

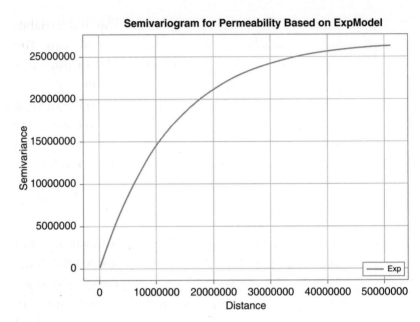

Figure 7.14 Semivariogram for permeability based on the exponential model

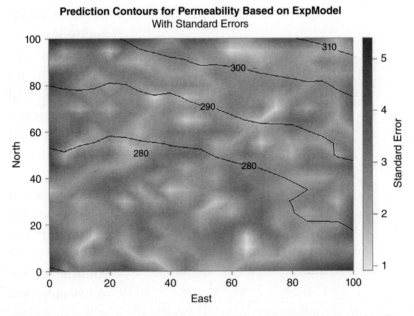

Figure 7.15 Kriging prediction for permeability values across reservoir using exponential model

the exponential model suggests a more limited spatial variability in adjacent locations as contours become less smooth. The lack of a nugget effect in the exponential model justifies this behavior. Also, the exponential model predictions seem less inclined to deviate farther away from the near-zero mean than the Gaussian-Gaussian model predictions. The prediction error reaches higher upper values in the exponential model, though its low values are slightly smaller in the exponential model.

GEOSTATISTICAL INVERSION

The petrophysicist and geophysicist can put their heads together and extrapolate the wireline parameters at each well location, implementing the 3D seismic data, invariably post-stack migrated data, as a roadmap to credible reservoir property values across the entire field under exploration. Geostatistical Inversion delivers an unconstrained, quantitative context for this extrapolation methodology. The geostatistical inversion technique performs an extrapolation of the petrophysical variables via stochastic simulation techniques (Haas and Dubrule, 1994) or Monte Carlo methods. Geoscientists often pick up on the idea that Monte Carlo is related to Bayes' theorem. And the Markov Chain Monte Carlo (MCMC) methodology (Geyer, 1992) is a general workflow to estimate sample distributions and relevant integrals and averages of the petrophysical properties throughout the reservoir.

The algorithm implemented for a geostatistical inversion workflow invariably uses an iterative simulated annealing approach. This method enables us to pinpoint a local minimum of the study data misfit function. Plots such as histograms and spatial variograms provide a visual and deterministic appreciation for the lateral evenness of the resulting petrophysical property values between existing wells.

Geophysical Attribute: Acoustic Impedance

The analytical methodology relies on the premise that acoustic impedance is correlated to the petrophysical variable of interest. We express this statistical relationship as a joint probability distribution function (PDF) that is fashioned from histograms of the dataset observations under study. The extrapolation is undertaken with a vertical sampling interval that is consistent with the joint PDF. The chosen sampling interval invariably falls between the well-log and the seismic data vertical resolution.

Every control point in our spatiotemporal window of the study had a measurement of both the acoustic impedance and a local PDF version of this geophysical attribute.

At the outset of the algorithm, the PDF at a given control point is estimated from global measurements of acoustic impedance. The first objective is to determine a local PDF at the point where a value of acoustic impedance is to be simulated. This local PDF is determined from the PDFs associated with the available control points by a standard kriging technique.

Having estimated the local PDF, we can use the associated cumulative PDF, or CDF, to create a random assessment of the acoustic impedance, implementing a Monte Carlo technique.

In general, the solution to the inverse problem is non-unique. The seismic data and wireline data are honored by multiple distributions of the acoustic impedance measurements. All geostatistical inversion runs provide an autonomous approximation of the acoustic impedance measurement.

Petrophysical Properties: Density and Lithology

The power and flexibility of geostatistical inversion are appreciated mostly when petrophysical parameters are correlated either directly or indirectly with acoustic impedance. A joint probabilistic density function describes such correlations. From the viewpoint of geostatistical inversion, it is desirable to enforce a relationship between the acoustic impedance and the petrophysical properties. The correlation can constrain the petrophysical simulations between existing wells to honor stacked seismic data.

We estimated the lithology PDFs from lithology logs. After calculating the density PDFs for each lithology type, a variogram workflow analyzed all wireline data and acoustic impedance data generated from the inverted traces. Finally, the simulation runs identified individual sand packets after the geostatistical inversions had completed with a vertical resolution of 2 milliseconds.

The reservoir in our study was populated by numerous wells strategically located, and this process enabled the geostatistical inversion methodology to estimate an accurate earth model.

KNOWLEDGE SYNTHESIS: BAYESIAN MAXIMUM ENTROPY (BME)

Let us reference a geostatistical framework (Christakos et al., 2005) entitled "Knowledge Synthesis" as depicted in Figure 7.16.

Kolovos et al. adopted the Knowledge Synthesis as a practical framework for spatiotemporal prediction. It implements physical principles in the context of a data analysis from a space–time continuum perspective. It is critical to express with rigor all spatiotemporal distances in a three-dimensional continuum of two spatial dimensions and time, adhering to all significant study conditions and appropriate geometry. In the case of a reservoir, the geophysicist and petrophysicist must describe the space and time variables applicable to each geoscience in the context of the structural and stratigraphic subsurface geometry across the field. The *Theoretical Foundation* embraces the key logical methodologies of space–time prediction. Other critical workflows incorporate the slackening of all restrictive modeling assumptions to ascertain a suite of *abstract principles*. The *openness* inherent in the framework

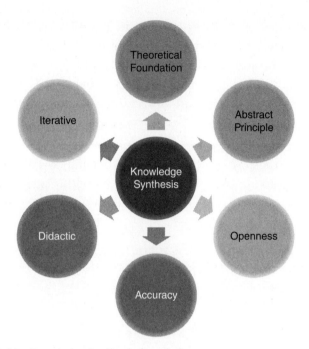

Figure 7.16 Knowledge Synthesis foundation

integrates multiple knowledge sources across varying scales in the space–time domain. An important step is to ensure rigor and mathematical *accuracy* in the functional relationships for all significant dependent and independent variables. It is imperative to generate ever-decreasing prediction errors across the space–time continuum. The *didactic* aspect increases the scope of potential solutions by harnessing the distributions as an outcome, rather than single predicted values. Finally, the *iterative* facet of the Knowledge Synthesis framework derives extant methodologies as its cases within a general framework. One of the more common techniques under the Knowledge Synthesis framework is *Bayesian maximum entropy* (BME).

The BME methodology includes traditional geostatistical methods as individual cases and extends their features and functionality in a way that liberates analysis from restrictive assumptions, and enables integrating information in more forms than sampled data values.

The suggested framework encourages unshackled method-ologies to enable a more realistic physical model. Gaussianity in the distribution of many petrophysical parameters is an assumption that can lead to significant bias in the analytical study. Something that is far from Mother Nature's reality.

Characterizing a hydrocarbon reservoir from a geostatistical perspective invariably means the adoption of kriging methods. Kriging embraces several techniques that ingest sampled data, and uses the spatial locations of the measurements to determine a distance-based correlation among the observed values of an attribute. A theoretical covariance function approximates the empirical correlation. The fitted covariance defines our current knowledge of the oil and gas field and is employed to predict attributes at unsampled locations between the cored and logged wells. Kriging variants, such as simple, ordinary, universal, and indicator kriging, to name but a few, have been used exten-sively in the Oil and Gas industry. Relevant references for krig-ing include Journel and Huijbregts (1978), Christakos (1992), Cressie (1993), Olea (1999), and Chilès and Delfiner (1999). In parallel, software tools that facilitate kriging-based spatial analy-sis are available as stand-alone packages such as GSLIB (Deutsch and Journel, 1992).

Essentially, kriging is more precise than analytically basic spatial analysis techniques such as Thiessen polygons and inverse distance interpolation (Tabios and Salas, 1985) as well as remote sensing technologies (Lee et al., 2012). However, when related to geostatistical analysis, kriging considers spatial covariance, variogram models, and observed attribute values. By only accepting observed single values as input data, other forms of knowledge bases that might be available to assist and improve prediction, such as applicable laws or conceptual mod-els, are ignored. Additionally, observed data might not always comprise accurate measurements. Kriging has had imperfect outcomes in integrating uncertain data in an accurate and effec-tual way, for example, Savelyeva (2010) whose approach on *kriging with measurement errors* necessitates expectations about the measurement errors under consideration. Such boundaries impact the accuracy of kriging-based prediction and its aptitude to extrapolate (Christakos, and Serre, 2000).

Bayesian Maximum Entropy (Christakos, 1990, 2000) postulated a new methodology to address these fundamental shortcomings of classical methods like kriging. It adopted a more encompassing epistemic framework for Geostatistical analysis and mapping. BME counts on the theoretical Knowledge Synthesis (KS) framework. KS is a knowledge-centered method that integrates different sources of various information content based on a more general, yet rigorous academic support for improved prediction accuracy (Christakos 2000, 2010). As an example, assessing the oil yield at a drilling site presumes the collection of borehole data to sample, for instance, monthly return. Accuracy in this analysis can be tentatively improved by including additional useful information about the soil type, composition, and characteristics at some location because these factors could influence the yield. BME provides the foundation to integrate such knowledge bases either as additional observed data or in universal knowledge forms such as physical laws, first principles, and empirical models (Kolovos et al. 2012). This is an attractive feature in the contemporary data-driven analytical environments because BME serves as an enabler to generate and integrate data from universal knowledge bases that might be otherwise left unused (Kolovos et al. 2002). Figure 7.17 details the workflows that implement BME on a Knowledge Synthesis platform. As opposed to general knowledge, observed hard data (single observations that are considered to have exact values in the context of a study) and soft data (observations with nontrivial measured uncertainties) are considered as case-specific knowledge in the BME framework. BME is also free of additional limitations and restrictions that burden other geostatistical methods; for example, the BME analysis is

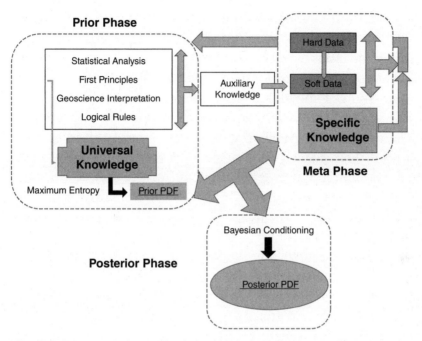

Figure 7.17 Knowledge Synthesis implementing Bayesian maximum entropy methodology

independent of the data distribution. As such, for instance, it can account for non-Gaussian data distributions, whereas kriging is unable to accurately handle heavy tailed data (Christakos et al. 2001).

The MetaPhase refers to observed data and relevant data workflows required to transform the data. All data Quality Control (QC) steps are implemented in the MetaPhase. The geophysicists and petrophysicists can evaluate, identify, and discriminate all the spatial and temporal data into hard and soft segments. The soft data is generated through a suite of traditional interpretation workflows, invariably based on first principles and engineering concepts.

The Posterior Phase updates the prior Probability Density Function (PDF) with the available case-specific knowledge.

The BME methodology links the maximum entropy theory with operational Bayesian statistics to strengthen its mathematical foundations for spatiotemporal analysis (Christakos, 1990). The maximum entropy theory enables the ability to manage multi-sourced knowledge bases from a general and case-specific perspective. BME also creates an underpinning to integrate all knowledge bases. Maximization of data input helps to coalesce a priori knowledge. We can specify a logical rule set to filter, integrate, and optimize a description of the general attribute characteristics. Additionally, the Bayes' rule maintains the prior knowledge by connecting the set of existing case-specific hard and soft data to generate a model that reflects a fundamental truth.

The core value of BME for oil and gas exploration is in its borrowed characteristics from statistics (Bayes' rule) and information theory (information maximization through maximum entropy). Unlike the data-driven classical statistics paradigm that is based solely on observed measurements, BME extends its analytical features and flexibility by enabling integration of a much broader range of knowledge types and by embracing informational content in uncertain data. These characteristics make BME-based geostatistical analytics very beneficial.

The preceding discussion about BME is presented in additional detail in He and Kolovos (2017). Of interest, He and Kolovos classify BME as part of the larger family of Bayesian Hierarchical Modeling (BHM) methods, known as model-based analysis approaches that can also handle various types of certain and uncertain input. BHM has been accordingly applied in many disciplines and offers the foundation for both spatial and space-time analysis (e.g., Banerjee et al., 2004; Le and Zidek, 2006). Compared to other BHM methods, BME is a nonparametric method that utilizes the Bayesian rule operationally. The BME edge lies in using maximum entropy as the conditionalization principle, and this enables BME to avoid distributional assumptions.

REFERENCES

Anselin, L., "The Moran Scatterplot as an ESDA Tool to Assess Local Instability in Spatial Association." In: Fischer, M., H. Scholten, and D. Unwin (eds.), *Spatial Analytical Perspectives on GIS*, Taylor & Francis, London (1996), pp. 111–125.

Banerjee, S., B. P. Carlin, and A. E. Gelfand, *Hierarchical Modeling and Analysis for Spatial Data*, Chapman & Hall/CRC, Boca Raton (2004).

Chilès, J. P., and P. Delfiner, *Geostatistics-Modeling Spatial Uncertainty*, John Wiley & Sons, New York (1999).

Christakos, G. "A Bayesian/Maximum-Entropy View to the Spatial Estimation Problem," *Math. Geol.*, 22 (1990): 763–777.

Christakos, G. *Random Field Models in Earth Sciences*, Academic Press, New York (1992).

Christakos, G., *Modern Spatiotemporal Geostatistics*, Oxford University Press, New York (2000).

Christakos, G., *Integrative Problem-Solving in a Time of Decadence*, Springer, New York (2010).

Christakos, G, and M. L. Serre, "BME Analysis of Spatiotemporal Particulate Matter Distributions in North Carolina," *Atmos. Environ.*, 34 (2000): 3393–3406.

Christakos, G., M. L. Serre, and J. L. Kovitz, "BME Representation of Particulate Matter Distributions in the State of California on the Basis of Uncertain Measurements," *J. Geophys. Res. Atmos.*, 106 (2001): 9717–9731.

Christakos, G., R. A. Olea, M. L. Serre, L. L. Wang, and H. L. Yu, *Interdisciplinary Public Health Reasoning and Epidemic Modelling: The Case of Black Death*, Springer, Berlin (2005).

Cliff, A. D., and J. K. Ord, *Spatial Processes: Models and Applications*, Pion Ltd., London (1981).

Cressie, N., "Fitting Variogram Models by Weighted Least Squares," *Mathematical Geology*, 17, no. 5 (1985): 563–570.

Cressie, N., and D. M. Hawkins, "Robust Estimation of the Variogram: I," *Mathematical Geology*, 12, no. 2 (1980): 115–125.

Cressie, N. A. C., *Statistics for Spatial Data*, John Wiley & Sons, New York (1993).

Deutsch, C. V., and A. G. Journel, *GSLIB: Geostatistical Software Library and User's Guide*, Oxford University Press, New York (1992).

Fergal, P. Casey, Joshua J. Waterfall, Ryan N. Gutenkunst, Christopher R. Myers, and James P. Sethna, "Variational Method for Estimating the Rate of Convergence of Markov Chain Monte Carlo Algorithms." Physical Review E 78, 046704, October 20, (2008).

Geyer, C. J., "On the Convergence of Monte Carlo Maximum Likelihood Calculations," Technical Report 571, School of Statistics, Univ. Minnesota (1992).

Grijalba-Cuenca, A., C. Torres-Verdín, and H. Debeye, "Geostatistical Inversion of 3D Seismic Data to Extrapolate Wireline Petrophysical Variables Laterally Away from the Well," SPE 63283, paper presented at the SPE Annual International Technical Conference, Dallas (October 1–4, 2000).

Haas, A., and O. Dubrule, "Geostatistical Inversion: A Sequential Method of Stochastic Reservoir Modeling Constrained by Seismic Data," First Break, 12, no. 11 (1994): 561–569.

He, Junyu, and Alexander Kolovos, "Bayesian Maximum Entropy Approach and Its Applications: A Review," *Stoch. Environ. Res. Risk Assess.* DOI: 10.1007/s00477-017-1419-7, Springer-Verlag Berlin, Heidelberg (2017).

Journel, A., and C. Huijbregts, *Mining Geostatistics*, Academic Press, London (1978).

Kolovos, A, G. Christakos, M. L. Serre, and C. T. Miller, "Computational BME Solution of a Stochastic Advection-Reaction Equation in the Light of Site-Specific Information," *Water Resour. Res.*, 38, no. 12 (2002): 1318–1334.

Le, N. D., and J. V. Zidek, *Statistical Analysis of Environmental Space/Time Processes*. Springer, Berlin (2006).

Lee, S.-J., M. L. Serre, A. van Donkelaar, R. V. Martin, R. T. Burnett, and M. Jerrett, "Comparison of Geostatistical Interpolation and Remote Sensing Techniques for Estimating Long-Term Exposure to Ambient PM2.5 Concentrations across the Continental United States," *Environ. Health Perspect.*, 120, no.12 (2012): 1727–1732.

Matheron, G., "The Theory of Regionalized Variables and Its Applications," Centre de Geostatistique de l'Ecole des Mines de Paris, Les Cahiers du Centre de Morphologie Mathematiques, Fasc. 5, 1970.

Olea, R. A., *Geostatistics*, Kluwer Academic Publication, Boston (1999).

Savelyeva, E, S. Utkin, S. Kazakov, and V. Demyanov, "Modeling Spatial Uncertainty for Locally Uncertain Data," *Geoenv. VII Geostat. Environ. Appl*, 16 (2010): 295–306.

Tabios, G. Q., and J. D. Salas, "A Comparative Analysis of Techniques for Spatial Interpolation of Precipitation," *JAWRA J. Am. Water Resour. Assoc.*, 21 (1985): 365–380.

Yu, H. L., A. Kolovos, G. Christakos, J. C. Chen, S. Warmerdam, and B. Dev, "Interactive Spatiotemporal Modeling of Health Systems: The SEKS-GUI Framework," *Stochastic Environmental Research and Risk Assessment*, 21 (2007): 555–572.

Yu, H.-L., S.-J. Ku, and A. Kolovos, "Advanced Space-Time Predictive Analysis with STAR-BME," *Proceedings of the 20th International Conference on Advances in Geographic Information Systems*, ACM (2012), pp. 593–596.

Yu, H. L., S. C. Ku, and A. Kolovos, "A GIS Tool for Spatiotemporal Modeling under a Knowledge Synthesis Framework," *Stochastic Environmental Research and Risk Assessment*, 30 (2016): 665–679.

Zagouras A., A. Kolovos, and C. F. M. Coimbra, "Objective Framework for Optimal Distribution of Solar Irradiance Monitoring Networks," *Renewable Energy*, 80 (2015): 153–165. DOI: http://dx.doi.org/10.1016/j.renene.2015.01.046.

CHAPTER 8

Artificial Intelligence: Machine and Deep Learning

"The language of probability allows us to speak quantitatively about some situation which may be highly variable, but which does have some consistent average behavior. Our most precise description of nature must be in terms of probabilities."

Richard Feynman

INTRODUCTION

Artificial intelligence (AI) has captured the imagination of a global audience. We have been obsessed with the idea of simulating human intelligence and witnessing machines emulate our everyday activities. Hollywood, of course, has painted a multicolored celluloid representation on the big screen. So, what is the reality? We accept that AI has been integrated into expert systems, speech and face recognition solutions, and robotic process automation. John McCarthy, who introduced us to the concept in 1956, coined it as an umbrella term to reflect the vast array of robotics that could be realized to automate our lives. Today, we witness a rapid adoption and proliferation of AI and machine learning (ML) across all business verticals. Why? The answer is *big data*. The explosion of data volumes, varieties, and velocities across hitherto-siloed engineering groups within E&P has opened the doors to ML, a version of AI. In the Oil and Gas (O&G) industry we are searching for patterns in big data, both spatial and temporal as well as structured and unstructured. And ML teaches computers how to learn without the burden of overt programming. It paves the road to solving critical exploration and production (E&P) business problems through data analysis. Data-driven methodologies often ignored by statisticians are at the core of ML. Some of these soft-computing techniques include pattern recognition, causality, nonlinearity, clustering or segmentation, and parallelization. Moving beyond vanilla statistics, we follow the ML curve to mature algorithmic problems with computational efficacy that optimize data engineering and address ultimately business issues.

It is often said that figures don't lie, but liars do figure. When it comes to finding patterns in data, figures do not have to lie to suggest things that are not true. We depend so profoundly on patterns in our daily routines that we tend to see them even when they are not there. When we observe the night sky we see not a random arrangement of stars, but the Big Dipper or the Southern Cross. The widespread acceptance of conspiracy theories is further evidence of that human desire and need to find patterns.

The challenge is to decide which patterns are useful. Let us describe data mining (DM) as a technical process, shifting from identifying business problems to translating business problems into DM problems.

Mining pieces of data to transform them into information/knowledge expands into several topics, including hypotheses testing, model building, and pattern discovery. DM is a way of learning from the past to make better decisions in the future.

Avoid:

- Learning things that are not true
- Learning things that are true but not useful

Artificial intelligence (AI) adds smarts to automation across all industries. The oil and gas vertical business has witnessed automated processes and methodologies during the past decade as the evolution of the Digital Oilfield of the Future (DOFF) has gained traction across E&P. But automation is not smart. Not until AI soft-computing techniques educate the DOFFs' implementations can geoscientists claim their solutions have intelligence. The brain has been trained to think with its mind. AI constitutes a paradigm shift. We have moved from manual workflows to automated workflows, and now AI is providing multiple possibilities across E&P to address complex automated systems. The traditional E&P engineering groups are compartmentalized, and even though the boundaries are gradually collapsing, the adoption of AI accelerates a more efficient interdisciplinary work ethic. AI encapsulates a multifaceted approach to deriving business value from raw data across E&P. The data scientists who play in the AI arena may come from various backgrounds such as signal processing, statistics, mathematics, physics, and neuroscience.

DATA MANAGEMENT

Data management is critical to delivering a robust and quality-controlled dataset for data-driven analytics. ML techniques are ideal for analyzing massive datasets, and piecemeal the same workflows are being implemented in a data quality suite of methodologies across multiple industries such as drug development and an array of engineering verticals. Sustaining data reliability across a siloed industry such as O&G is a resource-intensive chore and an almost impossible task to resolve, no matter how good the intentions. We tend not to address the data issues until an operational undertaking sheds light on the poor data quality under interpretation. Big data adoption only manifests the issues as being more critical and invasive. Machine learning offers an alternative way to rectify data quality problems. Let us discuss three aspects of a data management system where machine learning can play a useful role:

1. Data quality quantification
2. Data matching accuracy
3. Data enrichment

MACHINE LEARNING METHODOLOGIES

In Figure 8.1, we define a taxonomy of "Machine Learning algorithms in which supervised, unsupervised, and semi-supervised

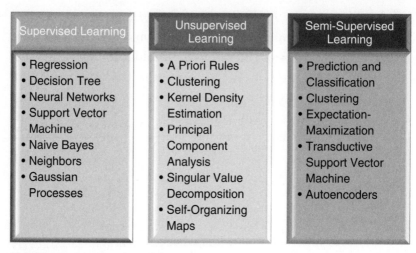

Figure 8.1 Machine learning taxonomy

learning algorithms lie at the intersection of the Machine Learning and Data Mining fields" (Hall, Dean, Kabul, and Silva, 2014).

Supervised Learning

Algorithms that fall into this group are trained with labeled datasets. *Labeled* refers to the prior knowledge of the desired output from a given input. An example in petrophysics would be a fluid parameter such as porosity labeled either "H" (Highly porous) or "L" (Low porosity). The algorithm learned from a suite of input data and associated expected or accurate output data. By equating the actual output with the expected outputs, we can ascertain errors in prediction. The errors then adjust the model's set of rules. Supervised learning techniques like regression, classification, and gradient boosting adopt a pattern identification logical workflow to forecast the values of the label on unlabeled data. Invariably in geophysics and petrophysics, we have stored historical data that can be analyzed for signatures and patterns. These past events are harbingers to future occurrences. Supervised learning techniques are conducive to these types of workflows. For example, a supervised learning method can perform a sample-to-sample prediction across a 3D seismic cube to identify every sample with a lithological parameter.

Unsupervised Learning

When the data has no historical labels, we adopt the family of unsupervised learning techniques. In such instances, the algorithm is left in the dark and doesn't know the correct answers. Instead, the algorithm has to determine the output for itself with no a priori guidance. The purpose is to uncover some hidden structure for all the observations that make up the input space. Unsupervised learning can enable seismic facies analysis. Thus, it would provide a very robust and efficient workflow to estimate reservoir properties. This results from an accurate mapping of various seismic attributes to reservoir properties through pattern recognition algorithms. Modern techniques include self-organizing maps (SOMs), nearest-neighbor mapping, k-means clustering, and singular value decomposition (SVD).

Semi-Supervised Learning

The semi-supervised techniques are ideal candidates for many applications that are modeled by the supervised algorithms, the difference being that both labeled and unlabeled datasets are fair game as simultaneous input. Invariably, the input dimension for semi-supervised algorithms consists of a small amount of labeled data and a larger quantity of the less expensive unlabeled data. Classification or clustering techniques are semi-supervised methods that fit the labeled and unlabeled soup of multivariate data. We can classify features by applying semi-supervised methods to subsurface seismic profiles.

DL is an innovative branch of ML that endeavors to corral the intricacies and nuances of all ML back into the pen labeled *artificial intelligence* (AI). DL is essentially a suite of algorithms designed to model high-level abstractions hidden in the data.

The complexity inherent in the number of layers escalates owing to the iterative nature of the DL algorithms. A large volume of data is a prerequisite to train the networks, and thus there is a lot of computational power required to address business problems in E&P from a deep learning perspective.

DL workflows have been ascribed the stamp of a black-box methodology compared to the traditional analytical steps advocated by linear and nonlinear regressions. It is critical therefore to set aside a portion of the data to test and validate the DL algorithm used for analysis. Invariably, it is challenging to persuade geophysicists and other siloed upstream engineers to appreciate the intrinsic business value and possible knowledge that can be garnered from DL workflows. However, the dynamic nature of DL methodologies and their ability to continuously advance and accommodate variations in the underlying patterns offer an incredible convenience to advocate a less deterministic and a more data-driven perspective of analytics.

An image can be expressed as a vector of intensity values for each pixel. Look at a color seismic profile, and immediately your brain abstracts a three-dimensional (color) property space overlapping onto shared space. When we look at a picture composed of multiple pixels we see there are two spatial coordinates x and y that locate each pixel horizontally and vertically in Euclidean space. If we were to view the picture as a frame of an animated video, we could introduce the t variant or temporal location, thus determining the three values x, y, and t for space–time definition. But what about the pixel's color? If you imagine a three-dimensional (color) property space atop the ordinary space (Figure 8.2), then we can extend the pixel characteristics by introducing a symmetric shape such as a cube for color definition. As James Clerk Maxwell taught us, we must specify the intensities of three color sources—red, green, and blue—and these intensities are depicted as R, G, and B. Now we have six numbers: x, y, t, R, G, and B to identify the pixel.

The RGB (Figure 8.3) color cube illustrates the color selections you have at each pixel in the seismic image to substantially

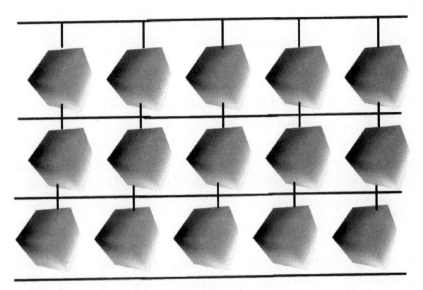

Figure 8.2 Concrete and colorful property space concept

Figure 8.3 Red, green, and blue (RGB) color cube

illuminate the picture element. The three-dimensional cube is a real description of the property space as it lends credence to the range of the possible intensities spanning from zero to one.

DEEP LEARNING TECHNIQUES

Deep learning (DL) is a subset of machine learning (ML). DL implements large neural networks that support various hidden layers to identify features in the input data that have robust predictive capabilities. DL neural networks evolved from the basic artificial neural networks, taking advantage of both unsupervised and semi-supervised techniques. The evolution has witnessed the adoption of erudite optimization algorithms and groundbreaking computational platforms to achieve state-of-the-art accuracy.

After a data preparation suite of automated or semi-automated workflows, it is essential to adopt an exploratory data analysis suite of workflows that via intuitive visualizations expose hidden patterns, correlations, and trends in the underlying datasets. In the case of seismic analysis, you could aggregate multiple attributes from a pre- or post-stack perspective dependent on the objective function or business problem under study, for example, production optimization or effectiveness of an enhanced oil recovery technique such as water-alternating-gas (WAG). The data-driven methodology supplements the traditional interpretation of 3D immersive visualization workflows. Figure 8.4 depicts the method that post–model building ensures the correct operationalization of the model(s) deemed appropriate for seismic attribute analyses in a reservoir characterization study.

Some of the deep learning techniques under consideration for E&P are:

- Deep forward neural network
- Convolutional deep neural network

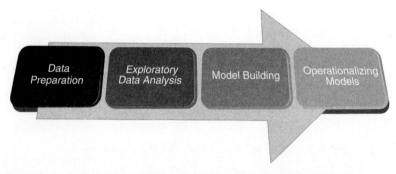

Figure 8.4 Typical open workflow based on derived seismic attributes

■ Recurrent deep neural network

■ Stacked denoising autoencoder

We shall implement some of the soft-computing techniques enumerated in Figure 8.1 under the headings: Supervised, Unsupervised, and Semi-Supervised. Figure 8.5 provides more details for each of these taxonomies.

Semi-Supervised Learning

Data scientists across many business verticals have discovered that the aggregation of unlabeled data with a limited amount of labeled data generates a marked improvement in the accuracy of the learning algorithms in the FL family.

Use some labeled data (hard to get) and a lot of unlabeled (easier to get) in combination with predictions/classification and clustering. Get around the cold-start problem in recommendation engines. Semi-supervised models are proposed.

Some single algorithms, like autoencoders, are also capable of semi-supervised learning. We notice the data forming discrete groups or clusters. Members of the same cluster share a

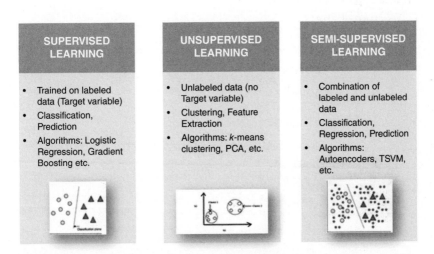

Figure 8.5 Supervised and unsupervised data mining techniques in deep learning

common label, but of course, this is not a strict law. When a label represents a cluster, we are essentially implementing a smoothing technique that yields an efficient feature learning method for the data in a study. Whereas support vector machines for supervised learning seek a decision boundary with a maximal margin over the labeled data, the goal of TSVM (Transductive Support Vector Machines) is a labeling of the unlabeled data. The decision boundary has a maximal margin over all the data.

Supervised Learning

Target:
- Regression = simple supervised learning
- Prediction
- Classification

Examples: regression, LASSO regression, logistic regression, and ridge regression

- Decision tree: gradient boosting and random forests
- Neural networks, naïve Bayes, support vector machines

Unsupervised Learning

No Target:
- k-means = primary unsupervised learning
- Clustering
- Feature selection
- Feature extraction (provide some structural organization into the data)
- A priori rules
- Clustering
  - k-means clustering
  - Mean-shift clustering
  - Spectral clustering

- Kernel density
- Principal component analysis: kernel and sparse
- Self-organizing maps

Several architectures are built on neural networks, and a few are not necessarily deep unto themselves but are stackable to emulate deep. Deep learning is essentially a subset of machine learning, which itself is a subfield of artificial intelligence. It has been said that deep learning is "where machine learning shakes hands with big data." I would describe deep learning as a paradigm shift that applies to the siloed datasets from the various upstream E&P sectors:

- Learning feature representation instead of feature engineering (don't engineer; discover!).
- Fundamentally understand the world around us (see, hear, read, touch, gesture).
- Learn to represent the world as a nested hierarchy of concepts.
- Describe problems as layers of abstractions.
- Perform a task by training, not by applying rules and policies.
- Build complex ideas out of simpler representations.
- Improve with experience and data.

DEEP NEURAL NETWORK ARCHITECTURES

Deep Forward Neural Network

The architecture of a deep forward neural network, as depicted in Figure 8.6, is appropriate to identify approximations to the *estimated ultimate recovery* measurements and to determine probabilistic measures for inter-well reservoir properties derived from seismic attributes. It is a discriminative model with a flat architecture that is suitable for regression and classification workflows. It is, however, difficult to scale to large-pixel matrices.

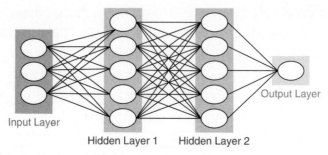

Figure 8.6 Deep forward neural network

The number of hidden layers that process the input data consistently exceeds the single-hidden-level architecture that we traditionally implement in a vanilla artificial neural network. In deep learning neural networks, the data is sent through a multistep sequence of pattern recognition processes. Each layer is trained by a discrete suite of features that are influenced by the preceding layer's output. Thus, the complexity of the features' characteristics is more compliant and recognizable the further the data move through the stacked hidden layers owing to the aggregated learning of the features in each layer of neurons. This feature hierarchy takes on more complexity and abstraction as data progresses to the output layer. This type of architecture enables the handling of high-dimensionality datasets with literally billions of parameters.

Another advantage inherent in deep forward neural networks is the ability to surface latent structures in all unlabeled and unstructured datasets. The clustering or grouping of input data to identify similarities on unlabeled data is unsupervised learning at its most effective, generating more accurate models proportional to the amount of data. Unlike most machine learning algorithms, deep learning neural networks accomplish automatic feature extraction without the engineers' or domain experts' intervention.

Like the restricted Boltzmann machines (RBMs), each hidden layer of a deep forward neural network that trains on unlabeled data learns feature characteristics automatically by iteratively reconstructing the input whence it elicits its samples. This process strives to minimize the difference between the network's estimates and the probability distribution of the input data. We can then identify correlations between features defined a priori as significant to the solution of our business problem. The role of the output layer is to intuitively act as a logistic classifier that ascribes a probability to an outcome or label.

Convolutional Deep Neural Network

The word *convolve* finds its etymology in the Latin root *convolvere,* which means to roll together. From a mathematical perspective, a convolution is "the integral" that quantifies the overlap between two functions as they pass over each other. A convolutional deep neural network (CDNN), as detailed in Figure 8.7, can be implemented to classify images and group them by similarities. They also carry out object recognition within the larger image such that a geophysicist could identify a seismic pinch-out (a type of stratigraphic trap) across a 2D seismic section. These network architectures are ideal for finding visual stratigraphic or structural features that are key production indicators. Convolutional deep neural networks also intersect with text analysis implementing a sequence of optical character recognition (OCR) techniques. These are ideal methodologies when integrating daily field reports during seismic acquisition. Are there surface anomalies noted in the logs that impact static shifts in the seismic traces across an anticline?

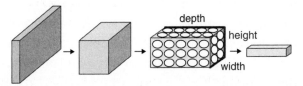

Figure 8.7 Convolutional deep neural network

The CDNN is ideal to improve the signal-to-noise ratio in seismic images and act as a seismic feature detector across the 3D input space. The architecture characteristic of the CDNN is often preferred to improve the picture and video processing, so there are E&P workflows suitable to analyze not only seismic profiles but also logging while drilling (LWD) and measurement while drilling (MWD) images and video. The CDNN is also ideal for natural language processing and has been applied with some success to daily rig reports. The wide-ranging learning algorithms implemented in a CDNN for NLP are established on statistical inference. The algorithms are taught a suite of rules via the analysis of real-world business issues that occur at rigs during daily activities. The annotated daily rig reports serve as input datasets that are derived from the rules grounded in the engineers' experience. Thus, we are moving away from the decision trees that generated rigid if-then rules to a more sophisticated algorithm founded on statistical models that offer a soft-computing technique via machine learning to establish a range of probabilistic hypotheses. These methods provide the gain of stipulating the relative certainty of the multiple possible outcomes as opposed to a single deterministic result.

A CDNN, like a single-hidden-layer multilayer perceptron (MLP), is a biologically motivated architecture. Think about the incredible visual processing power inherent in an animal's visual cortex. The CDNN is one design that strives to emulate nature from the perspective of maximally identifying edge-like patterns within the limited receptive field as well as imitating the multiple cells in a wider receptive field that position patterns exactly in a locally invariant manner.

Essentially a CDNN is a type of neural network implementing many duplicate reproductions of the same neuron. The duplication method is an identifying characteristic of CDNN. Other neural networks such as recurrent and recursive neural networks can adopt this architecture. However, one main advantage the many duplicate copies implementation offers is the ability to define computationally large models while limiting the number of actual input variables that describe the neurons' behavior. Many copies of the same neuron are equivalent to the abstraction of mathematical functions in computer science. The analogy of writing a function or algorithm once and calling it multiple times across different parts of the code is descriptive of a CDNN being taught by learning a neuron once and then using it in various places. The CDNNs serve a wide array of purposes, including image and video pattern recognition and natural language processing.

In the case of seismic images, we could implement a CDNN as an efficient architecture to identify geophysical features across a 3D suite of inlines and crosslines. We can identify stratigraphic traps, subtle facies changes, velocity anomalies that are indicative of rock properties, and shale inclusions. The CDNN can advocate germane tags for these features. Let us explore the LeNet1 architecture popularized in the late 1980s by Yann LeChun, who pioneered the network that kickstarted the field of deep learning. The current flavors of CDNN are very like the original LeNet architecture.

There are four critical algorithms in a CDNN:

1. Convolution
2. Nonlinearity
3. Sub-sampling
4. Classification

A seismic profile image, like all images, can be represented as a matrix of pixel values. Some of the conventional nomenclature discussed requires translation:

- *Channel* refers to a particular component of an image. Color plots of seismic sections have three channels: red, green, and blue (RGB). These are depicted as 2D matrices stacked on each other (one matrix per color) and each signifying pixel values in the range 0 to 255.

■ A *grayscale image* of a color seismic section entertains just one channel. So, we shall convert color seismic images to grayscale via a Python script to ensure we only have a single 2D matrix representative of the image under study. The value of the pixel in this array will also range from 0 to 255: 0 is indicative of black and 255 represents white.

Convolution

Convolution fundamentally extracts the seismic features from all the input images. It also conserves the spatial relationship between pixels by learning image features consuming small squares of input data. Let us look at a 5 × 5 image, Figure 8.8, and consider the matrix of pixel values can only be set to 0 and 1. Recall a grayscale image has a matrix with pixel values ranging from 0 to 255.

Now consider another matrix, this time of a 3 × 3 dimension. The convolution of a 5 × 5 seismic image shown in Figure 8.8 and a 3 × 3 matrix can be computed, resulting in the 3 × 3 matrix that is colored red in Figure 8.8. We only move the orange matrix from the top left of the 5 × 5 image and pass one pixel at a time to the right, also known as sliding. We then *slide* down one pixel and again move from the left to the right, convolving and computing the output matrix as we slide across the image as an element-wise matrix multiplication and addition between

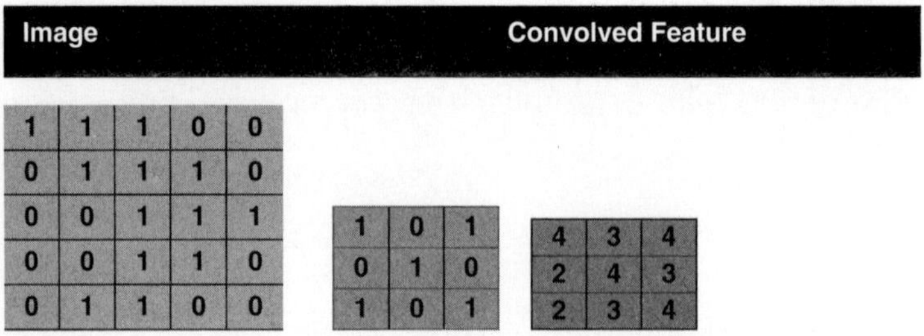

Figure 8.8 5 × 5 seismic image convolved with a 3 × 3 matrix to generate another 3 × 3 matrix of pixel values

the two matrices. The orange 3 × 3 matrix is considered a *filter* or feature detector, and the *convolved function* or *activation/feature map* is the resulting output of the matrix multiplication.

It is intuitive that different filters that slide across the input seismic image will generate different activation maps depicting the features from a different perspective. Some of the operations that can be accomplished with various filters can be enumerated:

- Edge detection
- Sharpen
- Box or Gaussian blur
- Curve detection

The CDNN architecture mostly learns the values of the possible filters by itself during the training phase. We can control some of the critical parameters that initiate the convolutional process, such as the number of filters, the filter size, and the overall architecture of the CDNN. Thus, the more filters we implement, the more image features that can be extracted, and this in turn ameliorates the network to distinguish patterns in hitherto-unseen seismic images.

We can constrain the size of the feature map using three parameters invariably implemented in the convolution algorithm:

1. *Depth*, which correlates to the number of filters.
2. *Stride*, which reflects the number of pixels driving the movement of the filter matrix across the seismic image.
3. *Zero-padding*, which is the custom of padding zeros around the border of an input image. This enables the application of the filter across all extreme locations of the input seismic image.

Nonlinearity

There is an additional operator of nonlinearity that is applied to each pixel. It essentially replaces all negative pixel values in the feature map with a zero value. Convolution is a linear operation: element-wise matrix multiplication and addition. We thus account for the fact that seismic data is nonlinear by implementing a nonlinear function. Some of the nonlinear functions executed by the algorithm include ReLU, tanh, and sigmoid.

Sub-Sampling

To reduce the dimensionality of the feature maps and at the same time retain the critical knowledge garnered from such maps, it is important to implement a sub-sampling function. There are several instantiations of sub-sampling or pooling common among the current array of CDNNs: for example, Max, Average, and Sum.

If we applied the max-pooling function, Figure 8.9, it would delineate a spatial neighborhood and elicit the largest element from the *rectified* feature map within the window under

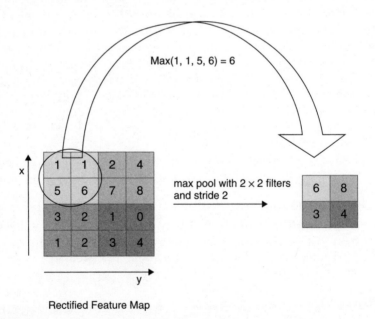

Figure 8.9 Max-pooling function applied to demarcate a spatial neighborhood

study. It has been shown that ReLU with max-pooling is more sensitive and robust when analyzing seismic images.

The pooling operation is implemented discretely to each feature map representing a distinct seismic characteristic or signature. Thus, the idea behind pooling is to piecemeal contract the spatial dimension of the input space and ensure feasibility to manage the features with a smaller number of parameters and network computations. This in turn reduces the possibility of overfitting the model.

Finally, the *fully connected* layer is the traditional multilayer perceptron. By fully connected, we refer to the implication that every neuron in the previous layer has a connection to all neurons in the following layer.

The convolution and pooling layers combine to act as feature extractors from a seismic input image. A fully connected layer performs the classification process:

Step 1: All filters and parameters are initialized with a random generator function.

Step 2: We train the CDNN with an input seismic image: either an inline or crossline 2D profile detailing some of the exciting seismic features. The network implements the forward propagation step (convolution, ReLU nonlinear, and max-pooling operations combined with forward propagation in the fully connected layer). The output probabilities are ascertained for each classification.

Step 3: The total error is calculated at the output layer by summing all the classifications:

$$\text{Total Error} = \Sigma \tfrac{1}{2} (\text{target probability} - \text{output probability}) 2$$

Step 4: Backpropagation is implemented to calculate the gradients of the error on all weights in the network. Gradient descent is used to adjust all filter values/weights and parameter values to reduce the error in the output layer. The weights are restructured in proportion to their contribution to the total error. Classification of a seismic image is deemed correct when the CDNN has learned to automatically change the weights/filters, resulting in a much-reduced error on the output layer. It is important to appreciate that the key network parameters such as some filters and filter sizes along with network architecture are fixed before Step 1. The training process does not impact these parameters; it only adjusts the values of the filter matrix and the weights.

Step 5: We repeat Steps 2 through 4 with all the seismic images in the inline and crossline direction to coalesce a 3D perspective of the active seismic acquired across the field. Running the trained CDNN (Steps 1–5) against new unseen seismic images would kick off the forward propagation step and generate a probability for each classification. If the training dataset is sufficiently large, the CDNN should generalize successfully and thus classify them into related and robust categories.

Recurrent Deep Neural Network

The recurrent deep neural network (RDNN), as shown in Figure 8.10, is an ideal architecture to model sequential data. It has the advantage to remember information in their hidden state. Thus, RDNNs are excellent at analyzing time-series data such as seismic traces as well as the nonstationary production data to forecast well performance.

There may be multiple types of feedback loops in a recurrent deep neural network. We implemented two examples:

1. Input delays
2. Feedback delays

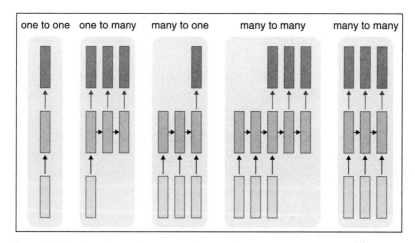

Figure 8.10   Recurrent deep neural network

The number of input nodes is impacted by each type of delay, mostly increasing the nodal count. Hence, delayed information coalesces with any current information.

Input Delays

There are many consecutive feature time steps input to the network concurrently.

Feedback Delays

During the implementation of feedback delays, the network delivers the output of the model to the input nodes simultaneously with the previous data. The delivery process can be attained by either a closed or an open loop. The former connects the output directly to the input layer and the latter ensures the known output is provided as an input to the network. In the estimated final recovery case study we trained and forecasted one-step-ahead with open loops. To make a prediction further into the future, we would require the use of closed loops. However, we noted that closed loops resulted in a 10 percent increase in error owing to clipping of peak and trough demand.

Stacked Denoising Autoencoder

Deep neural networks are commonly created by stacking autoencoders. An autoencoder is a kind of single-layer neural network. The denoising version of the autoencoder is trained by a random corruption of the input matrix. Autoencoders use the training examples as target variables as opposed to the training example labels. This behavior renders them as semi-supervised techniques. The output of one layer in the autoencoder architecture trains the subsequent layer. The training inputs kick off the layered training sequence as feedstock to the first layer in the autoencoder neural network. The neural network is initialized by the weighting factors of each individually trained layer. Then all the layers are retrained simultaneously by the original training examples. If a large number of inputs is consumed by a less significant number of hidden layers, we notice that the extracted features of the hidden layers are a nonlinear projection of the training examples projected onto a lower-dimensional space. These features have very accurate predictive tendencies for a training example's class label.

Figure 8.11 depicts a stacked denoising autoencoder. When we train a stacked denoising autoencoder, we use the original labels, the unlabeled training inputs, and slightly corrupted copies of the unlabeled training inputs. Every layer that consists of hidden units is trained separately on the output of the previous layer. Finally, the entire network is retrained. We can use those features output by the middle layer (layer h3) as inputs to subsequent predictive models.

The artificial neural network (ANN) defines and trains a denoising autoencoder. There are five hidden layers. The pixels that are corrupted represent the input training data, and the original pixels are the labels for the training of entry data. We ignore the actual class labels. How do we ascertain an accurate

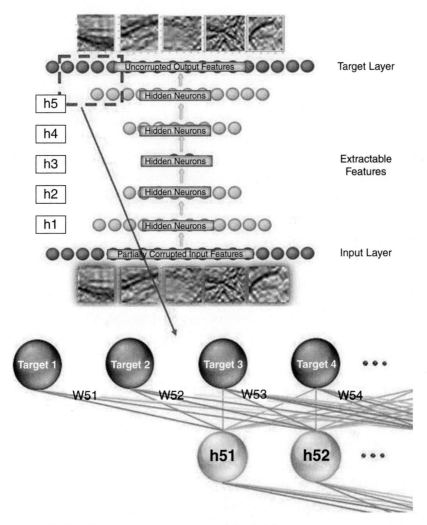

Figure 8.11 Stacked denoising autoencoder details

or useful number of hidden layers and neurons? Some of the key influencing characteristics are:

- Properties of the training data
- Amount of the training data
- Available optimization algorithms
- Anticipated predictive results

The odd number of layers in the hourglass architecture generates a single low-dimensional middle layer. This enhances feature extraction efficiency. Invariably, we see a higher level of predictive accuracy associated with designs exhibiting a larger number of both input features and examples in tandem with more layers and neurons. However, we must be aware of overfitting the DL neural network as more layers and neurons are added to the architecture. Sometimes a more sophisticated optimization algorithm will mitigate this problem. This study determined that a five-hidden-layer neural network struck the best balance between overfitting and the optimization abilities for the input seismic profiles.

We can ascertain the dimension of the space of the weights because it must be the same as the targets that are generated by a dictionary of filters combined with the input data.

The partially corrupted input seismic features can be either:

A. *A dataset that consists of 3D volumes.* Assume X_i is a volume of size ($p1 \times p2 \times p3$). For each volume, we need a label (target variable Y_i, which is binary) that indicates whether there is a feature of interest. The dataset is a collection of volume/label pairs $\{(X\_1, Y\_1) \ldots (X\_n, Y\_n)\}$. Note that $p1 \times p2 \times p3$ could also be a sub-block of a larger volume. So, for example, if the big volume is $100 \times 100 \times 100$ voxels, we could have X_i correspond to $8 \times 8 \times 8$ blocks. There needs to be one Y_i for each X_i.

B. *Exactly like the previous option, but the dataset consists of 2D images.* Assume X_i is an image of size ($p1 \times p2$). The dataset is a collection of volume/label pairs $\{(X\_1, Y\_1) \ldots (X\_n, Y\_n)\}$. And again, $p1 \times p2$ could also be a sub-block of a bigger image, and we still need one Y_i for each X_i.

Thus, either annotated volumes (Option A) or annotated images (Option B) are provided as input. The annotated volumes could be in CSV format while the images could be in

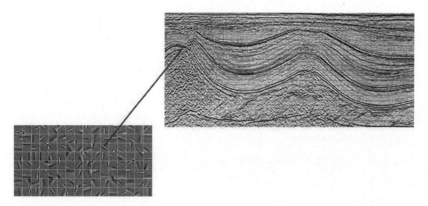

Figure 8.12 Seismic features generated for deep learning methodology

either CSV or some standard image file format (TIFF, PNG, etc.) It would be better to avoid JPG due to compression artifacts. Figure 8.12 illustrates the seismic features that were used as input to the stacked neural networks implemented for the deep learning methodology.

The annotations contain the Y_i labels. These annotations can be in a text file (say annotations.txt) that has two columns: <filename>, <label_value>. Each row corresponds to one of the X_i, which is either a (sub-block of a) volume or (a sub-block of) an image.

Alternatively, if it is not practical to create an annotations.txt file, it is feasible to use images/volumes that have the features of interest marked in a unique color. For instance, mark the interesting features/cracks/lines with red pixels in a gray image. Or mark them as (−1) voxel values in a CSV volume file, providing the information can be extracted automatically.

Stacked denoising autoencoders (SdAs), as shown in Figure 8.13, are implemented to extract features from a large dataset. It is applicable in the exploration phase to mine key performance indicators that identify direct hydrocarbon indicators in a 4D seismic dataset.

The building blocks for SdAs are autoencoders as implemented by Bengio et al. 2007.

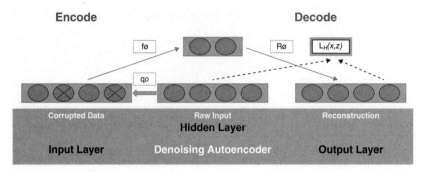

Figure 8.13 Stacked denoising autoencoder

An autoencoder takes an input x and first maps it to a hidden representation:

$$y = f\theta(x) = s(Wx + b)$$

Parameterized by $\theta = W, b$

The resulting latent representation y is then mapped back to a *reconstructed* vector $z \in [0, 1]^d$ in input space $z = g_{\theta'}(y) = s(W'y + b')$. The weight matrix W' can optionally be constrained such that $W' = W^\wedge T$, in which case the autoencoder is said to have tied weights. The network is trained so as to minimize the reconstruction error (the error between x and z).

During training, the denoising autoencoder algorithm corrupts x into $\tilde{x}$, where $\tilde{x}$ is a partially destroyed version of x employing a stochastic mapping. Afterwards y is computed as before (using $\tilde{x}$), $y = s(W\tilde{x} + b)$ and z as $s(W'y + b')$. The reconstruction error is now measured between z and the uncorrupted input x, which is computed as the cross-entropy:

$$\sum_{k=1}^{d} [x_k \log z_k + (1 - x_k) \log(1 - z_k)]$$

A denoising autoencoder tries to reconstruct the input from a corrupted version of it by projecting it first in a latent space and re-projecting it afterward back in the input space (Vincent et al., 2008). If x is the input, then Equation (1) computes a partially destroyed version of x using a stochastic mapping q_D. Equation (2) computes the projection of the input into the latent space. Equation (3) computes the reconstruction of the input while Equation (4) computes the reconstruction error.

$$\tilde{x} \, q_D(\tilde{x}|x) \tag{1}$$

$$y = s(W\tilde{x} + b) \tag{2}$$

$$x = s(W'y + b') \tag{3}$$

$$L(x, z) = \sum_{k=1}^{d} [x_k \log z_k + (1 - x_k) \log(1 - z_k)] \tag{4}$$

We initialize the dA class by stipulating the quantity of visible units (the dimension d of the input), the number of latent units (the dimension d of the latent space), and the corruption level. The constructor obtains symbolic parameters for the input, weights, and bias. Such symbolic variables are useful when, for example, the input is the result of some computations, or when weights are shared between the SdA and an MLP layer. When dealing with dAs, the dA on layer 2 receives the output of the dA on layer 1, and the weights of the dA are implemented during the second stage of training to build an MLP.

Mainly the architecture accommodates a stacking of multiple denoising autoencoders to form a deep neural network. To create a network that could appreciate the subtle intricacies inherent in the various levels of abstraction found in the petrophysical, geophysical, and geological data variables, we had to implement a data-driven methodology that incorporated a stacked denoising autoencoder (SDAE) (Vincent, Larochelle, Lajoie, Bengio, and Manzagol, 2010). To avoid complexity and to reduce uncertainty, it is customary to fix the input and the preferred output values to the same dataset. During the training step, you can taint the input data by adding Gaussian noise and omitting certain variables. This behavior forces the network to reconstruct the original data. Each level of abstraction is rebuilt. The encoder and decoder algorithms ensure the deconstruction of the input data and the transformation back into the original data respectively. See Figure 8.13 for a pictorial representation of the SDAE method. The principle behind the denoising autoencoder is simplistic by nature: to identify more vigorous seismic or petrophysical features and to avoid the hidden layers from only learning the identity of these features. This is achieved by reconstructing the input from a degraded version of it.

SEISMIC FEATURE IDENTIFICATION WORKFLOW

Efficient Pattern Recognition Approach

Let us walk through a simple set of preprocessing steps using DL techniques to identify features in seismic profiles. Initially, we must generate multiple small image patches from the larger images that represent the pre-stack or post-stack seismic sections output from a traditional processing suite of the acoustic wavelets as depicted in Figures 8.14 and 8.15.

The set of small image patches allows us to define a limited range of geophysical features to represent an image. This decreases the amount of training time required to learn subtle

Figure 8.14 Convert pixels of interest to grayscale

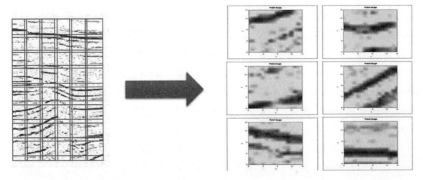

Figure 8.15 Break grayscale images into thousands of overlapping patches

patterns within the images. A classifier is trained to identify patches of focal interest when a training label is accessible. Geophysicists can implement a stacked autoencoder network to generate a dictionary of appropriate patches if selecting an unsupervised methodology. This method can be applied to pattern recognition problems in general, and we shall discuss an example from the unconventional reservoirs in the United States.

When analyzing seismic profiles by implementing DL workflows, we shall build deep neural networks (DNNs), which are artificial neural networks (ANNs) with multiple hidden layers of neurons. The DNN architectures encompass compositional models where objects are defined as layered image primitives. These additional layers build piecemeal composite features from lower layers.

These slides explain how the DNNs work for unsupervised learning to generate dictionaries that provide accuracy in defining faint and nonlinear patterns.

Having decomposed a greyscale image, in this case a seismic post-stack inline section, into overlapping patches, we generate relevant blocks of adequately small size for valuable processing. The patches enable compelling dimensionality reduction as well as highlighting relevant local insights across the spatial regions of the seismic image under study.

We also create a dictionary consisting of a set of representative patches reflecting a generalization of a basis in vector space. The dictionary of patches facilitates feature extraction in a deterministic way that allows the patches to be studied in an unsupervised workflow without training labels. Dictionary learning for images is a critical issue and underpins the foundation of several state-of-the-art compression and reconstruction methods (Lee et al., 2006).

We shall discuss stacked autoencoders as detailed in current literature (Bengio, Courville, and Vincent, 2013) as being suitable candidates for unsupervised learning of dictionaries. It is also important to advocate forward k-means clustering and DNN classification methodologies for analytical workflows of the raw image patches and the image features extracted by the denoising autoencoder.

Methods and Technologies: Decomposing Images into Patches

Let us study a seismic image S of size H × W pixels. The pixel at the ith row and jth column of the image are denoted $S(i, j)$. In the case of a grayscale image, $S(i, j)$ has an intensity value, which is usually an integer between 0 and 255. In the case of a color image in the red-green-blue (RGB) coordinate system, $S(i, j)$ is a tuple that consists of three integer values: $S\_R(i, j), S\_G(i, j), S\_B(i, j)$. These values invariably fall between 0 and 255. A grayscale image of resolution 2560 × 1920 consists of nearly 5 million pixels, an inordinate number of features for most of the predictive algorithms to use directly as input.

We adopt a general practice in image processing dividing our image into square sub-images, also called patches or tiles. Let P be a patch of size B × B. For example, if B = 2, then P contains 4 pixels, which is far more suitable for analysis. In general, B is an important tuning parameter, and you should select B large enough to capture recognizable patterns in the image. Patches are often allowed to overlap to avoid block artifacts or visual discontinuities. These defects occur along the boundaries of patches after they are processed. In Figure 8.16, patches P and P' have size B × B, and they overlap.

Patches can be represented as a set of linear combinations of the elements under study, also called dictionary atoms. The number of dictionary atoms is dependent on the size represented by the number represented by B. You can vectorize a patch by rearranging all the pixels into a row vector of size B^2, denoted $x = vec(B)$. See Figure 8.17 for an example.

Representing Patches with a Dictionary

Like any vector of dimension B^2, $vec(B)$ can be represented as a linear combination B^2 of orthonormal basis elements. We implement a *dictionary* instead of a *basis* in this example. The dictionary is a generalization where the elements (called *atoms*) are not required to be orthonormal. Dictionaries tend to be more efficient as a representation. Figure 8.18 shows an example of a

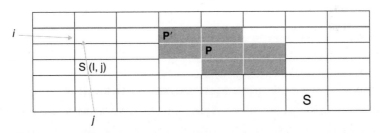

Figure 8.16 Illustration of overlapping patches in an image

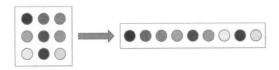

Figure 8.17 Patch vectorization rearranges pixels as a row vector in lexicographic order

Figure 8.18 Example of a dictionary that has 12 atoms

dictionary. Each atom is itself a sub-image that has the same dimensions as depicted by a patch.

The mathematical expression for the representation of a patch P is

$$x = vec(P) = \sum_j \alpha_j d_j$$

where each α_j is a scalar coefficient and each d_j is a vectorized dictionary atom.

A comprehensive dictionary contains atoms that are similar to the image patches so that the atoms can be represented using as few non-zero coefficients as possible. This kind of representation is deemed as sparse and provides a standard mechanism to reduce the dimensionality and thus act as a picture summarization technique.

Stacked Autoencoder

You can train a deep, unsupervised neural network to learn a composite dictionary of a few images that represent the most important features of the patches. To train a stacked denoising autoencoder, the target neurons should be equal to the original input neurons. The multiple layers tend to form the shape of an hourglass with a bottleneck in the middle layer. Thus, the network is required to learn a smaller dimensional, internal representation of the inputs before reconstructing them in the subsequent layers. Every layer of hidden units is usually trained separately on the output of the prior layer, and then the entire network is retrained. The features that are output by the middle layer (layer h3) can be used as inputs to subsequent predictive models.

Because of the hourglass shape of the network, the top layer weights will be the same dimension as the original patches, and this configuration forms a single low-dimensional middle layer suitable for extraction of features. These weights compose the dictionary of representative images. Figure 8.19 illustrates a stacked neural network with five hidden layers. The corrupted pixels act as training inputs. The original pixels are the training

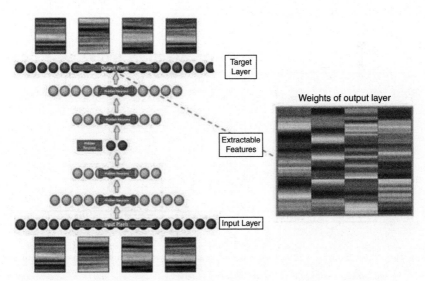

Figure 8.19 Schematic of a stacked autoencoder. Outputs are set equal to input patterns and the learned weights of the output layer from the dictionary

labels while the actual class labels are ignored. Several drivers dictate the ideal number of hidden layers and neurons:

- The training data
- Available optimization routines
- The desired outcome

Invariably, the greater the number of input features, the more hidden layers of neurons are requisite for more precise and quantifiable accuracy. However, it is important to avoid overfitting during this increase in neurons.

Refer to current literature covering these topics: DNNs and stacked autoencoders in Bengio, Courville, and Vincent (2013) and a *neural* algorithm used to train autoencoders in Hall et al. (2014).

To enhance the knowledge garnered from the original input images in an unsupervised manner, it is often necessary to perform a cluster analysis step on the image patches by implementing the k-means algorithm. It is feasible and probably more efficient to run a cluster with the low-dimensional projections generated by the middle hidden layer of an autoencoder. The optimum number of clusters, k, can be estimated by the *aligned-box criterion*. In addition to unsupervised training, you can also solve supervised classification or regression problems by using DNNs whenever targets are available in the training dataset.

REFERENCES

Bengio, Y., A. Courville, and P. Vincent, *IEEE Transactions on Pattern Analysis and Machine Intelligence*, 35, no. 8 (August 2013).

Bengio, Yoshua, Pascal Lamblin, Dan Popovici, and Hugo Larochelle, "Greedy Layer-Wise Training of Deep Neural Networks," *Advances in Neural Information Processing Systems 19 (NIPS 2006)*, MIT Press (2007), pp. 153–160.

Hall, Patrick, Jared Dean, Ilknur Kaynar Kabul, and Jorge Silva, "An Overview of Machine Learning with SAS® Enterprise Miner™," paper SAS313-2014, SAS Institute Inc. (2014).

Hinton, G. E., and R. R. Salakhutdinov, "Reducing the Dimensionality of Data with Neural Networks," *Science*, 313 (July 28, 2006): 504. DOI: 10.1126/science. 1127647.

Holdaway, Keith R., *Harness Oil and Gas Big Data with Analytics: Optimize Exploration and Production with Data-Driven Models*, John Wiley & Sons, Hoboken (May 2014).

Lee, H., A. Battle, R. Raina, and A. Y. Ng, "Efficient Sparse Coding Algorithms." In: *Advances in Neural Information Processing Systems 19 (NIPS 2006), Proceedings of the Annual Conference on Neural Information Processing Systems* (2006), pp. 801–808.

Vincent, P., H. Larochelle, Y. Bengio, and P. A. Manzagol, "Extracting and Composing Robust Features with Denoising Autoencoders," *ICML* 2008, pp. 1096–1103.

Vincent, P., H. Larochelle, I. Lajoie, Y. Bengio, and P. A. Manzagol, "Stacked Denoising Autoencoders: Learning Useful Representations in a Deep Network with Local Denoising Criterion," *Journal of Machine Learning Research*, 11 (2010): 3371–3408.

CHAPTER 9

Case Studies: Deep Learning in E&P

"When you have excluded the impossible, whatever remains, however improbable, must be the truth."

Sherlock Holmes (Sir Arthur Conan Doyle)

INTRODUCTION

Machine learning (ML) encapsulates a methodology for data analysis to automate the building of advanced analytical data-driven models. The algorithms iterate through a learning cycle sourced by disparate datasets. Ultimately, ML enables computers to surface hidden trends, insights, and patterns with no a priori knowledge programmed into their directives. The iterative nature of ML algorithms ensures the models are capable of independently evolving and thus surviving as a valid and trustworthy means to discover similar patterns in new data. The array of current ML algorithms allows geophysicists to automatically generate models against bigger, more complex data, delivering faster and more accurate results on an enormous scale of input data.

Thomas Davenport is a luminary in the field of academia, focusing on advanced analytical techniques. It is he who emphasized the necessity of automated and rapid predictive modeling, endorsing the application of automated DL architectures.

RESERVOIR CHARACTERIZATION

Interesting subsurface geophysical features in hydrocarbon exploration are three-dimensional. Salt-diapirs, unconformities, folded and overthrust belts, anticlines, deltaic sands, and reefs are a few examples of oil and gas stratigraphic and structural traps. Reliable interpretations and deterministic geologic models of the subsurface can be formalized when experienced geophysicists have adequate migrated 3D datasets to visualize. Seismic data are thus critical for the upstream exploration sector as well as brownfield redevelopment strategies and tactics to hone reservoir characterization for enhanced oil recovery techniques.

Efficient and robust reservoir characterization is critical to production optimization. Some of the key business value propositions that can be addressed by marrying traditional seismic interpretation and advanced data-driven deep learning analytics can be enumerated thus:

- Attain maximum reservoir contact.
- Identify well interference patterns.
- Discover additional satellite compartments.
- Implement deep learning methodologies.
- Custom-built advanced space–time analytics.
- Scalable computing in a big data framework.

Many modern applications exist for reservoir characterization. Alas, not all software offerings can harness the knowledge of the primary production indicators. To gain valuable insight, you need this understanding in a broad, spatiotemporal context across the entire areal hydrocarbon play.

For mature fields, you need to consider big datasets collated from well tests, petrophysical data, and high-resolution mapping of seismic attributes to reservoir properties. Exploratory data analysis is an important component of this task to ensure consistent data integration, aggregation, and management. Advanced tools in geostatistics and multivariate analysis can further boost your space–time analysis and uncertainty quantification; specific methods in deep learning and convolutional and recurrent neural networks can help you improve the signal-to-noise ratio and detect subtle features in data.

Figure 9.1 illustrates a suite of iterative DL workflows customized for reservoir characterization. We are trying to:

- Enrich and accelerate the knowledge garnered from traditional interpretation with scientific core principles, data-driven operations research, and advanced analytics.

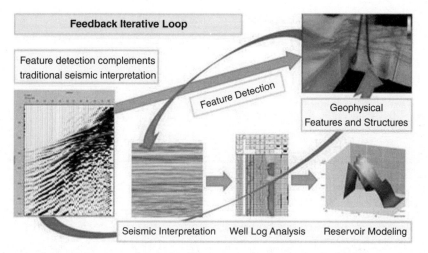

Figure 9.1 Reservoir characteristic workflows using DL technologies

- Generate an accurate description of formations and their content to identify economic reservoir units.

Existing approaches either lack scientific foundation or depend heavily on data analysis. There is nothing unfair in using core science, advanced analytics, and new technologies to your best benefit. We are putting forward our expertise of longer than 20 years in these fields to back an application that will help you understand your reservoir better and thus best position you to optimize its lifetime performance.

The key elements of our approach are:

A multidisciplinary methodology: We operate across disciplines to incorporate rock physics, geopressure, and geomechanics. Although different methods exist to create empirical and numerical mechanical earth models (MEMs), we use our particular expertise to aggregate field knowledge and technologies to create for the first time an innovative, integrated MEM. Our model is a unique, customizable solution that leverages empirical well-centric analyses to constrain interrelated criteria. To put it modestly, our MEM is the most robust model you can use to optimize unconventional plays.

Focused and advanced analytical workflows: We employ customized analytical approaches to address the array of business problems centered on reservoir characterization. Our analytics have solid roots in a science-based *knowledge synthesis* (KS) foundation that goes beyond mainstream statistical modeling. By observing critical details such as physical-based interpretation of natural quantities and using models free of restrictive assumptions, we enable more accurate modeling of interdependencies and space–time prediction.

Some of the challenges facing a data-driven analytical methodology when adopting deep learning techniques on seismic data range from mapping the traces to a spatial location to define features such as faults in their exact spatiotemporal dimension. We are primarily dealing with a very complex nonlinear functional relationship where the output space is structured. Even though deep neural networks address these issues from a modeling perspective, we need to consider the large input data dimension required to train the networks. We could, of course, generate a suite of randomly synthesized training datasets that aggregated both geophysical and petrophysical parameters and attributes.

Let us illustrate some practical case studies implementing ML and DL workflows across exploration and production.

CASE STUDY: SEISMIC PROFILE ANALYSIS

Supervised and Unsupervised Experiments

We executed two experiments to validate the unsupervised and supervised aspects of a patch-based analytical methodology on images or pictures. We created a dictionary of representative image patches, using one of the unsupervised deep neural network architectures. The input images were high-resolution seismic profiles across the producing reservoir in a mature

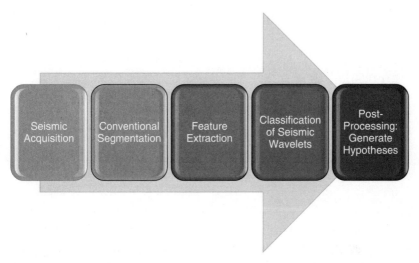

Figure 9.2 Classification as applied to the interpretation of seismic facies (Duda et al., 2000)

unconventional field. These same images were analyzed by another unsupervised method, k-means cluster analysis. Figure 9.2 depicts the DL workflow stages to segment the input seismic data and classify the wavelets. k-means clustering was used to both segment the seismic input data and classify the seismic wavelets.

We adopted the aligned-box criterion option to automate the number of clusters. Figure 9.3 illustrates examples of the high-resolution seismic images used in the study.

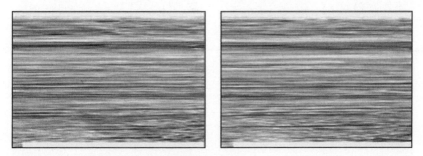

Figure 9.3 High-resolution seismic images

Unsupervised Results

Twenty-four high-resolution seismic images were converted to grayscale and split into 50 × 50 pixel patches using a 25-pixel stride length. Patches were then downsampled to 20 × 20 pixels to increase processing efficiency. The patching process resulted in a training set containing 30,459 input sub-images like those in Figure 9.4.

A neural network algorithm was implemented to train a 5-layer autoencoder with 50 latent units in the first layer, 25 latent units in the second layer, 10 latent units in the third layer, 25 latent units in the fourth layer, and 50 latent units in the fifth layer (50-25-10-25-50). Since the autoencoder contained 50 latent units in the fifth and top output layer, 50 dictionary images were created.

Following Hall et al. (2014) the autoencoder was instigated, employing layer-wise pre-training. All layers were concurrently trained to convergence. Conjugate gradient optimization was implemented to train all the network layers.

Input patches were also clustered to reveal different segments of interest in the original input images. A clustering algorithm was used to cluster the input patches by the k-means algorithm. The k-means algorithm usually results in spherical

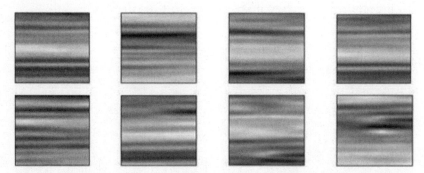

Figure 9.4 Sample 20 × 20 pixel patches created from high-resolution seismic images

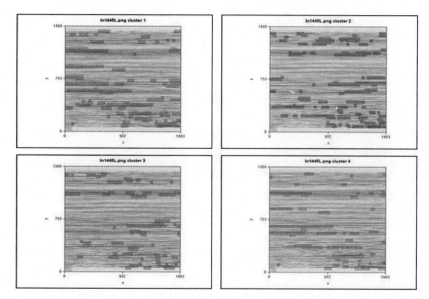

Figure 9.5 Four clusters of patches overlaid onto a single original inline 2D seismic image

clusters. However, the clustering patches are sufficient to populate complex clusters in the original image as can be seen in Figure 9.5.

In general, you apply some filters and some other preprocessing techniques to extract useful features from the images. Then you use these features for your modeling. It is usually hard to find out these features because you cannot know which feature will be useful for the modeling. On the other hand, using this framework, you can obtain these features/dictionary without worrying about this. In this example, you can see that the deep neural network learned some features about the input images. Train a deep, unsupervised neural network to learn a composite dictionary of a few images that represent the most important features of the patches.

Because of the hourglass shape of the network, the top-layer weights will be the same dimension as the original patches, and this configuration forms a single low-dimensional middle layer suitable for extraction of features. These weights compose the dictionary of representative images. The corrupted pixels act as training inputs. The original pixels are the training labels while the actual class labels are ignored.

Several drivers dictate the ideal number of hidden layers and neurons:

- The training data
- Available optimization routines
- The desired outcome

Invariably, the greater the number of input features, the more hidden layers of neurons requisite for more precise and quantifiable accuracy. However, it is important to avoid overfitting during this increase in neurons.

The dictionary can be used to efficiently identify areas of interest in new images, as depicted in Figure 9.6.

Figure 9.7 illustrates a sample of 32 dictionary images learned from 100 stochastic gradient descent (SGD) epochs, inputs corrupted at 25 percent, random weight dropout at 5 percent.

Figure 9.8 illustrates a sample of 32 dictionary images learned from 200 SGD epochs, inputs corrupted at 25 percent, weights below 1 dropped, and many filters trained to all 0s.

Deep learning (DL) has evolved from machine learning (ML) to gather the latter back into the realm of artificial intelligence (AI). DL is underpinned by a stack of algorithms that are designed to model high-level abstractions inherent in datasets. There are several architectural possibilities compatible with DL as we transcribe an observation such as an image into its composite representation as a vector of intensity values for each pixel:

1. Deep forward neural networks
2. Convolutional deep neural network
3. Recurrent deep neural network
4. Stacked denoising autoencoder

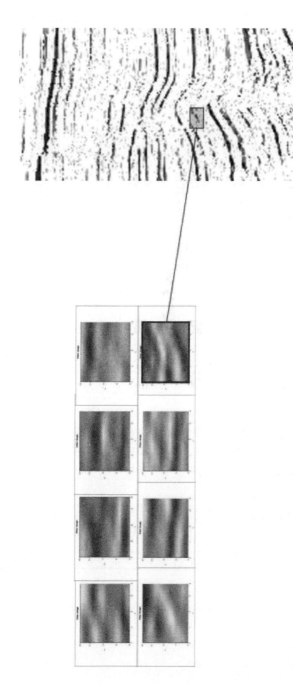

Figure 9.6 Dictionary defines new direct hydrocarbon indicators (DHIs)

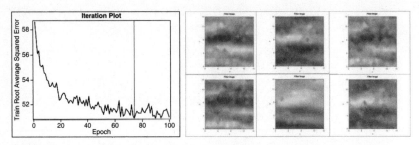

Figure 9.7 Single-layer autoencoder trained by stochastic gradient descent optimization

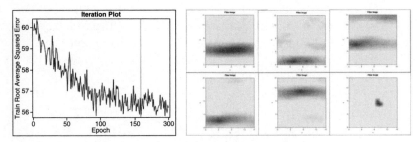

Figure 9.8 Sample of the dictionary images

DL is essentially synonymous with neural networks as research in this branch of ML strives to improve representations through the development of soft-computing models from unlabeled big data. Invariably the neural networks consist of many hidden layers designed to gain insight into specific features that offer substantive predictive capabilities. DL embraces two major learning paradigms, semi-supervised and unsupervised, that are coupled with advanced optimization approaches. This implementation of neural networks enables extraction of characteristic features from a suite of training data. One way to achieve feature learning is to stack a type of single-layer artificial neural network (ANN) known as an autoencoder or Diablo network.

Patrick Hall et al. (2014) describe the stacked denoising autoencoder implementation for feature extraction:

> Autoencoders are trained by using the same unlabeled inputs as both training examples and target labels. A denoising autoencoder is trained by randomly corrupting the input matrix of the autoencoder. Because autoencoders do not use the training example labels as targets but instead use the training examples themselves, they have been categorized as a semi-supervised learning technique. Each layer of the deep network is usually trained separately by using the output of the prior layer, or by using the training inputs in the case of the first layer. The weights of the individually trained layers are then used to initialize the entire deep network, and all layers are trained again simultaneously on the original training examples. When many inputs is used in conjunction with a much smaller number of hidden units, the features that are extracted as outputs of the hidden units are a nonlinear projection of the training examples onto a lower-dimensional space. Such features can be highly predictive of a training example's class label.

The original unlabeled training inputs are used to train a stacked denoising autoencoder. A stacked training workflow enables each layer of hidden neurons to learn in isolation from the output of the lower layer.

Deep learning enables engineers to develop soft-computing models that represent the geophysical data in multiple processing tiers that are stacked to determine representations of said data with multiple levels of abstraction (LeCun, Bengio, and Hinton, 2015). We have witnessed vastly improved understanding in several areas that have adopted these methodologies, such as speech recognition, object detection, visual object recognition, and drug discovery, as well as genomics. Geophysicists can surface complex and hidden features such as structural and stratigraphic traps in large 3D seismic datasets by utilizing a backpropagation algorithm. Such a deep learning workflow can identify how to adjust the internal parameters used to calculate the representation for every layer based on the representation for each previous layer. We have seen how deep neural networks (DNNs) have led to quantum leaps in processing video, high-resolution images, and speech and audio files.

CASE STUDY: ESTIMATED ULTIMATE RECOVERY

We present a geophysics data-centric methodology for a reservoir characterization study that develops a prediction model for multistage hydraulically fractured horizontal wells in tight gas and oil reservoirs. The innovative application of DNNs can be realized owing to new progress in the study of deep learning and concurrently the adoption of big data. A DNN was trained to appreciate the relationship between geophysical attributes and the average *estimated ultimate recovery* (EUR, estimated by traditional decline curve analysis).

The model is ideal and significant during the exploration sector since it only necessitates geophysical and geologic data. This is key as type curve field segments require production data to be analyzed and are thus not readily available until the wells have been producing for some minimum period.

We can programmatically evolve a DNN that reflects the complexity inherent in the structures and levels of abstraction from the geophysical data. We adopt a methodology coined by the most important algorithms: stacked denoising autoencoders. Instead of forecasting EUR from the geophysical data, the algorithm establishes both the input and the anticipated output to the same data. We pollute the input data during the training stage of the workflow by either deleting variables or adding noise, thus making the DNN reconstruct the original data and in the process discovering and building all the levels of abstraction. There are ostensibly two separate components to the DNN: an encoder and a decoder. The former breaks down the geophysical data into the complex structure with multiple levels of abstraction while the latter converts the data into its original format.

Deep Learning for Time Series Modeling

We successfully implemented a deep learning architecture for forecasting EUR using seismic attributes garnered from active seismic across an oil and gas field. Linear and kernelized regression techniques produced robust results for our given data. We found that owing to the huge dataset it was feasible to implement complex nonlinear models without encountering many problems of overfitting. The deep neural networks supported significant complexity in the model.

Many papers commend the benefits of greedy layer-wise unsupervised training for deep neural network initialization (i.e., stacked autoencoders and restricted Boltzmann machines). Contrast this philosophy to the extreme scaling properties of either polynomial regression or even nonparametric Gaussian processes, which scale O (m^3) with data.

This case study shows the application of a data-driven deep learning suite of methodologies to ascertain the EUR of a field that constitutes part of the Eagle Ford shale region. We used reservoir properties, geologic parameters, and seismic attributes generated from active 3D seismic reflection data acquired by vibroseis. The attributes were produced from pre-stack depth-migrated data. The input data parameters included those shown in Table 9.1.

It is imperative before executing any data-driven advanced analytical workflows to ensure the quality of the input data. An exploratory data analysis (EDA) suite of visualizations (Figure 9.9) is critical to surface correlations, trends, and hidden

Table 9.1 Input Data for EUR Study

Name	Role	Level
Acoustic_Impedance	Input	Interval
Brittleness_Index	Input	Interval
Bulk_Modulus	Input	Interval
Density	Input	Interval
Fluid	Input	Nominal
FracFluidVol	Input	Interval
FracStages	Input	Interval
Gas_Saturation	Input	Interval
LateralLength	Input	Interval
Name	Classification	Nominal
NetThicknessPay	Input	Interval
PROD_AVG	Input	Interval
PhiE	Input	Interval
PhiSH	Input	Interval
PhiT	Input	Interval
Poisson_s_Ratio	Input	Interval
Prod_date	Time_ID	Interval
ProppantVol	Input	Interval
Qg100	Target	Interval
SUM_of_GAS	Input	Interval
Shear_Modulus	Input	Interval
TOC	Input	Interval
T_MON	Input	Interval
Type	Input	Nominal
VitriniteRefl	Input	Interval
VpVs	Input	Interval
Water_Saturation	Input	Interval
WellID	ID	Interval
Young_s_Modulus	Input	Interval
month	Input	Interval
Year	Input	Interval

Figure 9.9 Exploratory data analysis visualizing the histograms of key variables

relationships as we strive to not only reduce the dimensionality of the input space but also identify the statistically most relevant variables that impact the target or dependent variable. In our study, we identified Qg100 as the appropriate target variable as it represented the cumulative gas production 100 days post the collection start date of the production logging tool data. This enabled us to normalize all the input wells under study since the spud date varied across the array of wells. The histograms in Figure 9.9 illustrate the distribution of the individual variables, allowing us to identify anomalous data points such as unwanted outliers and predominant noise caused by poorly recorded measurements. The ability to select one bar in a histogram such as a high value of Qg100 and simultaneously see the corresponding values of the other variables is a very efficient way to define rules in the context of profiling extensive ranges of values expected in this case for high Qg100 measurements.

Scaling Issues with Large Datasets

This calculation-intensive process of feature creation was wasteful since a full polynomial expansion resulted in multiple features that bore limited statistical significance. We adopted a suite of subset selection methods such as a forward–backward stepwise methodology. Smaller subsets of the seismic data were computationally agreeable to this approach, potentially at the expense of losing valuable training knowledge. We implemented k-means cluster analysis to maximize information credibility and to enable more complex measurements or functional calculations.

Conclusions

It was prohibitively slow when we ran the algorithm until convergence. Nevertheless, we obtained sound and useful results with some expedited heuristics. Using different numbers of clusters and performing a naive "nearest-centroid" classification we saw improved results as we increased model complexity. We implemented feedforward neural networks on large datasets to analyze model parameters and then expanded these simple architectures with the recurrent architecture to advance forecasting accuracy.

Using a simple feedforward network, we ignore some of the temporal structures present in the time series data. This structure can be exploited using recurrent neural networks where we explicitly construct a sequential representation of our data.

Building on the literature, we trained feedforward neural networks with stacked autoencoders. Greedy layer-wise training has been shown to improve network performance in scenarios where large amounts of unlabeled data are available, but minimally labeled data. While all the data used in this study are labeled, we implemented the layer-wise training protocol to ascertain if it would mitigate local-non-global minima in the optimization problem. However, results with this technique were discouraging, with no significant performance gain but added computational complexity.

CASE STUDY: DEEP LEARNING APPLIED TO WELL DATA

Introduction

Reservoir engineers rely heavily on traditional methodologies such as empirical *decline curve analysis* (DCA) to forecast possible rates of flow of oil, gas, and water in mature fields. Several critical assumptions are made as to the values of the primary reservoir parameters impacting the production of the hydrocarbons. The type curves such as exponential, hyperbolic, and harmonic that are fitted against the historical well production data are at best somewhat useful but deterministic in nature. Owing to the inherent complexities of a heterogeneous reservoir system, such empirical assumptions lead invariably to over- or underflow rate estimation. This case study adopts a probabilistic methodology that implements a suite of deep learning neural network architectures. The DL algorithms that are proposed have been very efficient at pattern recognition and feature classification. The DL aspect relies on the concept of moving information from the input layer to the output layer via multiple stacked hidden layers that represent the features under study in matrices. Each layer is processed with varying mathematical operators. Our aim is to ascertain the best DL methodology to model the sequential production time series data generated at five different wells across a conventional sandstone oil and gas reservoir.

This case study describes the applicability of the neural networks we architected to forecast well performance. It is also important to clarify the dataset and preprocessing workflows that enabled the training and testing phases of the methodology. The final discussion reports the observed results and conclusions.

The time series oil and gas production data collated at several wells within a reservoir features as the input datasets for a deep learning analysis to generate a predictive model. We shall explore the advantages and draw out any disadvantages from the following data-driven analytical techniques:

1. Restricted Boltzmann machines (RBMs)
2. Deep forward neural networks (DFNNs)
3. Convolutional deep neural networks (CDNNs)
4. Recurrent deep neural networks (RDNNs)

Restricted Boltzmann Machines

The restricted Boltzmann machine is a generative graphical model representing a probability distribution. The *restricted* nature of the Boltzmann machine implies a simplification of the learning problem by an imposition of constraints on the adopted network topology. The graphical model characteristic refers to the undirected Markov random fields. The architecture we took consists of a visible layer and a hidden layer with connections between these two layers. The data is ingested through the input or visible layer and pushed upwards, propagating to the hidden layer. The input data is then reconstructed and sent back down to the visible layer. The primary goal of the thinking for implementing an RBM is to determine if there are a discrete number of feature patterns in the production time series data. The activation function used was a sigmoid function that trained the RBM by adjusting the weights between the two layers: visible and hidden. See Figure 9.10 for a pictorial expression of the RBM used in the study.

The following columns represent the variables in each of the 150 well datasets aggregated to generate one input dataset for study.

Date: Date measurement was on the last day of the month

Field: Anonymous field name where reservoir and wells located

Formation: Lithological rock formation top for the reservoir

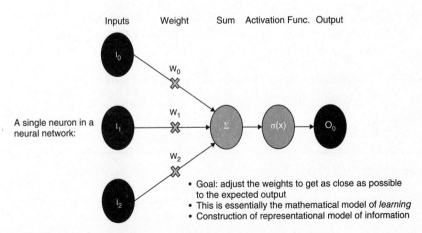

Figure 9.10   RBM architecture implemented to predict output

Well name: First two letters of field name followed by formation and index

Oil: Monthly oil production

Water: Monthly water production

Gas: Monthly gas production

The wells under study had varying amounts of production data
owing to different spud dates and timing of well tests (PTA
and RTA).

Each dataset was sampled and zero production values were
imputed by determining the average of the month prior and post
the missing data point.

- Transpose the well datasets into sectors.
- Normalize sectors.
- Divide datasets into training, validation, and test datasets.

Transpose the Well Datasets into Sectors

- Some machine learning algorithms only take fixed-size
  input.
- *Advantage:* There is sufficient training data.
- The study implemented the following data criteria:
  - Input size: 48 months (4 yrs.)
  - Output size: 12 months (1 yrs.)
  - Step size: 6 months

We adopted a supervised methodology.

Normalize Sectors

Step 0: Subtract the mean value and divide by the standard
deviation.

Step 1: Center the data sectors about 0 and then distribute
equally.

Divide Datasets into Training, Validation, and Test Datasets

To do machine learning, we split our data into training and validation sets:

1. Train neural networks using training set.
2. Test how well it works on novel input using validation set.
3. Set aside the third dataset, the testing set, which contains predictions for the wells at future dates.

Avoid overtraining: After a certain number of training steps, you continue to get better predictions on data the network has seen, but not on new data.

Mathematics

The mathematics behind a single neuron represents the evaluation of the activation functions at the value yielded by the dot product of the weight vector and the input vector.

$$O_0 = \sigma\left(\begin{bmatrix} w_0 \\ \vdots \\ w_n \end{bmatrix} \cdot \begin{bmatrix} I_0 \\ \vdots \\ I_n \end{bmatrix}\right) = \sigma\left(\overrightarrow{W_0} \cdot \overrightarrow{I}\right) \text{ where } \overrightarrow{W_0} = \begin{bmatrix} w_0 \\ \vdots \\ w_n \end{bmatrix}, \ \overrightarrow{I} = \begin{bmatrix} I_0 \\ \vdots \\ I_n \end{bmatrix}$$

Extending this idea for multiple output nodes turns the dot product into a matrix product of the weighting matrix (consisting of the weight vectors for each output stacked vertically as rows) and the input vector.

$$\overrightarrow{O} = \sigma(W\overrightarrow{I}) \text{ where } W = \begin{bmatrix} \cdots & \overrightarrow{W_0} & \cdots \\ \cdots & \vdots & \cdots \\ \cdots & \overrightarrow{W_n} & \cdots \end{bmatrix}$$

So how do you adjust the weighting matrix to get the algorithm's output to match the predicted output? First define loss function $L(W^\wedge k.\overrightarrow{I}, \overrightarrow{O})$ where $W^\wedge k$ is the weighting vector at iteration k. $\overrightarrow{I}$ is one of the input sets from the training data, and $\overrightarrow{O}$ is the output given $\overrightarrow{I}$.

For time series prediction, we define loss as square error: $L(W^\wedge k, \overrightarrow{\ }, \overrightarrow{\ }) = \|W^\wedge k, \overrightarrow{I}, -\overrightarrow{O}\|^\wedge 2.$

CASE STUDY: GEOPHYSICAL FEATURE EXTRACTION: DEEP NEURAL NETWORKS

Let us build piecemeal a CDNN to consider a seismic image or a single 2D inline from a 3D seismic data cube. We want to identify a seismic feature or attribute such as a flat-spot as visualized in Figure 9.11.

This feature invariably cuts across the stratigraphy imaged in the seismic profiles of oil and gas reservoirs. It can be thought of as a *direct hydrocarbon indicator* owing to its frequent presence in hydrocarbon reservoirs. Why do we see a flat-spot from a geophysicist's perspective? An increase in acoustic impedance can be characteristic of a flat-spot appearing when limestone or sandstone pores contain gas overlying a liquid-filled rock that has a higher acoustic impedance. If we can characterize a subtle flat-spot located on a seismic image post-drilling, we can then recognize other similar flat-spots across the 3D images at an earlier stage and ultimately reduce the risk of dry holes.

We can extract pixel attributes at each common depth point and time across the flat-spot. We can aggregate these pixel characteristics with the seismic attributes across the flat-spot: acoustic impedance, Z (product of seismic velocity and density), frequency, and amplitude content as well as instantaneous phase. These flat-spot characteristics across the lateral extent as well as the temporal domain can be sampled and then classified with a neural network.

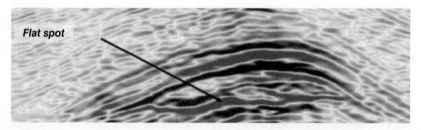

Figure 9.11 Flat-spot is a seismic attribute anomaly depicted as a horizontal reflector

CDNN Layer Development

The simplest methodology is to connect the attributes to a fully connected layer in the neural network. As depicted in Figure 9.12 we have a suite of different neurons and each input connects to every available neuron.

We can adopt a more elegant design that inherently recognizes a symmetry in the seismic properties under study. As geophysicists, we put great emphasis and value on localized seismic attributes within the data. What are the flat-spot characteristics for a given spatiotemporal location? And what are these features at all points in the spatiotemporal seismic images?

We can generate a group of neurons, A, that focus on a small window of the seismic traces in space and time. A can scan all the segments or windows, determining features. The output of this convolutional layer acts as input to a fully connected layer F.

A is an assemblage of neurons that individually might detect different aspects of a flat-spot. One neuron might identify a vertical edge while the adjacent neuron might detect a horizontal edge to the flat-spot. All color contrasts and amplitude variations can also be ascertained and distinguished across the neurons in layer A.

In Figure 9.13, A analyzes only segments consisting of two points. This is obviously not sufficient. Invariably, in a CDNN, a convolution layer's window would be more extensive.

The key architectural components of a CDNN are the convolutional layers and their representation as composite layers. Thus, the output of one convolutional layer can feed into another layer, and the network can distinguish higher-level, more abstract features.

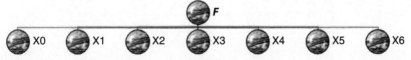

Figure 9.12 Simple neural architecture for flat-spot identification

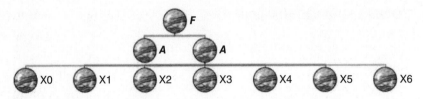

Figure 9.13   Introduction of layer A focused on a small time–space window

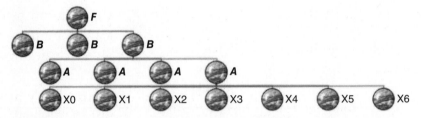

Figure 9.14   Layer of neurons B adds a convolutional layer for focused analysis

In Figure 9.14, we depict another group of neurons; B is used to produce an additional convolutional layer stacked on top of the preceding one, A.

Pooling layers are frequently interlaced with convolutional layers, and there is one type of layer named a *max-pooling* layer that has garnered much support for implementation in a CDNN architecture (Figure 9.15). We can take advantage of the max-pooling layer when identifying seismic features such as flat-spots within a spatial–temporal window within a seismic image. The advantage gained lies in the concept of taking the maximum of features within small blocks of a preceding layer.

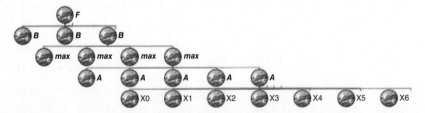

Figure 9.15   A max-pooling layer helps to identify seismic features

We are advised as to whether a feature was existing in a section of the prior layer, but not exactly where. Thus, there is a type of "zooming" behavior implemented by a max-pooling layer. Subsequent convolutional layers can manage much larger sections of the seismic data since a small patch post the pooling layer maps to a much greater patch before it.

We have examined CDNNs built with one-dimensional convolutional layers. However, higher dimensions of data can be addressed. Often a two-dimensional convolutional layer is popularized such that the neural network can analyze patches in addition to small windows in space and time.

If a patch of seismic imaging data is selected, it is feasible to ingest it into a multidimensional version of Figure 9.15 with max pooling in two dimensions. This ensures a maximum of seismic features within a small patch.

This architecture is ideal when interpreting a complete 2D seismic image, be it an inline or crossline within the 3D seismic data cube. Why? It is not necessary to concern ourselves about an exact location of an edge at the pixel level when identifying a flat-spot. It is sufficient to appreciate where it is located within a few pixels.

When thinking about convolutional neural networks, it is easier to formulate the implementation of a CDNN from a mathematical perspective. There is an operation well-known to processing geophysicists called *convolution*. It is a potent device often seen in the learning of partial differential equations. Geophysicists often apply *de*convolution operators on the recorded seismic data to reverse the effects of the Earth's convolved signatures. The convolutional operator in CDNNs offers multiple benefits when looking for features such as flat-spots in a complete 3D seismic cube. The first advantage enables far more efficient implementations of the convolutional layers and the second value removes a significant amount of confusion from our formulation. The third benefit lies in the pointedly different perspective for cogently thinking about convolutional layers.

CASE STUDY: WELL LOG DATA-DRIVEN EVALUATION FOR PETROPHYSICAL INSIGHTS

There are many sources of well-log data collated from a spatial, temporal, and physical dimension (Figure 9.16). We need to marry some of the more valid traditional interpretations of these datasets with a data-driven suite of analytical methodologies. This hybrid approach will encompass a far greater percentage of existing data and provide more insight and generate more efficient and robust knowledge for decision making. The predetermined and subjective interpretations inherent in the current deterministic workflows often fall short of the critical knowledge requisite of successful field development. Fluid and rock models fixed by biased analyses a priori limit the value garnered from an ever-increasing dimension of the multivariate parameters and measures taken from well logs.

When we study rock formations, there is little surprise that there are complexity, heterogeneity, multivariate, and multivariant issues simply because of the notion that geological time has played havoc with the first sedimentary environment in which the rocks stratified.

Petrophysicists study the underlying measured quantities (hard data) to ascertain lithology, fluid types, as well as porosity and permeability of the rock matrix. These raw measurements obtained in the field via a compendium of varying well logs act as feedstock for the interpretation step that is primarily based

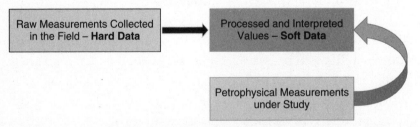

Figure 9.16 Workflow details the acquisition of raw hard data from logging tools that are used to determine petrophysical properties

on first principles and calibrated to deliver a model quantified by the established laws of Newtonian physics and Gaussian mathematics. Marrying the hard and soft datasets into a data-driven methodology implementing regression or machine learning techniques provides a more robust understanding of the complexity inherent in the rock matrix.

One standard statistical workflow that is growing in popularity is the probability theory behind Bayes' law. This soft-computing technique defines the likelihood of an event occurring based on conditions deemed probably correlated with the event. Bayes' theorem (Reverend Thomas Bayes, 1701–1761) is represented mathematically by the following equation:

$$P(A \mid B) = P(B \mid A)P(A)/P(B)$$

Where:

A and B are events and $P(B) \neq 0$.

$P(A)$ and $P(B)$ are the probabilities of witnessing A and B independent of each other.

$P(A \mid B)$ is a conditional probability such that the likelihood of seeing event A given that event B is true.

$P(B \mid A)$ is thus the probability of seeing B given A is true.

From the petrophysicist's perspective, we can apply Bayes' law to quantify the likelihood that a particular fluid distribution is witnessed based on a priori knowledge of a few of the hard data collected in well logs.

Bayesian Inference

What exactly does Bayesian inference mean? We know that *inference* is a synonym for "educated guess." Thomas Bayes was a Presbyterian minister in London during the colonial days, and as a nonconformist, Bayes dabbled in probability.

There is no mystery inherent in Bayesian inference. The mathematics often obfuscates the simple concepts and Bayesian inference is no exception. In short, Bayesian inference enables engineers to ascertain more robust results from an ever-burgeoning array of complex data across E&P.

We are overrun by a litany of different well logs currently collating these hard datasets: nuclear, NMR, acoustics (DAS), mud logging, resistivity logs, sonic logs, geomechanical logs, as well as spatial dimensions for depth that range across 3D electromagnetic propagation and 2D images. The time series datasets enhance these data above sets, especially the 4D time-lapse data. We quickly move into more complex scenarios with multiple wells, horizontal and vertical.

Many soft-computing workflows incorporate machine learning and deep learning methodologies as well as the more commonly recognized suite of data-driven models based on regression, supervised and unsupervised networks (ANNs and SOMs), decision trees, and ensembles of different models. The two critical characteristics that promote confidence and acceptability of applying these data mining models can be defined as:

1. Scalable
2. Idempotent

The first is important since invariably more data will be collected and added to the models. The idea of implementing an idempotent workflow is sound in the field of mathematics and computer science as it ensures that no matter how many times a functional relationship is executed via a data-driven methodology, the results are consistently the same when applied to the same dataset.

Let us explore possibilities of applying these techniques to surface knowledge of the fluid distribution in the pores of a rock matrix and ascertain the facies changes using nuclear magnetic resonance (NMR) logs. The NMR response for a formation enables petrophysicists to calculate both porosity and permeability that are primarily continuous recordings of these rock properties along the length of a wellbore. We are manipulating the *magnetic moment* of hydrogen abundant in rocks as water saturation. Thus, the signal amplitude measured by the NMR log reflects the number of hydrogen nuclei present in the rock formation. Calibration then provides readings for porosity devoid of lithology effects. Petrophysicists can determine permeability by studying the rate of decay of the NMR signal amplitude. The rock properties impact the two-dimensional measurement of an NMR value (depth and relaxation time T2) that interests petrophysicists.

The Workflow

1. Build a data-specific soft-computing model:
   a. Identify the number of noteworthy types in data containing T2 distribution across a depth interval.
   b. Find the unique types and characterize them as T2 distributions of fundamental poro-fluid components.
   c. Implement exploratory data analysis and surface patterns and trends that correlate to poro-fluid constituents' spatial distribution across the depth dimension. Assign depths to poro-fluid facies.
2. Perform an inversion for all quantities under study:
   a. Calculate T2 cutoffs for all poro-fluid constituents.
   b. Invert for all the volumes of the poro-fluid constituents for permeability transforms.
   c. Describe each facies by its mean T2 distribution, pseudo-capillary pressure, and saturation height functions.

The magnetic moment represents the torque experienced by a magnet in an external magnetic field. An electron orbiting an atomic nucleus is an example of this phenomenon.

CASE STUDY: FUNCTIONAL DATA ANALYSIS IN RESERVOIR MANAGEMENT

Oil companies always strive to enhance the quality and accelerate the process of active reservoir management decision making to derive necessary exploitation strategies and tactics. We must consider the complex and heterogeneous reservoirs of very mature fields. Such decisions are based on classical and exploratory data studies to garner robust and reliable knowledge of critical uncertainty factors within the reservoir's segmented regions. It is imperative to assess risk inherent in field engineering operations and quantify the uncertainty of the primary reservoir properties deemed important in the decision-making cycles.

Big-data analytics provide potential answers to questions related to risk and uncertainty, as well as endorsing reserves information, ensuring that exploitation plans are adhered to by predefined targets.

This case study provides insight into a water-drive project in a giant Saudi carbonate field using a set of analytical workflows to classify wells, extract original indicators of production, and divide the field into areas exhibiting high water-cut or poorly drained zones.

What we are proposing in this case study is a nonparametric statistical approach that is essentially replicating some of the workflows advocated in the functional data analysis (FDA) methodology (Ramsey et al., 2005), as illustrated in Figure 9.17. FDA is a branch of statistics ideally suited to analyze data and generate knowledge about curves and surfaces over a space–time continuum. The functional component proposes that a mathematical function represents each sample element across the field under study. The physical continuum can be established simply as time or as a spatial location, wavelength, or even statistical probability.

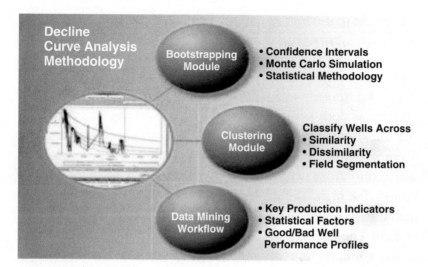

Figure 9.17 Functional data analysis

In FDA production data (oil, gas, and water) is modeled as temporal data consisting of a summation of weighted smooth analytical basis functions. Instead of assuming a model, the data teaches us the model by jointly fitting all production profiles across the segmented field. *Functional principal component analysis* (fPCA; Ramsey et al., 2005) transforms time-varying data into lower-dimensional score data. We can represent the entire production dataset by 2 to 3 functional principal components (PCs). Lower-dimensional-score data is ideal for subsequent data mining workflows and sensitivity studies to surface a better appreciation of the key production indicators (KPIs). Building regression relationships between geological parameters and completion variables and functional PC scores enables forecasting production of the different liquids at new well locations with different geological/completion parameters.

It is understood that in a fractured reservoir, water-cut and the recovery factor relationship may show a significantly different characteristic. Hence, with the objective of generating new insight about the fractures of the Saudi field we started analyzing the distribution of the water-cut.

The bootstrapping module enables engineers to build reliable confidence intervals for production rate forecast and reserves estimates over the lifecycle of the wells. The clustering module allows engineers to deal with a plethora of different upstream data generated from an extensive portfolio of wells by providing a means for classifying the wells on the strength of similar characteristics, tactical or strategic, aggregated with reservoir properties and geomechanical parameters. The goal of the data mining step is to introduce the reservoir team to an innovative approach that analyzes massive amounts of data, surfacing hidden patterns and trends and identifying correlations and relationships in a complex multivariate subsurface system. The intention is to underscore the KPIs as new engineering plans are drawn up for a mature field, reducing the decision-making cycles quantified under uncertainty.

There are different water-cut behaviors in homogeneous and highly fractured reservoirs. Thus, a plot of water-cut against the recovery factor indicates fracture intensity close to the wellbore. Wells located at various locations tend to exhibit different fracturing intensity values and thus may exhibit different water-cut against recovery factor characteristics.

Classify wells by dividing the field into regions:

- Modeling daily production
- Smoothing of water-cut and GOR
- Identifying indicators of production
- Multivariate (principal component analysis)

Clustering:

- Classifies wells to production indicators
- Identifies production mechanisms (best producers)

Cluster analysis, depicted in Figure 9.18, can be used to segment wells into distinct groups based on type curve shapes (patterns) and other properties.

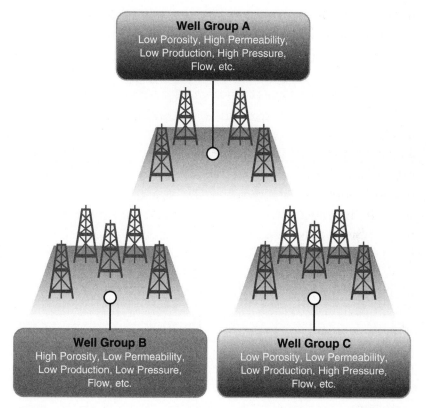

Figure 9.18 Cluster analysis to segment the well portfolio in a brownfield

Clustering is a data mining methodology to categorize and analyze partitions of data observations sharing comparable attribute characteristics. We can plot the clusters of well profiles and provide a visual perspective of a field's distribution by common well characteristics. Where are the best performing wells? Where are the wells with the highest water-cut?

The well clustering workflow generates the first round of similar wells based on the characteristics that underpin the business problem under study. The next analytical step compares the average of the clusters to the remaining wells to generate a second set of clusters. This workflow iterates until an acceptable point of business value is achieved. The hierarchical cluster technique is reliable and produces a higher resolution of results than the *k*-means method. One output is a displayed dendrogram providing a means to optimize the number of clusters for subsequent runs.

It is plausible to segment the field into discrete areas to accelerate business decisions for field reengineering. These are some of the analytical steps that enrich the process:

- Interpolation and smoothing algorithms
- Nonlinear multivariate regressions
- Principal component analysis
- Cluster analysis
- Discrimination analysis

The FDA process analyzes data that is infinite from a dimensional perspective. Oil and gas production data is discretely sampled over the time series under study. These discrete measurements are taken on a regular or irregular periodicity across the time domain ($t\,\epsilon\,(\mathrm{l}, \mathrm{T})$), assuming the measurements originate from a smooth process corrupted by noise.

$$f_{\text{observed}}(t) = f_{\text{true}}(t) + \epsilon(t) \,\cdots\, t\,\epsilon\,(\mathrm{l}, \mathrm{T})$$

We transform the discrete measurements into continuous approximations of the accurate fundamental function. Essentially, raw measurements of the functional data are estimated with a "scaled sum of smooth analytical basis functions" (Grujic et al., 2015) that cross the same time domain as the original data.

There are several forms of basis systems or logical basis functions. Selecting the optimal basis function is dependent on the business problem under study and the characteristics of the input dataset. If you are dealing with periodic temporal data, then a Fourier basis function is appropriate. The production data in our case study has an inherent nonstationary and aperiodic characteristic. We selected the B-spline basis function.

Ramsey et al. discussed multiple types of basis functions, recommending the B-splines to analyze non-periodic data. An aperiodic signal does not repeat its signature or pattern after certain time periods.

Having selected the B-splines basis function, we had to determine scaling coefficients to minimize the mean squared error of the fit. It is important to avoid overfitting and attain a smooth variation of a fitted function (Ramsey et al., 2005; Hastie et al., 2008).

The fPCA process provides three visualization steps:

1. A scree plot to identify cumulative variance by the first PCs
2. A plot to illustrate the perturbation of the PCs about the mean function
3. A score plot of the functional principal components

Each point in the score plot represents a production profile. Euclidean distances illustrate similarities and emphasize variances among the different production profiles. We could visually classify those geophysical and petrophysical attributes that impacted the production statistically. We achieved this insight by coloring the points depicted in the score plot by the parameter values. Any systematic color changes observed in the score plot may represent an underlying trend indicative of a parameter's sensitivity and influence on the production.

The functional methodology is an innovative suite of advanced analytical workflows that expands the functional basis to represent oil and gas production decline across a reservoir. We make no a priori assumptions about the underlying physical mechanisms or any empirical decline models. Please reference the work conducted by Grujic, Da Silva, and Caers in 2015 for a more detailed case study that studied an unconventional reservoir in North America.

REFERENCES

Bengio, Y., A. Courville, and P. Vincent, "Representation Learning: A Review and New Perspectives," *IEEE Transactions on Pattern Analysis and Machine Intelligence*, 35 (2013): 1798–1828.

Bengio, Yoshua, Pascal Lamblin, Dan Popovici, and Hugo Larochelle, "Greedy Layer-Wise Training of Deep Neural Networks," *Advances in Neural Information Processing Systems 19 (NIPS 2006)*, MIT Press (2007), pp. 153–160.

Duda, R. O., P. O. Hart, and D. G. Stork, *Pattern Classification*, 2nd ed., John Wiley & Sons, New York (2000).

Grujic, Ognjen, Carla Da Silva, and Jef Caers, "Functional Approach to Data Mining, Forecasting, and Uncertainty Quantification in Unconventional Reservoirs," paper SPE 174849, SPE Annual Technical Conference and Exhibition, Houston (September 28–30, 2015).

Hall, Patrick, Jared Dean, Ilknur Kaynar Kabul, and Jorge Silva, "An Overview of Machine Learning with SAS® Enterprise Miner™," paper SAS313-2014, SAS Institute Inc. (2014).

Hall, Patrick, Ilknur Kaynar Kabul, Jorge Silva, Keith Holdaway, and Alex Chien, "An Efficient Pattern Recognition Approach with Applications," paper SAS3100-2016, SAS Institute Inc. (2016).

Hastie, T., R. Tibshirani, and J. Friedman, *The Elements of Statistical Learning, Data Mining, Inference, and Prediction*, 2nd ed., Springer (2008).

Hinton, G. E., and R. R. Salakhutdinov, "Reducing the Dimensionality of Data with Neural Networks," *Science*, 313 (July 28, 2006): 504. DOI: 10.1126/science. 1127647.

Krizhevsky, A., I. Sutskever, and G. E. Hinton, "ImageNet Classification with Deep Convolutional Neural Networks." In: *Advances in Neural Information Processing Systems 25 (NIPS 2012), Proceedings of the Annual Conference on Neural Information Processing Systems* (2012), pp. 1097–1105.

LeCun, Yann, Leon Bottou, Yoshua Bengio, and Patrick Haffner, "Gradient-Based Learning Applied to Document Recognition," *IEEE* (November 1998).

LeCun, Yann, Yoshua Bengio, and Geoffrey Hinton, *Nature*, 521 (May 28, 2015): 436–444. DOI: 10.1038/nature14539.

Lee, H., A. Battle, R. Raina, and A. Y. Ng, "Efficient Sparse Coding Algorithms." In: *Advances in Neural Information Processing Systems 19 (NIPS 2006), Proceedings of the Annual Conference on Neural Information Processing Systems* (2006), pp. 801–808.

Ramsey, J., and B. W. Silverman, "Functional Data Analysis," *Springer Series in Statistics* (June 8, 2005).

Glossary

Acoustic Impedance   It is the ratio of the pressure over an imaginary surface in a sound wave to the rate of particle flow across the surface.

ANN   In computer science and related fields, artificial neural networks are computational models inspired by animals' central nervous systems that are capable of machine learning and pattern recognition. They are presented as systems of interconnected "neurons" that can compute values from inputs by feeding information through the network.

ARIMA   In time series analysis, ARIMA stands for Autoregressive Integrated Moving Average and is used to predict future trends.

ASCII   American Standard Code for Information Interchange—the widely used standard for encoding human-readable characters and symbols for computation.

AVO   Variation in seismic reflection amplitude with a change in distance between shot point and receiver that indicates differences in lithology and fluid content in rocks above and below the reflector. AVO analysis is a technique by which geophysicists attempt to determine thickness, porosity, density, velocity, lithology, and fluid content of rocks.

Bayes' Theorem   It describes the probability of an event based on prior expertise or knowledge of the constraints or conditions that might impact the event.

Binary Variable   A binary variable has only two distinct values. A binary variable can be legitimately treated as nominal, ordinal, interval, or sometimes ratio.

CAPEX   Capital expenditures are expenditures creating future benefits. A capital expenditure is incurred when a business spends money either to buy fixed assets or to add to the value of an existing fixed asset with a useful life extending beyond the taxable year.

Categorical Variable   A categorical variable is used for mutual exclusivity. It is not an ordered category. For example, geophysicists might compare different seismic attributes. We can code these attributes with numeric values if the order is arbitrary and any estimates are worthless.

CDP In multichannel seismic acquisition where beds do not dip, the common reflection point at depth on a reflector, or the halfway point when a wave travels from a source to a reflector to a receiver. In the case of flat layers, the common depth point is vertically below the common midpoint.

CEP Event processing is a method of tracking and analyzing (processing) streams of information (data) about things that happen (events) and deriving a conclusion from them. Complex event processing (CEP) is event processing that combines data from multiple sources to infer events or patterns that suggest more complicated circumstances.

Class Variable A class variable is a categorical target variable, and classification means assigning cases to categories of a dependent variable. A class variable is a categorical variable, either an input or a target.

CRM Customer relationship management is a model for managing a company's interactions with current and future customers. It involves using technology to organize, automate, and synchronize sales, marketing, customer service, and technical support.

DAS Distributed acoustic sensing (DAS) systems take advantage of the fiber-optic cables that consist of one or several optical fibers used to transmit light. It is an emerging technology that finds its roots across the Department of Defense.

Data Mining Data mining is the process of discovering patterns in datasets. The goal is to create soft-computing models to enable pattern recognition workflows to address business problems based on data alone.

Data Science Data science is a discipline based on scientific methods, processes, and systems that extract actionable knowledge from raw data. The data can be structured, unstructured, spatial, and temporal in nature. It implies the implementation of data-driven methodologies using soft-computing models.

DCA Decline curve analysis. An empirical determination of the type curves based on historical production data to forecast well performance and estimate ultimate recovery.

Deduction Deductive reasoning represents the process linking premises with logically certain conclusions.

Decision Tree Decision trees are models to enable classification of observations based on nominal, binary, or ordinal targets. It is a hierarchy with each segment called a *node* of a tree.

Deep Learning   The study of artificial neural networks in a multilayered architecture.

DHI   In reflection seismology, a bright spot is a local high-amplitude seismic attribute anomaly that can indicate the presence of hydrocarbons and is known as a direct hydrocarbon indicator.

Discriminant Analysis   Discriminant analysis classifies rows of data defined by values of continuous variables into clusters or discrete segments.

DOFF   Digital Oilfields of the Future is defined by how the petroleum industry deploys its technology, people, and processes to support optimizing hydrocarbon production, improving operational safety, protecting the environment, and maximizing and discovering reserves.

DTS   Distributed temperature sensing (DTS) systems enable downhole temperature measurements to be collected at multiple points simultaneously by way of fiber optics.

Ensemble   The ensemble methodology generates models by uniting the posterior probabilities or the predicted values from multiple precursor models. The ensemble model is used to score new data.

E&P   Exploration and production chain that covers all the steps in the upstream: exploration, appraisal, development, production, and intervention.

EDA   In statistics, exploratory data analysis is an approach to analyzing datasets to summarize their main characteristics, often with visual methods.

EOR   Enhanced oil recovery is a generic term for techniques for increasing the amount of crude oil that can be extracted from an oil field.

EUR   Estimated ultimate recovery from a field, reservoir, or well.

Factorized Machine Learning   Factorized machines (FMs) can model the entire family of possible interactions between the variables by adopting factorized parameters. Using FMs enables geophysicists and petrophysicists to estimate interactions in sparsely populated datasets.

FFT   A fast Fourier transform is an algorithm to compute the discrete Fourier transform (DFT) and the inverse. A Fourier transform converts time (or space) to frequency and vice versa; an FFT rapidly computes such transformations.

FL   Fuzzy logic is a form of many-valued logic; it deals with reasoning that is approximate rather than fixed and exact. Compared to traditional binary sets (where variables may take on true or false values) fuzzy logic variables may have a truth value that ranges in degree between 0 and 1.

GA   In the computer science field of artificial intelligence, a genetic algorithm is a search heuristic that mimics the process of natural selection.

Geophysics   The study of the physics of the earth. Reflection seismology implements geophysical techniques to map the acoustic response of hydrocarbon reservoirs.

Gradient Boosting   An example of an ensemble methodology is gradient boosting that generates a resultant model from a suite of weak predictive models in a stepwise and sequential process.

Induction   Inductive reasoning provides the premises as strong evidence for the truth of a conclusion.

Internet of Things   Smart sensors in wells, reservoirs, and surface facilities enable real-time streaming data to be analyzed owing to the connectivity across massive networks of upstream data. The Industrial Internet of Things encapsulates this innovative paradigm.

Interval Variable   An interval variable reflects a meaningful difference in measurement between two variables.

LAS   Log ASCII Standard is the data interchange format for well logging data. Maintained here: http://www.cwls.org/las/.

Machine Learning   A branch of artificial intelligence that provides data scientists the ability to develop algorithms that learn from a data-driven workflow and predict based on historical patterns.

NMO   The effect of the separation between receiver and source on the arrival time of a reflection that does not dip.

Nominal Variable   A numeric or character categorical variable. The categories are unordered. The values of each category carry no supplementary information beyond the category membership.

NPT   Nonproductive time when oil and gas wells are not producing owing to maintenance or shut-in for testing.

OOIP   Original oil in place is the total hydrocarbon content of an oil reservoir and is often abbreviated *STOOIP*, which stands for Stock Tank Original Oil In Place, or *STOIIP* for Stock Tank Oil Initially In Place, referring to the oil in place before the commencement of production.

OPEX Operating expense is an ongoing cost for running an oil-and-gas strategy across the exploration and production value chain.

Ordinal Variable The order is important, but any differences between the values are immaterial. For example, a petrophysicist might express the hardness of a rock using Moh's scale of 1 to 10. However, a score of 8 means a harder rock than one scored at 6, and that is more than 4, but the difference between 8 and 6 is not the same as that between 6 and 4.

OWC *Water contact* is a term used in the hydrocarbon industry to describe the elevation above which fluids other than water can be found in the pores of a rock. In most situations in the hydrocarbon industry, the term is qualified as being an oil–water contact (OWC) or a gas–water contact (GWC). Often there is also a gas–oil contact (GOC).

Partial Least Squares Partial least squares is a methodology that is useful for extracting the latent input variables that account for the greatest variation in the predicted target.

PCA Principal component analysis is a statistical procedure that uses orthogonal transformation to convert a set of observations of possibly correlated variables into a set of values of linearly uncorrelated variables called principal components.

Petrophysics The study of the physical and chemical properties of rocks and the interactions with hydrocarbons and other fluids.

Poisson's Ratio It is the ratio of transverse contraction strain to longitudinal extension strain in the direction of stretching force.

Random Forests A random forest collates a group of decision trees that each represent a randomly associated subset of the original data and then determine a predictive result from the ensemble methodology.

Ratio Variable A ratio variable is like an interval variable and carries a defined value of 0.0. The weight of proppant in a hydraulic strategy is a ratio variable, but the temperature is not, as 100° C is not twice as hot as 50° C, but 1000 lbs. is twice as much as 500 lbs.

Regression Linear regression strives to predict the value of an interval target as a linear function of one or more independent inputs. However, the logistic regression method predicts the probability that an ordinal or binary dependent variable will attain the event under study as a function of one or more independent inputs.

Rules-Based   Rules-based techniques fall into the same family of soft-computing methods as the decision trees. However, there is no rigid hierarchical partitioning of the training set for rules-based workflows.

SAGD   Steam-assisted gravity drainage is an enhanced oil recovery technology for producing heavy crude oil and bitumen.

Soft-Computing Techniques   The workflows and methodologies that bring together the requisite steps to build a probabilistic model. The definition enables upstream geoscientists to sample data, explore the data for patterns, modify the data for statistical compliance, and then generate models.

SOM   A self-organizing map or self-organizing feature map (SOFM) is a type of artificial neural network (ANN) that is trained using unsupervised learning to produce a low-dimensional (typically two-dimensional) discretized representation of the input space of the training samples, called a map.

Support Vector Machine   Support vector machines (SVMs) use linear conditions to isolate classes from each other. The methodology known as SVM executes binary linear classification as well as a nonlinear classification. It uses a mapping of the input geophysical and petrophysical data into a high-dimensional feature space.

TOC   Total organic compound is the amount of carbon in an organic compound such as hydrocarbons.

UCM   The model decomposes temporal data into trends, cycles, and regression effects.

WAG   The WAG injection process aims to squeeze more oil out of a reservoir. It was originally intended to improve sweep efficiency during gas flooding, with intermittent slugs of water and gas designed to follow the same route through the reservoir.

Young's Modulus   A measure of elasticity, equal to the ratio of the stress acting on a subsurface to the strain produced.

About the Authors

Keith R. Holdaway is advisory industry consultant and principal solutions architect at SAS, where he helps drive implementation of innovative oil and gas solutions and products. He also develops business opportunities for the SAS global oil and gas business unit that align SAS advanced analytics from exploratory data analysis and predictive models to subsurface reservoir characterization and drilling/production optimization in conventional and unconventional fields.

Prior to joining SAS, Holdaway was a senior geophysicist with Shell Oil, where he conducted seismic processing and interpretation and determined seismic attributes in 3D cubes for soft-computing statistical data mining.

* * *

Dr. Duncan H. B. Irving has been a leading consultant in oil and gas for Teradata since 2010. Prior to that he researched and instructed in petroleum geoscience at the University of Manchester, and provided freelance upstream data management consulting. Throughout his career he has worked on data acquisition, integration, and analytics around oil reservoir, subsurface, and sensor data in data centers, in extreme field conditions, and in general upstream workflow and data management.

Duncan has led and supported projects across the oil and gas and wider manufacturing industries, consulting at strategic and operational levels. Projects in these industries span scientific, technical, and business domains, and Duncan stays wide in his approaches, for example, marrying modern data science paradigms to longstanding supercomputing-driven workflows.

He has slowly swapped Perl for Python and PowerPoint for data art. He has a PhD in glacial geophysics, publishes and speaks regularly on oil industry data and analytics challenges, and enjoys being at the forefront of the emerging analytical ecosystem in upstream oil and gas.

Index